Stained Glass
FOR
DUMMIES®

by Vicki Payne

WILEY

Wiley Publishing, Inc.

Stained Glass For Dummies®

Published by
Wiley Publishing, Inc.
111 River St.
Hoboken, NJ 07030-5774
www.wiley.com

For general information on our other products and services, please contact our Customer Care Department within the U.S. at 877-762-2974, outside the U.S. at 317-572-3993, or fax 317-572-4002.

For technical support, please visit www.wiley.com/techsupport.

Wiley also publishes its books in a variety of electronic formats. Some content that appears in print may not be available in electronic books.

Library of Congress Control Number: 2010935561

ISBN: 978-0-470-59132-1

Manufactured in the United States of America

10 9 8 7 6 5

WILEY

About the Author

Vicki Payne has hosted the internationally syndicated show *Glass with Vicki Payne*, on PBS, for more than two decades. With her husband Chris, she owned and operated one of the largest stained-glass teaching and supply centers in the Midwest. She has produced more than 50 stained-glass DVDs, authored nine bestselling books about the art-glass craft, and invented and developed some very helpful tools for glass workers.

Vicki is also the host of *For Your Home,* the second-most-aired home-and-garden series on television and has hosted the *Handmade Gifts* and *DIY Crafts* television series on the DIY Network. She's also a frequent guest on other national and regional home-improvement and craft shows. In addition, she's an accomplished educator and a much sought after speaker at the International Hardware Show, Builders Show, and International Furniture Market in High Point. As the creative force behind Charlotte, North Carolina–based Cutters Productions, Vicki has made her name synonymous with the how-to industry. She also serves as a consultant to companies in the home-improvement and furnishing industries, where her innovative development and marketing strategies are fully embraced.

Dedication

This book is dedicated to my mom, Mary James. She was an accomplished glass artist who never failed to encourage me to pursue my dreams and to do what I love. Thanks Mom, I miss you.

Mary James
1924–2010

Author's Acknowledgments

I want to thank my husband, Chris Payne, for coming out of retirement to help me create all the projects and samples in this book. It was great fun to share the studio together again.

I would like to thank the folks at Glass Accessories International for their great glass cutters. They always make me look like a pro. Thanks to Lori at Glastar Corporation, Glass Accessories International, and Copper Tools for their unwavering support for more than 20 years. I appreciate the glass manufacturers Spectrum Glass Company, Bullseye, and Uroboros Glass for providing me with glass photos. Thanks to Randy and Carole Wardell at Wardell Publications and Ron Bovard for helping me track down more photos.

A special thank you to all my girlfriends, staff, and family who had to listen to me turn down invitations and new projects because "I have to work on my book!" You guys are great friends and allies. Special thanks to Dan Rutter for picking up the slack so I could play in my studio and to my daughter Sloan Rutter for her help and support.

I also want to thank my acquisitions editor, Erin Calligan Mooney , my project editor, Chrissy Guthrie, my copy editor, Amanda Langferman, and everyone else from Wiley who helped make this book what it is today.

Thank you to Mike LoBiondo for his great photos that really make this book pop! Next time, Mike, let's do the photo shoots when it isn't 95 degrees in the studio!

Publisher's Acknowledgments

We're proud of this book; please send us your comments at http://dummies.custhelp.com. For other comments, please contact our Customer Care Department within the U.S. at 877-762-2974, outside the U.S. at 317-572-3993, or fax 317-572-4002.

Some of the people who helped bring this book to market include the following:

Acquisitions, Editorial, and Media Development

Senior Project Editor: Christina Guthrie

Acquisitions Editors: Mike Baker, Erin Calligan Mooney

Copy Editor: Amanda Langferman

Assistant Editor: David Lutton

Technical Editor: Beverly S. Precious

Editorial Manager: Christine Meloy Beck

Editorial Assistants: Rachelle Amick; Jennette ElNaggar

Art Coordinator: Alicia B. South

Cartoons: Rich Tennant (www.the5thwave.com)

Composition Services

Project Coordinator: Sheree Montgomery

Layout and Graphics: Samantha K. Cherolis, Nikki Gately, Brent Savage

Special Art: Interior photos by Michael LoBiondo

Proofreaders: Laura Albert, Betty Kish

Indexer: Johnna VanHoose Dinse

Publishing and Editorial for Consumer Dummies

Diane Graves Steele, Vice President and Publisher, Consumer Dummies

Kristin Ferguson-Wagstaffe, Product Development Director, Consumer Dummies

Ensley Eikenburg, Associate Publisher, Travel

Kelly Regan, Editorial Director, Travel

Publishing for Technology Dummies

Andy Cummings, Vice President and Publisher, Dummies Technology/General User

Composition Services

Debbie Stailey, Director of Composition Services

Contents at a Glance

Table of Contents

Introduction

F or centuries, art glass has been ever-present in many parts of life; you find it in homes, churches, public spaces, and even restaurants. You can probably picture one or two beautiful pieces of glass that you've seen at some point, either up close and in person or in an art book. At first glance, you may think only true artists can create such magnificent works as these, but truth be told, glass working is more about craftsmanship than artistry. In this book, I introduce you to this fascinating art medium and help you develop the craft skills you need to create your own glass masterpieces.

About This Book

Art glass is a big umbrella that encompasses several different techniques, including stained glass and warm glass. The two most recognized stained-glass techniques are lead came and copper foil. You can use either construction method to create most stained-glass projects. In this book, you find instructions for both techniques, plus tips on choosing which technique to use for which project.

Warm glass, often called *fusing*, is all about heating glass to form it into different projects. One popular fusing technique, called *slumping*, actually involves shaping the glass into vases, bowls, jewelry, and other neat projects. Because more and more glass workers are embracing these warm-glass techniques, I dedicate a whole part of this book to warm glass and the unique project opportunities it presents.

So if you're interested in giving art glass a try, you've come to the right place! Although hands-on instruction is a great way to learn new glass-working techniques, finding an art center where you can take glass classes is becoming increasingly difficult. That's why I've written this book — to be the next best thing to having your own personal instructor. Sometimes a good book is even better than one-on-one instruction because it gives you the opportunity to go back and review particular steps or processes again and again until you master them. In addition to my written instructions, I include numerous full-color photos throughout this book that make it easy for you to see exactly what you need to do to get rolling with your new hobby.

Before I jump into the nitty-gritty of art glass, I help you set up your studio and fill it with all the necessary tools of the trade. Then I cover the basic techniques of working with glass from using a pattern to cutting your own glass to putting the pieces together. I give you plenty of step-by-step instruction to help you master the basics and then show you how to build on your skills to create fun and beautiful projects. With all the hands-on practice you get in this book, you may be surprised by how quickly you can develop your glass-working skills.

With more than 25 years of stained-glass instruction under my belt, I'm excited to get to share my love and knowledge of this beautiful art form with you. Although this book covers a lot of information, it's easy to follow, and you can adapt it to fit your current skill level. As you get ready to dive into the awesome world of art glass, I encourage you to concentrate on only one goal: to make your next project better than your last one. That way, you'll always be proud of your work.

Conventions Used in This Book

The techniques and projects in this book are meant to help you develop and improve your glass-working skills. To make the text easy to follow, I use the following conventions:

- Although I recommend that you use clear glass when you're first getting started (because it's more affordable), I use colored glass in this book's photographs to make it easier for you to see what I'm demonstrating.

- I include lots of project patterns in this book, and in case your space needs aren't quite the same as mine, I also provide instructions for enlarging these patterns if you want to do so.

- I use *italics* to point out new terms or add emphasis.

- I use **boldface** to indicate key words in bulleted lists and the action parts of numbered lists.

  Any extra explanatory text that helps you get a better handle on a particular step appears in roman text after the boldface step.

- Throughout the book, I use the terms *art glass, stained glass,* and *leaded glass* interchangeably.

- When writing measurements, I list the width first, followed by the height. (For example, a 4-x-5-inch piece of glass is 4 inches wide and 5 inches tall.)

- I indicate all temperatures in this book in degrees Fahrenheit.

- I use `monofont` to make Web sites stand out.

  When this book was printed, some Web addresses may have needed to break across two lines of text. If that happened, rest assured that I haven't put in any extra characters (such as hyphens) to indicate the break. So, when using one of these Web addresses, just type in exactly what you see in this book, pretending as though the line break doesn't exist.

What You're Not to Read

Throughout this book, I include a bit of information about the history of art glass because I think it's interesting to know more about how the medium became what it is today. Feel free to skip over this information if you want to cut to the chase and focus only on working with glass.

You'll know information is skippable if it appears in a sidebar (gray shaded box) or is marked with a Technical Stuff icon.

Foolish Assumptions

In writing this book, I made some assumptions about you:

- ✔ You have an appreciation for stained glass and other forms of art glass and want to know how to create your own stunning pieces.

- ✔ You have a space in your home to safely contain your new craft.

- ✔ You realize that you're working with glass, hot irons, kilns, and lead-based products that require special handling and safety precautions, including wearing safety glasses whenever you're working in your studio and following the manufacturer's recommendations regarding all power tools, like soldering irons and kilns.

- ✔ You may have some basic woodworking skills and want to build your own storage bins and work boards. For you, I include some step-by-step construction guidelines.

- ✔ You have an unlimited budget when it comes to investing in what I like to call "all the bells and whistles." Just kidding. Add to your collection of equipment as you have the money and inclination to do so. Note, though, that I introduce you to all the latest tools and equipment that will make this hobby as easy as possible for you with total disregard to your budget. Sorry!

How This Book Is Organized

I've organized this book like I do my classes. I start simple with the supplies and space you need to practice your new art form and go from there. Each part of the book focuses on a different aspect of working with glass. You can easily refer to the specific parts and chapters that contain the answers you're looking for at any particular moment without having to read the entire book. Of course, I secretly hope you read it cover to cover several times, but know that you don't have to. You can skip around to the topics that most interest you.

Part 1: Glass, Glorious Glass

Part I is more of an overview than a step-by-step manual. Here, I outline the tools and supplies you need to get started with your new glass-working hobby and show you how to set up your studio. I also introduce the two basic techniques used to create stained glass — copper foil and lead came — and tell you a little about warm glass, the hottest craze in glass studios today. And because the beauty and essence of this art form is the glass itself, I spend some time going over the various types of glasses you'll be working with and provide suggestions for how to work with them.

Part II: Easing Your Way into the Art: Basic Stained-Glass Techniques

This part is all about hands-on practice. In Chapter 4, I jump right into working with patterns for stained-glass projects. I realize you may not be an artist, so I supply lots of resources for finding designs and making them your own with little to no artistic ability required.

After you know how to use a pattern, I show you how to cut your glass pieces to fit it. Although glass cutting can be the scariest part of the hobby, it doesn't have to be. In Chapters 5 and 6, I share plenty of tips, techniques, and ideas to help you master the art of cutting glass and show you how to fine-tune your glass shapes to make them fit your patterns perfectly.

When you're ready to heat things up, I show you how to solder in Chapter 7. By following my helpful tips and tricks, you're sure to be a first-class solder master before you know it. To help keep you safe, I also talk about how to make your work environment a healthy and safe one when soldering.

Part III: Practice Makes Perfect: Stained-Glass Projects Aplenty

It's time to start building the stained-glass projects you've been dreaming about since you picked up this book. In Chapter 8, I show you how to tackle copper-foil projects, including how to work with foil, run the perfect solder bead, and use wire and patina to spice things up a bit. Then it's on to lead-came projects in Chapter 9, where I show you how to prepare your design, work with lead came, solder the perfect joints, and cement your finished panel to give it strength and beauty.

At the end of this part, stained-glass becomes three-dimensional as I show you how to create stunning stained-glass boxes and panel lampshades in Chapters 10 and 11. I also include a few additional project patterns in Chapter 12 so you can get some more practice with both copper and lead techniques. I just know you'll find a project that you can't wait to make next.

Part IV: Adding a Little Heat to the Mix: Working with Warm Glass

This part switches from traditional stained-glass techniques to warm-glass fusing. Because fusing is a whole new way of working with glass, you need to add some new equipment (most importantly, a glass kiln) and safety guide-lines to your studio. Don't worry, I cover everything you need to know about tools, supplies, and safety in Chapter 13 so you can start fusing right away!

Because most fusers don't work with patterns, I jump right into the nitty-gritty of warm glass in Chapter 14. I cover the importance of using compatible glass and introduce you to some fun, preformed glass shapes, like stringers, noodles, and frit, that you can use to decorate your projects. I also walk you through the basics of firing your glass to fuse the pieces together.

In Chapter 15, I show you how to take your fusing projects to the next level by using some more-advanced fusing techniques like stacking, weaving, and incorporating wire and fiber paper. When you're ready to raise the bar even higher, take a look at Chapter 16, where I show you how to use molds to slump and drape your glass into bowls, platters, and vases.

Part V: The Part of Tens

Soldering is the most difficult skill for most beginners to master, so I spend Chapter 17 going over ten strategies that can help you improve your soldering skills fast. To help you get a better feel for stained glass as an art as well as grow your own skills and techniques, I include a list of my favorite Louis C. Tiffany glass projects in Chapter 18. (In case you don't know, Louis C. Tiffany is the number-one, all-time master of stained glass.) Take some time to study these works; trust me, you'll see a big difference in your projects after you do!

Icons Used in This Book

In the margins of almost every page of this book, you find icons. They serve to direct you to particular types of information, including tips, practice exercises, technical tidbits, and more. Here's what the different icons mean:

 This icon contains important information that you want to file away for future use. The info marked with this icon often applies to more than one technique or process and is something you definitely don't want to forget as you build your glass projects.

 Just to keep the technical critics happy, I've included some fascinating albeit technical data that you don't absolutely have to know to be a successful glass artist. If you're in a hurry or just want to cover the basics, feel free to skip stuff marked with this icon.

 This icon points out important, time-saving ideas or suggestions you can use to improve your glass-working skills and make your projects go more smoothly.

 I use this icon to tell you when it's time for you to stop reading and have a little fun trying out a new technique.

 I use this icon a lot to point out when you need to pay attention for your safety's sake. Art glass naturally involves some hazardous materials that can be especially dangerous if you don't handle them properly. The last thing I want to happen is for you to hurt yourself or destroy a project, so when you see this icon, read the information that follows. Your safety — and the well-being of your project — depends on it!

Where to Go from Here

Stained glass is an art form that progresses step by step. So if you've never worked with glass before, I recommend that you start at the beginning and read at least through Chapter 8. At that point, you'll have enough knowledge to create a stained-glass window using the copper-foil technique. If you want to find out more about the lead-came technique, feel free to read through Chapter 9.The chapters on stained-glass boxes and lampshades are important if you're interested in making either one of those types of projects.

Part IV is all about warm-glass fusing, so you don't have to go there if you want to focus only on stained glass right now. But if you're most interested in warm glass, I suggest that you also read Chapter 5 about glass-cutting techniques so you don't hurt yourself or your glass as you begin your first fusing project.

Basically, just let your experience, skill level, and interests be your guide. For example, if you're an experienced glass worker but have been struggling with soldering, turn to Chapter 7 for an overview of soldering basics, and then look through Chapter 8 for copper-foil-specific instructions and Chapter 9 for lead-came instructions. Also take a look at Chapter 18 for some strategies for improving your soldering skills.

Part I
Glass, Glorious Glass

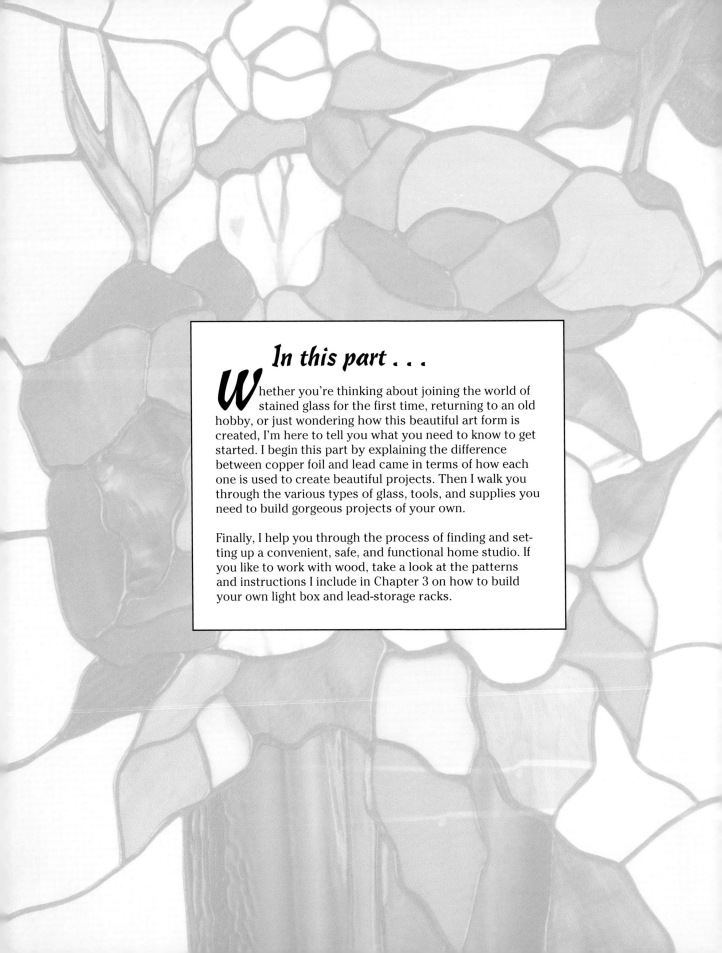

In this part . . .

Whether you're thinking about joining the world of stained glass for the first time, returning to an old hobby, or just wondering how this beautiful art form is created, I'm here to tell you what you need to know to get started. I begin this part by explaining the difference between copper foil and lead came in terms of how each one is used to create beautiful projects. Then I walk you through the various types of glass, tools, and supplies you need to build gorgeous projects of your own.

Finally, I help you through the process of finding and setting up a convenient, safe, and functional home studio. If you like to work with wood, take a look at the patterns and instructions I include in Chapter 3 on how to build your own light box and lead-storage racks.

Chapter 1

Welcome to the World of Glass

In This Chapter

▶ Discovering the different construction techniques used in stained glass

▶ Examining what's new in this traditional craft — warm glass

▶ Identifying various types and textures of glass

Glass is magical. It surrounds you in your home, office, place of worship, and many of the commercial establishments you visit on a daily basis. Although glass serves a very practical purpose today, in some cases, it also makes an important decorative statement (and that's where this book comes in).

The creation and history of glass itself has always held a certain mystery. As a super-cooled liquid, glass has the unique ability to capture light and glow from within. Even with such an awesome feature, though, the chemistry behind glass is really very simple — sand transformed by heat. The various colors you see in glass come from metallic salts and oxides: Gold produces red, silver produces yellow and gold, cobalt produces blue, and copper produces the greens and dark reds.

This vast array of glowing colors in glass enchants craftsman and artisans alike. So, too, does its permanency. After all, glass never fades and its colors never dull. This awesome feature allows the artist to literally paint an eternal image with glass.

In this chapter, you become familiar with the various craft styles used to create beautiful works of stained glass, and you get an introduction to the newest form of art glass: warm glass. Finally, you survey examples of the various types of glass available for you to work with.

A brief history of stained glass

The first real examples of stained glass appeared in the early European churches built around the tenth century. At that time, stained-glass windows became the storytellers of religious history. Artists used paint on glass to tell the stories of the Bible and other holy books.

In the 15th century, stained glass changed dramatically — not in the way the glass itself was made but in the way the artists created the finished products. With the rediscovery of silver stain during the Renaissance, glass paint colors went from dull black and gray to rich golden colors. (Silver stain is a paint that's applied to the surface of the glass and then fired in a kiln. The stain penetrates the surface and becomes a permanent part of the glass.) The Renaissance brought stained glass, with its many brilliant colors, into vogue for the next 300 years.

(continued)

(continued)

One of the best-known glass artists of all time, American Louis C. Tiffany, began his artistic career as a painter, but after he experimented with stained glass, he never went back to paint. As a young art student in Europe in 1869, Tiffany visited many of the churches and great buildings there. Inspired by the stained glass he saw, Tiffany embarked on a journey to find a glass that could both tell a story and glow from within (in other words, a glass that didn't have to be painted to shine with color). This journey toward colored glass required manufacturers to make glass in an infinite array of opalescent colors.

In the late 1800s, Thomas Edison, a good friend of Tiffany's, invented electric lighting. With this invention came an eagerness to show off the latest techno gadget — the electric lamp. Around the same time, Tiffany developed a stained-glass construction technique called *copper foiling*. Using this technique, he constructed stained-glass lampshades that surrounded the electric light and acted as a beacon for this new status symbol. Over the next 70 years, Tiffany's studio — together with dozens of other highly active studios throughout the eastern and midwestern United States — created thousands of beautiful stained-glass windows and lampshades.

As buildings changed over time, so did the art of stained glass. No changes are more obvious than the ones you see in the works of American architect Frank Lloyd Wright. He designed more than 1,000 stained-glass works. He called his glass works *light screens* because of their ability to shape the light in any space, much like the way Japanese rice-paper screens shaped light. Many of Wright's building designs incorporated stained-glass windows, doors, and lighting.

The arts and crafts movement embraced stained glass, too, but it made a few changes to the stained glass of Tiffany. In the stained-glass doors and panels that accented homes across the Midwest and California, clear glass replaced much of the heavy, opalescent glass. Designs were clean and geometric in style, fabricated from clear glass with just small touches of color. Many panels featured all-clear-glass designs. Thicker clear-glass pieces were facetted, creating bevel-shaped edges that captured the sunlight and sent a cascade of rainbows onto interior walls.

In the 1970s, stained glass made a comeback that incorporated larger-than-life splashes of brightly colored glass depicting such things as flowers and butterflies. With this comeback came the stained-glass hobby movement, which is where I (and you) come in.

Stained-Glass Techniques

Stained glass has many names, most common of which are *art glass, leaded glass,* and *copper-foiled glass.* The term *art glass* is interchangeable with stained glass, and both terms reference objects that you create using pieces of colored glass. Note that the colored glass used to create these projects is also called *stained glass* and *art glass.* Don't worry; because the terms are interchangeable, you can't really make a mistake referencing this art form.

The real difference comes in the terms *leaded glass* and *copper-foiled glass,* which describe the specific working techniques used to fabricate stained-glass projects. So what's the difference between these two techniques? The following sections are here to show you, so read on!

When you're ready to start your own stained-glass project, turn to Chapter 4 for tips on preparing your pattern, Chapter 5 for all the details on glass cutting, Chapter 6 for everything you need to know about grozing and grinding, and Chapter 7 for the ins and outs of soldering.

Leaded glass

Stained-glass artists generally use the leaded-glass technique for flat-panel works such as doors, windows, and screens. But you can also find examples of leaded-glass lampshades and boxes. This technique involves creating a leaded-glass panel by connecting pieces of glass together with strips of metal that have been shaped into *U-* or *H-*shaped profiles.

The metal strips used in the leaded-glass technique, called *cames,* come in a variety of widths and profiles, and they can be lead, brass, zinc, or copper. Metal cames are available in 6-foot lengths. Regardless of which metal makes up the came used to create a particular panel, all panels fabricated from cames are called *leaded-glass panels.*

As for which type of came is used for what, cames shaped into *U* profiles typically go around the perimeters of panels (see Figure 1-1 for an example). And cames shaped into *H* profiles link the interior glass pieces together (see Figure 1-2 for an example).

Each intersection where two or more cames meet is called a *joint* (see Figure 1-3). Each joint is soldered together on both the front and back sides of the panel. This double-soldering gives strength to the whole panel.

Head to Chapter 9 if you're interested specifically in leaded-glass projects.

Figure 1-1:
Lead came shaped into a *U* profile goes around the perimeter of a glass panel.

Figure 1-2:
Lead came shaped into an *H* profile links the interior pieces of a panel together.

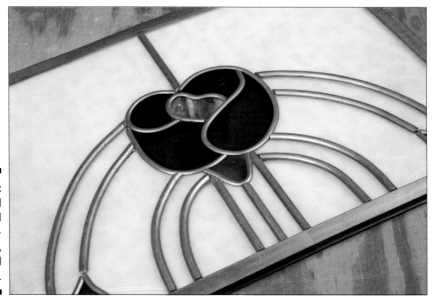

Figure 1-3:
Several unsoldered lead inter-sections, also called joints.

Copper-foiled glass

Using the copper-foil technique to create stained glass involves wrapping thin strips of copper-foil tape around the edges of each individual piece of glass. The foil is crimped around the edges of the glass, creating a copper frame (see Figure 1-4).

Figure 1-4:
Copper-
foiled glass
pieces.

The copper-foil technique revolutionized the way artists worked with glass (before its development, stained glass had been utilized only in flat panels and panel lamps). American artist Louis C. Tiffany employed the copper-foil technique to fashion his highly sought after lampshades. A hundred years later, stained-glass artists are still working to improve the method. Today, you can buy precut strips of copper foil in a variety of widths. The foil is much thinner and easier to manipulate than it was in Tiffany's day, and it comes with an adhesive already applied to the back of the foil, which allows it to adhere to the edges of the glass, making the whole application process much easier.

Copper foil allows the artist to use very small pieces of glass to execute the most detailed designs. Foiled glass pieces easily contour to fit almost any curved surface. The invention of this technique was critical in allowing Tiffany and other glass artists of the early 1900s to create not only beautifully formed lampshades but also to develop other practices such as double-plating glass pieces to create unique shading effects for panels and shades.

If copper foil sounds like fun, head to Chapter 8, where I feature several projects that use this technique.

Adding a Little Heat: Warm Glass

Art glass includes lots of different construction techniques and processes. One of today's most popular processes is *warm glass*. Warm glass uses some of the same basic skills that are needed in stained glass, such as glass cutting and fitting templates to patterns, but instead of using metal and solder to hold projects together, you heat warm-glass pieces in a kiln.

Although you can use many of the same tools for warm glass that you'd use for stained glass, you do need to purchase some special equipment — namely, an electric glass kiln. You also need to make sure you're using the proper glass, as well as make sure that all the glasses you're using are compatible with each other (glasses that aren't compatible will crack and fall apart during or after firing). Head to Chapter 13 if you're interested in what it takes to set up a functioning warm glass studio.

Warm glass basically breaks down into the following techniques:

✔ **Fusing:** When you're fusing glass, you heat the pieces of glass to the point that the glass "fuses" together to form a solid piece of glass.

Fusing can be as basic as attaching some decorative glass pieces to a small sheet of glass (see Chapter 14) or as complicated as layering different types and colors of glass into a particular picture or design (see Chapter 15).

✔ **Slumping:** Slumping, or *shaping,* involves using molds to turn glass into bowls, platters, vases, and other three-dimensional shapes. Depending on the type of mold and type of project, you either slump the glass around the mold or into it.

Slumping is done at a lower temperature than fusing, so you first fuse your glass pieces together to get the desired coloring and design, and then you slump them to achieve whatever shape you want (assuming you want something three-dimensional). Figure 1-5 shows a vase that's been both fused and slumped.

Warm glass is usually more free-form than stained glass, so it appeals to a lot of people who don't want to mess with the precision and construction techniques that lead and copper-foil projects require. You can certainly jump into warm glass without figuring out how to do copper-foil or lead-came stained glass, but I recommend that you spend some time learning how to cut glass in Chapter 5 before you move on to Part IV, which covers warm glass in detail.

Figure 1-5:
Warm-glass techniques allow you to create vases like this one.

Warming up to the new kid on the block: A brief history of warm glass

In the middle of the 20th century, glass artists became fascinated with the possibilities of *sagging* (or bending) glass, a process that automakers had been using for years to make curved windshields. The first artists to experiment with bending glass primarily worked with methods that combined gilding, enameling, and laminating, often sandwiching other substances between layers of clear glass.

Then came Harriett Anderson, who spent most of her artistic career developing glass kilns that could be installed in residential settings. Kilns allow artists to take pieces of glass and refire them. While the glass is hot, artists can slump it into or over a ceramic mold to create bowls, platters, vases, and uniquely formed pieces of glass that the artists can then incorporate into traditional stained-glass panels.

In the early 1980s, a band of young glass makers in the northeastern United States began experimenting with this new glass-refiring process. To describe their work, they coined the term *fused glass*. The work of these young artists signified the beginning of the *Warm Glass* movement. Their backyard experiments lead to the development of new glass kilns, molds, materials, and finally a completely new glass-manufacturing process.

Getting to Know Glass

The art of stained glass primarily involves two categories of glass:

- **Cathedral glass:** This transparent glass is made from a clear base and then color is added; as a result, it's available in a vast array of colors. The glass's level of transparency ranges from clear to almost opaque. See Figure 1-6a.

- **Opalescent glass:** Glass with a white base is mixed with various minerals and compounds to create this type of glass, which is opaque in nature. Opalescent glass (also called *opals* for short) captures light within itself and transmits a glow from within. It can be a combination of two to five different colors of glass. See Figure 1-6b.

Figure 1-6: Cathedral glass versus opalescent glass.

Feeling the heat: Glass manufacturing

The manufacturing process used to produce sheets of art glass is still pretty basic. Glass is made up of melted silica sand combined with potash or soda ash and limestone. Glass makers heat this mineral mixture in a large glass furnace to a temperature between 1,700 and 2,500 degrees, at which point the mixture becomes a liquid. The makers remove some of the molten glass from the furnace and transport it to a steel table. They case the glass onto the surface. If the particular art sheet requires more than one color of glass, the makers add another scoop of molten glass from a different furnace. The molten glass then passes through a single metal roller, which flattens it into a thin sheet. (In case you're curious, America is the leading manufacturer of sheets of art glass today; many of the factories that started making glass more than 100 years ago are still family owned and operated.)

Stemming from these two major categories are dozens of varying hues, textures, and levels of transparency. For example, a sheet of glass can contain several colors within that one piece. The colors can appear transparent or semi-transparent. A texture on the backside of a piece of cathedral glass can make it impossible to see through but it is still considered cathedral. Sound confusing? Not to worry. It doesn't matter what the manufacturer labels his glass; what matters is the fact that you like it and want to use it in your project.

In this section, I introduce you to several types of art glass, so you can begin to get an idea of the vast array of choices that await you as you begin your new hobby. (Check out Chapter 4 for more suggestions on which types of glass to use for different types of projects.)

Surveying different glass types

The fact that you can to mix various colors, textures, and types of glasses together is what makes glass projects so interesting and unique. But don't forget that you can also create a wonderful stained-glass or warm-glass project using just clear, smooth glass. For each technique in this book I give you suggestions and ideas for working with many of these different types of glasses.

The following list not only introduces you to types of glass that work well for stained-glass and/or warm-glass projects but also alerts you to some types of glass that aren't suitable for use in art glass projects of any kind:

- ✔ **Float glass:** This clear glass is manufactured primarily for residential and commercial installation. It can vary in thickness from $\frac{1}{16}$ inch to 2 inches.

  Float glass makes for great practice glass when you're just starting to develop your glass-cutting skills because it's so affordable; it's also easier to see your score line on float glass.

- ✔ **Tempered glass:** Tempered glass, or *safety glass*, as it's sometimes called, is a type of float glass that has been put through a special annealing process (*annealing* refers to the temperature the glass was cooled to during the manufacturing process). When tempered glass is broken, it breaks into thousands of tiny pieces rather than large sharp shards of glass that could fall like a guillotine when broken. Large sheets of tempered glass are often used in commercial installations. ***Note:*** It *cannot* be used for stained glass or for fusing.

- **Laminated glass:** A thin sheet of plastic is laminated between two sheets of thin float glass to create this type of safety glass. When broken, laminated glass remains intact. The window shield of your car is made of laminated glass. You can't use this glass for stained-glass projects, but you can use it for slumping (a warm-glass technique done in a kiln that reshapes the glass).

- **Beveled glass:** To make beveled glass, the edges of ¼-inch-thick clear float glass are ground down to 45-degree angles using diamond wheels. The 45-degree angle catches the light and reflects it back into rainbow prisms that bounce around the walls. Beveled glass is beautiful for stained glass, but it can't be used for warm glass.

- **Wispy glass:** This glass can be either cathedral or opalescent. The glass has a base color of clear if it's cathedral and white if it's opalescent. Additional colors of glass are then added to this base color to create the finished product. Wispy glass can include one or more colors in the mix. You can use it in stained glass and in warm glass as long as it's compatible with the other glasses being used in that warm-glass project.

- **Mirrored glass:** The back of this glass is coated with a silver paint that's baked on. The result is reflective glass. Mirrored glass also comes in colors and various textures. It is used primarily for stained-glass projects, not for warm glass.

- **Iridescent glass:** To create iridescent glass, metallic oxide is sprayed onto the glass after it first comes out of the furnace while it's still hot. As a result, an iridescent finish is permanently adhered to the surface. You can use iridescent glass in stained glass and warm glass.

Touch and feel: Taking a look at textured glass

Glass makers create various glass textures while the glass is still molten (check out the nearby sidebar "Feeling the heat: Glass manufacturing" for more on the hot process used to make glass). Glass makers create most of these effects by passing molten glass through a textured roller. One side of the glass is left smooth, while the other side takes on the impression of the roller. Cathedral glass is the most commonly used glass, but opalescent glass can also be textured. The following list includes examples of textured glass. (Unless otherwise noted, the glass works for both stained-glass and warm-glass projects.)

- **Drapery glass:** Drapery glass has been manipulated while hot to create gentle folds, much like the ones you see in draperies. See Figure 1-7a.

- **Rippled glass:** Small wavy patterns appear on this glass's surface. The ripples are created as the glass passes though an embossing roller, and they can be formed into various shapes, including herringbone. See Figure 1-7b.

- **Hammered glass:** Small round dents appear on the back surface of this glass; this effect is created as the glass passes through an embossing roller. See Figure 1-7c.

- **Granite-back glass:** A random raised texture, like granules of sand, appear on the back side of this glass. See Figure 1-7d.

- **Crackled glass:** This glass is blown into a large cylinder and then dipped into cool water, causing a random crackling of just the surface layer of the glass. The cylinder is reheated, scored, and flattened to form a sheet of glass. The resulting texture looks a bit like crocodile skin. Crackled glass can be used in stained glass but doesn't do well in warm-glass projects. See Figure 1-7e.

- **Seedy glass:** Small air bubbles are injected into this glass before it's rolled into sheets. The air bubbles or seeds distort the clarity of the glass and provide an interesting texture that resembles little bubbles trapped inside the glass. It's available only in cathedral glass. See Figure 1-7f.

- **Fractured and streamered glass:** Small, thin chips of glass (called *fractures*) and thin glass strings (called *streamers*) are arranged on the steel casting table before hot glass is poured onto it. They stick to the surface of the glass and provide a beautiful effect. Famed glass artist Louis C. Tiffany likely invented this glass texture for use in his landscape windows. See Figure 1-7g.

- **Mottled glass:** To create this texture, crystal growth is allowed to occur inside opalescent glass. The result is ring-shaped areas of opacity scattered throughout the sheet of glass. See Figure 1-7h.

Be aware that textured glasses can lose some or all of their texture if used in warm-glass projects that are fired above 1,250 degrees. Always test a sample of the glass before using it in a warm-glass project.

All the various textures, types, and colors of sheet glass provide tools for the glass artist's imagination. The great joy of working with glass is the unlimited supply and variety of sheet glass you have to choose from as you create your different projects. I find myself collecting sheets of glass much like a quilter would collect fabrics. You never know when you might need a piece of pink and lime-green fractured glass to create the perfect backdrop for a spring landscape window.

The color of glass can change from batch to batch. Always make sure you purchase ample amounts of each glass color before you start a particular project so you don't run out of glass before you finish your project.

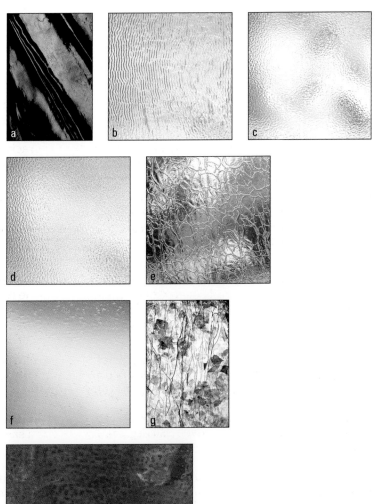

Figure 1-7: An assortment of available textures.

Chapter 2

Getting Started with the Right Tools

In This Chapter

▶ Selecting the glass-cutting tools and soldering equipment you need to get started

▶ Turning on the power with saws and grinders

▶ Choosing the right tools for lead-based versus foil-based projects

▶ Keeping it safe with the right safety equipment

▶ Adding some basic drafting supplies to your stained-glass toolbox

*B*efore you can start your first stained-glass project, you need to grab a few unique tools that you probably don't already have in your toolbox. Lucky for you, this chapter shows you exactly what you need and why you need it; it also explains a couple of different options you have, depending on which type of stained glass you plan to do.

When it comes to tools of the trade, I'm not a gimmicky kind of person — I like to stick to the basics whenever possible. However, I don't believe in skimping on quality. I learned this lesson the hard way when I first started working with glass. Because I was working on a limited budget and didn't know whether I'd excel or even like this hobby, I purchased really inexpensive tools. Within a couple of months, I had to replace those tools with ones of better quality. Turns out that a superior tool really does help you excel quicker and results in a lot less frustration. If you start with the right tools, you're sure to enjoy the experience much sooner than I did!

Knowing which tool is the right tool isn't always easy; the most expensive tool isn't always the greatest tool for the job. I do my best to help you decide which tools are right for you throughout this chapter. After you know which tools you need, you can purchase them through your local stained-glass retailer or online. I recommend that you shop with a local retailer, if possible, so that you can actually handle the tools before you buy them.

Getting a Handle on Hand Tools

Stained glass is a hands-on craft, so it's no surprise that you need to purchase a few hand tools before you can start making your projects. In general, the term *hand tools* refers to the nonpower tools you hold in your hand when creating stained-glass projects; they include glass cutters, pliers, and lead knives. I discuss cutters and pliers in the following sections. (For info on lead knives, go to the section "Looking at lead-specific tools.")

Take your time selecting your hand tools. You want them to fit your hands comfortably because you can easily spend eight to ten hours just cutting out glass shapes — and you don't want to be in pain the whole time. If the tools you buy hurt your hands after only a few minutes of cutting, imagine how much pain you'll feel after ten hours!

Glass cutters

Your glass cutter is the most important tool purchase you have to make. A *glass cutter* is a hand-held tool that houses a wheel that scratches the surface of the glass, releasing the tension in the glass and allowing it to break along the scratch (also called the *score line*). A quality glass cutter allows you to cut the glass shapes you need without excessive breakage.

Don't skimp on your glass cutter. Working with a poor-quality glass cutter will undoubtedly destroy your spirit and your checkbook. Invest in a good, brand-name, quality glass cutter, and you'll become a better glass cutter faster.

When I'm shopping for a new cutter, I go straight to the self-oiling glass cutters with carbide cutting wheels. A *self-oiling cutter* applies a small, consistent coating of cutting oil to the wheel as it rolls across the surface of the glass. The cutting oil keeps the score line lubricated and easier to break. The oil also protects your cutting wheel and makes it last longer. The *carbide wheel* is harder than the standard steel wheel and helps keep the edge of the wheel sharp for many quality hours of cutting.

You can find lots of different styles of self-oiling glass cutters anywhere from basic to quite high-tech (see Figure 2-1). The various styles of cutters, which I discuss in the following sections, are designed for different hand sizes and cutting techniques. They come with either stationary cutting heads or heads that swivel when you score curved lines. I prefer a swivel head because it makes scoring around curved pattern lines easier.

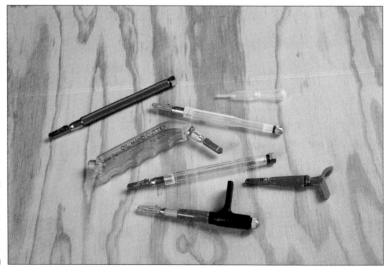

Figure 2-1:
A variety
of glass
cutters.

If possible, try out a few different glass cutters before you make your selection. After all, you want your cutter to feel comfortable in your hand when you're cutting glass, not just when you're holding it in the store!

Barrel cutter

The most common style of self-oiling cutter is the *barrel cutter* (see Figure 2-2). This cutter has a swivel cutting head and a barrel that's designed for comfort in your hand; the barrel serves as the oil reservoir. You can choose a barrel cutter with either a lightweight acrylic barrel or a heavier metal one; they perform equally well, so pick the one that's most comfortable.

My personal favorite is the TOYO Comfort Grip acrylic barrel cutter because the barrel is smaller and seems to be a better fit for my hand. I also like the fact that this particular cutter comes in a variety of bright colors so I can find it easily on my workbench.

Pistol-grip cutter

If you have arthritis or difficulty holding finger tension for extended periods of time, the *pistol-grip cutter* may be a good option for you. This cutter is designed to fit comfortably into the palm of your hand, taking the pressure off your fingers (see Figure 2-3). The pistol-grip cutter has the same swivel cutting head as the barrel cutter, so it cuts just as well.

Strip-and-circle cutter

A strip-and-circle cutter isn't a necessary tool, but I highly recommend getting one, especially if you want to make glass boxes or lampshades (see Chapters 10 and 11 for details). As its name indicates, you use the *strip-and-circle cutter* (also called just a *strip cutter*) to cut straight strips of glass and circles. You can adjust the tool to cut almost any size of glass strips from ½ inch up to 8 to 10 inches (see Figure 2-4a). It also easily converts into a circle cutter, allowing you to cut circles of glass (see Figure 2-4b).

Figure 2-2:
A barrel cutter and the proper way to position it in your hand.

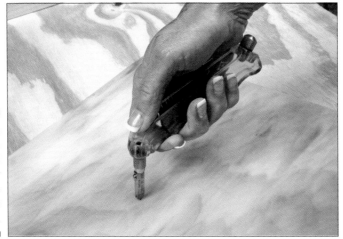

Figure 2-3:
A pistol-grip
cutter and
the proper
way to
position it in
your hand.

Figure 2-4:
The ver-
satility of
this cutter
makes it
a handy
addition to
your glass-
cutting
toolbox.

A variety of pliers

As you move through different stained-glass projects, you'll use a variety of different hand-held glass-breaking pliers. Each type of pliers provides you with the leverage you need when breaking glass. The following sections introduce you to the various types of pliers you'll need for all your projects.

Breaking pliers

The most basic pliers are the *breaking pliers,* which you can see in Figure 2-5. The inside of the pliers' jaws are smooth so they don't scratch the glass. Breaking pliers act as an extension of your hands when you're breaking smaller pieces of glass and need more leverage. For details on how to use breaking pliers to break and split glass, turn to Chapter 5.

I keep two pairs of breaking pliers in my studio for those times when I need to split a narrow strip of glass.

Running pliers

Compared to other types of pliers, *running pliers* provide more consistent leverage when breaking straight lines and larger sheets of glass. You can adjust them to accommodate varying thicknesses of glass simply by turning the set screw on the top of the pliers (see Figure 2-6). The pliers' curved jaws apply equal amounts of pressure simultaneously to each side of the score line. They're especially helpful when you use them in combination with a strip cutter. (Check out Chapter 5 to find out how to use running pliers.)

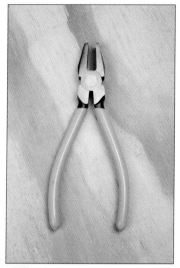

Figure 2-5:
Breaking
pliers.

Figure 2-6:
Running
pliers.

Grozing pliers

Grozing pliers, which are shown in Figure 2-7, are the glass cutter's best friend and a necessary tool to add to your stained-glass toolbox; you use them to smooth out your broken glass pieces. After you successfully cut the glass, small shards of glass remain along the edges. The ridges on the inside jaws of the grozing pliers act like a file to clean up any excess glass from your cut pieces. Turn to Chapter 6 to find out how to use grozing pliers.

Figure 2-7:
Grozing
pliers.

Don't skimp on your grozing pliers. Buy a pair that's made from quality steel so the ridges don't wear down too quickly. After all, a good pair of grozing pliers will save you hours of prep time on your projects.

Warming Up to Soldering Equipment

Next to selecting glass for my stained-glass projects, soldering is my most favorite task, but it's also the task that takes the most practice to perfect. The stakes are high when it comes to soldering because it's the skill that proves to other glass workers that you know your stuff. But don't worry — I have lots of easy-to-master techniques that'll have you soldering like a pro in no time. (Check out Chapter 7 for soldering tips and how-to info.)

In this section, I show you what tools you need to add to your toolbox to become a soldering pro. As you choose your soldering tools, keep in mind that quality is of utmost importance. Poor-performing soldering irons, unreliable *rheostats* (temperature controllers), or other low-quality pieces of equipment will crush your skills fast — so pay careful attention to the advice I offer in the following sections.

Soldering irons

Like a cook who uses a variety of pots and pans in the kitchen, I use several different soldering irons in my studio. Each one provides its own unique soldering experience.

When you think about soldering, the first image that pops into your head may be a soldering gun. Well, erase that image immediately! Stained-glass artists don't use soldering guns on their work because guns don't deliver constant, consistent heat. Instead, you need to use an 80- to 100-watt soldering iron on your stained-glass projects. In general, the faster you work, the higher wattage you want.

In addition to choosing an iron with the correct wattage, you have to decide which kind of temperature control you want in your iron. Your two choices are a thermostatically controlled iron or an iron controlled with an external rheostat; I describe the two types in the following sections. If you can afford only one type of iron, I recommend you start with a thermostatically controlled iron because it's a little easier to work with. Then, as your interest develops, so will your toolbox.

Thermostatically controlled iron

A *thermostatically controlled iron* uses a thermostat inside the soldering tip itself; this thermostat switches power on and off to the heating elements. The temperature is preset by the manufacturer. The iron heats up to that preset temperature and maintains it throughout the entire soldering process. If you want a higher temperature, you just change out the soldering tip for one with a hotter setting. Figure 2-8 shows a thermostatically controlled iron tip.

Weller soldering irons are my favorite ones to use because they perform consistently and last a long time. Figure 2-9 shows one of these irons.

Figure 2-8: A thermostatically controlled iron tip showing its temperature number.

External rheostat

The second way to control the temperature of your soldering iron is to use an external rheostat. You plug your iron into the rheostat and then make all your temperature adjustments via the rheostat. Figure 2-10 shows an iron that's connected to an external rheostat.

Some soldering iron manufacturers make matched sets, which means your soldering iron and the rheostat that comes with it are engineered to work perfectly together. If you don't want to buy a set, you can find a variety of 80- to 100-watt soldering irons that can be controlled with a rheostat.

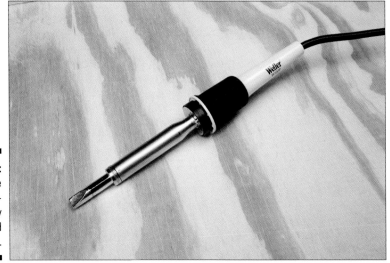

Figure 2-9:
An example
of a ther-
mostatically
controlled
iron.

Figure 2-10:
Soldering
iron with
an external
rheostat.

Be aware that a rheostat is only capable of reducing the amount of electricity flowing to the iron, thus slowing down the working temperature of the iron. The rheostat doesn't change the iron's temperature immediately, which is why it's always necessary to test your iron before you start soldering — especially when you're working with lead came.

Never ever plug a thermostatically controlled soldering iron into a rheostat. Doing so will ruin your iron.

Soldering iron tips

The key to the soldering iron's heat is the tip. Soldering iron tips come in a variety of sizes (see Figure 2-11). Which size tip you use with your iron depends on your iron's wattage. The bigger the wattage, the wider the tip you can use. For example, most lead-came soldering requires that you use a 100-watt iron with a tip that measures ⅜ inch wide; most copper-foil projects, on the other hand, use irons with more wattage with tips that are ¼ inch wide.

WARNING!

Don't mix brands of irons and tips. Stick with the recommended size and brand for your specific iron. Otherwise, you may void your iron's warranty or, worse, have an iron that doesn't perform at its maximum capability.

Soldering iron tips wear out over time, so if you have trouble keeping your soldering iron tip shinny when heated, you may need to replace it.

Figure 2-11:
Soldering
iron tips
come in
different
sizes.

Soldering iron stands

Although all irons come with small metal stands, I recommend that you purchase a sturdy, upright stand with a weighted bottom that will keep your iron from tipping over or rolling off the stand (see Figure 2-12 for an example of a sturdy stand). The best stands come with built-in spaces to hold a clean, damp sponge for cleaning your soldering tip while you work.

TIP

Soldering iron stands are one area where you can save some money. Select a quality iron stand that fits your iron, but don't go overboard. You'd be surprised by how many high-tech, high-priced stands are out there!

Tip cleaners

Fluxes, dirt, and oils collect on hot soldering tips. To keep your soldering iron tip looking good (and working well), you need to clean it often and gently with a clean, wet sponge called a *tip cleaner*. Be sure to always use a natural or cellulose sponge and never a synthetic sponge. You can keep your tip cleaner in your iron stand or in a separate waterproof container. Wherever you keep it, get in the habit of rinsing out your tip cleaner after each soldering session. When it begins to look dirty, replace it.

Figure 2-12:
Sturdy iron
stand with
weighted
bottom.

Don't use abrasive metals, like brass wool, or sal ammoniac to clean your soldering tip because they can damage the chrome plating on your tip.

Never clean a cold soldering iron tip. Always wait until it has heated up to a working temperature, and then wipe it across a clean, wet sponge. Be sure to wipe all four sides of the tip.

Solder

Stained-glass solder is a blend of tin and lead and has a solid core. The more tin content the solder has, the faster it melts. The kind of solder you need to use depends on the type of project you're working on. The two most common solder blends are 60 percent tin and 40 percent lead (called *60/40 solder*), which you use for copper-foil projects, and solder with equal amounts of tin and lead (called *50/50 solder*), which you use for lead-came projects.

Getting Turned On to Power Tools

In the 1970s, the stained-glass hobby movement really took off thanks to the invention of the diamond glass grinder and other power tools. Isn't it funny how a simple invention can make such a big difference in an art form? In the case of stained glass, the invention of these power tools made it possible for a novice to create beautiful works of art.

In this section, I introduce you to the power tools that are essential for stained-glass projects.

Glass grinders

Before you get started with any stained-glass project, you need to buy a *glass grinder* (a power tool that fine-tunes the cut shape of a glass piece so that it fits perfectly into your stained-glass project pattern). Grinders can be one of the more expensive investments you make, but don't worry too much; you only have to buy one.

Although all grinders essentially do the same job, they come in various sizes (see Figure 2-13); how big your grinder is depends on what types of projects you plan to make. If you want to make doors and windows, you'll need a pretty big grinder. But if lamps, jewelry, sun catchers, and boxes are more your style, save your money and buy a smaller grinder.

Figure 2-13: Glass grinders come in different sizes.

The part of the grinder that actually does the cutting is called the *grinder bit*. Grinder bits are nickel plated with diamond chips embedded into the plating. Bits come in a variety of sizes and shapes to match just about any glass-grinding job you can have (see Figure 2-14). I suggest that you always have on hand a standard ¾-inch bit for most grinding jobs and a ¼-inch bit for tough jobs that require getting into tight inside curves.

Don't throw away your old grinder bits when they start getting dull. Instead, save them and use them for projects involving soft glass that chips easily, like antique and mirror.

Figure 2-14:
Assortment
of grinder
bits.

Saws

When your stained-glass project requires that you cut out a really difficult glass shape or cut through metal or thick slabs of elaborately textured glass, such as drapery or rippled glass, you need to use a glass saw. As an added bonus, you can stack up layers of glass and use a glass saw to cut several pieces at once for production work or lamp making.

The two basic types of glass saws are the ring saw and the band saw, both of which are water cooled. A third, more advanced saw is the metal came saw. It's a real time saver when you're working with hard metals such as brass, zinc, and copper, and it allows you to cut angles fast and accurately.

These three glass saws are luxury tools. You don't have to have them, but they definitely make a nice addition to your studio. I discuss each saw in more detail next.

Ring saw

The most versatile glass saw is the *ring saw* (see Figure 2-15); you can use it to cut complex curves and any thickness of glass. The ring saw's round diamond-coated blade allows you to cut in any direction. As the blade rotates, it passes through a water reservoir, keeping it cool and keeping your glass from cracking. Ring saws aren't cheap, but their versatility and easy-to-use style makes them a great addition to your stained-glass toolbox. Plus, they save you money by reducing glass waste.

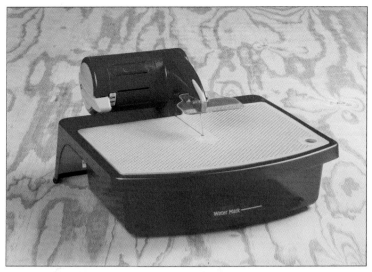

Figure 2-15:
A ring saw.

Band saw

If you want a glass saw but are working on a tight budget, consider buying a band saw. It's less expensive than the ring saw, but it's also a little more difficult to maintain. Because the saw blade is a flat metal blade with a diamond edge, you can cut in only one direction, and, if you force the blade, it'll break.

Metal came saws

I like to use hard metals when a project calls for joining together two or more pieces of glass because they provide additional strength and stability. The drawbacks are that you need a machine to bend hard metal and you have to use a metal came saw to trim the hard metal strips to size.

A *metal came saw* is a small, circular table saw that has a fiber blade (as compared to the metal blade in a wood saw). The fiber blade cuts through hard metals smoothly without leaving jagged edges. Metal came saws cost about the same price as a small glass grinder — less than $100 — and are fairly easy to maintain. The more expensive ones are safer to operate, and their blades are easier to set to position for different cutting angles. Replacement blades are affordable and available at glass shops and online.

Some of the metal came saws available today are a little too scary for me. They have a small work surface, it's hard to set cutting angles on them, and I'm always afraid I'm going to loose a finger or two when I use them. I prefer the came saws that are designed like small wood-chop saws. They have a feature that allows you to lock the cames into place, thus keeping your fingers away from the cutting action, and the angles are easy to set on them (see Figure 2-16 for an example).

The ends of the cames get really hot when cut, so be sure not to touch them until after they cool off. If the metal has small chips or jagged edges, you can file them off with a metal file after the metal has cooled.

Figure 2-16:
A metal
came saw.

When I first started working with glass, I used a hacksaw to trim the hard metals. Doing so took time and lots of elbow grease — after all, a simple window can easily have 30 to 100 cuts. But it got the job done.

If you don't want to buy a special metal came saw, you can use a hacksaw to make a few cuts when necessary. Just be sure to use a 32-tooth saw blade in your hacksaw. Doing so will make the work go faster.

Constructing Your Project with the Right Tools

When it comes to constructing your stained-glass project, you have two different techniques to choose from: leaded glass and foiled glass. Which technique you choose depends on the design of the project and the pattern you're using to create it. (See Chapter 4 for everything you need to know about project designs and patterns; see the later section "Assembling Basic Drafting Supplies" for details on what tools you need to design your project.)

No matter which technique you use to fabricate your stained-glass projects, the tools you use to get your glass ready to be fused together are basically the same. But when it comes to fabrication, you need separate tools for each technique.

Looking at lead-specific tools

The most traditional stained-glass construction method is called *leaded glass*. This technique involves assembling individual pieces of glass using lead strips with *U*- or *H*-shaped channels; these strips are called *cames*. Lead came strips come in 6-foot lengths and are very soft and pliable, and most of the tools you need for leaded-glass construction deal with these strips.

Lead vise and pliers

Before you can use lead-came strips to create your lead project, you need to stretch them to give them strength and straighten out any kinks or curves caused by being handled. That's where these first two tools — the lead vise and pliers — come in handy.

To stretch out the lead came, you need to mount a lead vise onto a counter-top or worktable (see Figure 2-17). The vise holds one end of the lead firmly in place while you grasp the other end with a pair of household pliers. You then pull or stretch the lead about 1 to 2 inches. Then you just have to trim the ends with a lead knife or pair of nippers (which I describe in the next section) and discard them.

Lead knives and nippers

Sounds like a chorus from a heavy metal band, right? Actually, you use these two tools to trim lead cames during the leaded-glass construction process. Each time one strip of lead intersects another strip, you have to trim or miter it to create a well-fitting joint. (In case you're wondering, *miter* means to cut an angle that follows the edge of the intercepting came strip.)

The more traditional tool for trimming lead cames is the lead knife (see Figure 2-18). Stained-glass artists angle the knife's blade to produce beautiful, long-flowing angles — which, to me, is where the real craftsmanship comes in. Keeping a sharp lead knife and using it to perfectly trim a lead came is the true mark of the stained-glass art.

You can use the lead inlay at the butt of the knife's handle to tap glass pieces into the came channels and to hammer in nails.

The better the lead intersections fit together, the easier it is to solder perfect joints. (See Chapters 7 and 9 for everything you need to know about soldering perfect joints.)

Figure 2-17:
Lead vise
mounted on
a worktable.

Figure 2-18:
A lead knife
and a cut
came.

You can also use *lead nippers* to trim the lead strips. Lead nippers are designed to trim the cames into various shapes and angles. One side yields a flat cut, the other a pointed cut (see Figure 2-19 for some examples of these cuts). By varying the position of the nippers, the artist can cut an unlimited number of angles.

Horseshoe nails and a wooden work board

During the leaded-glass construction process, you work on a wooden work board and use horseshoe nails and small pieces of lead (called *spacers*) to secure parts of the glass panel. Horseshoe nails are flat on two sides, so they're easy to hammer in and remove (see Figure 2-20). The flat sides keep the spacers from moving.

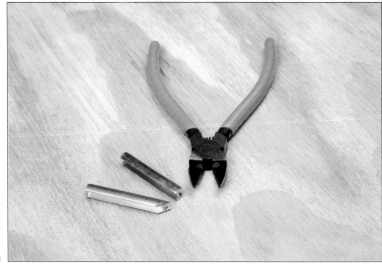

Figure 2-19:
Lead
nippers
and some
angles they
can cut.

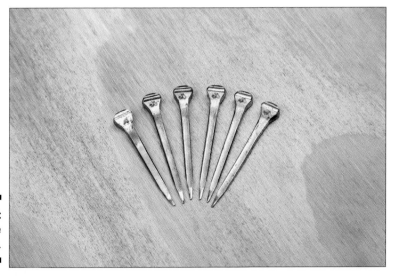

Figure 2-20:
Horseshoe
nails.

As far as the wooden work board is concerned, always build the biggest board your space allows (you'll be happy you did!). I built my studio work board from a 4-x-8-x-½-inch piece of plywood. I attached two 2-x-2-x-½-inch boards to the sides of the work board, creating a right angle. See Chapter 9 for more details on setting up a work board for your lead-came projects.

You can't build a stained-glass project that's larger than your work board.

Focusing on foil-specific tools

The other technique you can use to construct your stained-glass project is called *copper-foiled glass.* It uses copper foil rather than metal cames to join the glass pieces together, and it requires that you add a few more tools to your stained-glass toolbox. This section takes a look at what those tools are. (Check out Chapter 7 for tips on how to solder foil projects and Chapter 8 for instructions on how to build some complete foiled-glass projects.)

Rollers and lathkins

In foiled-glass construction, you have to handwrap and crimp the copper foil around the outside edges of each glass piece. This process is fairly labor intensive, but, with the right tools, it can be greatly improved.

The first tool you can use to make the copper-wrapping process easier is called the *Foilmate roller.* This simple hand tool, which I invented when I was a young glass worker, uses a curved wheel and a flat roller to smooth, crimp, and burnish the foil around the glass shape (see Figure 2-21).

You can also do this process with your hands and a Popsicle stick or a *lathkin,* a plastic or wooden tool that's used to burnish copper foil to the glass. Really, anything that helps you burnish the foil tightly to the glass will work here, although I've always thought the perfect foiling machine would be one into which you pour the glass and out of which comes the foiled glass — maybe someday!

Dispensers and storage

Because the size of the foil you use depends on the thickness of your glass, you need to have a variety of sizes of foil on hand at all times. To help you stay organized, keep your foil rolls in a foil dispenser or other similar container (refer to Figure 2-21 for an example).

The foil dispenser is easy to use, but you need to remember to store it inside a closed plastic storage bag or other airtight container. Oxygen tarnishes the foil, making it more difficult to solder. The adhesive backing on the foil is also subject to humidity and dampness.

Work board and layout blocks

After your glass pieces are cut, you need to wrap each one in foil and then lay out the pieces on a *Homasote work board* (which is made from compressed newspapers and comes in 4-x-8-foot-x-½-inch sheets). The material is available at your local lumber store and can be cut into any size sheet you need. Just remember that you can't build a stained-glass window that's larger than your work board.

To hold your glass pieces in place on the Homasote board during construction, use metal push pins. And to help you form right angles, use some affordable metal strips, called *layout blocks.* You can drill holes into one edge of the strips to accommodate the push pins (see Figure 2-22).

Notcher

Many copper-foil panels are framed in hard metals to give them stability. The most popular metal frame is made from a ⅛-inch *U*-shaped came. It's available in brass, copper, or zinc. You need a tool that helps you cut through the metal frame to get to the copper foil — which is where the notcher comes in. A *notcher* is a specially designed tool that allows you to cut perfect 45-degree angles in this particular frame came (see Figure 2-23). Trust me, it's a real time saver!

Figure 2-21:
Foilmate roller and foil dispenser loaded with rolls of foil.

Figure 2-22:
Homasote work board with project being constructed using layout blocks and push pins.

Figure 2-23:
A notcher with examples of came cuts.

If you're doing only a few panels a year that require this size of perimeter metal, you can use a pair of wire nippers to cut the came instead of buying a notcher. But don't use your lead nippers to cut hard metals. If you do, you'll dent the face of the cutting blade and render it useless for cutting lead cames.

Staying Safe: Purchasing the Right Safety Equipment for Glass Projects

Throughout this chapter, I talk about cutting and grinding glass, sawing metal, and hammering nails — just to name a few potentially dangerous tasks. Of course, I have to discuss safety, too.

You absolutely must have the following safety equipment in your stained-glass studio at all times (see Figure 2-24 for examples of each one):

✔ **Safety glasses:** The most important tool in your studio is your pair of safety glasses. Make sure you buy a pair that fits comfortably and allows you to see your work clearly. Of course, it doesn't hurt if they make you look cool, too. Maybe a stylish pair of safety glasses will remind you to wear them at all times. I have a pair of safety glasses that my optometrist made with my normal prescription and a stylish frame.

✔ **Gloves:** It's a good idea to wear safety gloves when cutting or handling glass. Make sure the gloves fit you well and are designed for handling slippery, sharp objects.

✔ **Fume extractors and respirators:** During the soldering process, you need to have a way to remove fumes from your work area. You may want to buy a commercial fume extractor that sits on the counter near your work area and draws the fumes through a filter to clean the air; you can also wear a respirator. Just make sure it's designed for soldering.

The outdoors provides the best working environment. If possible, work outdoors, or open up your studio windows and door while you work. Don't be afraid to let the fresh air in!

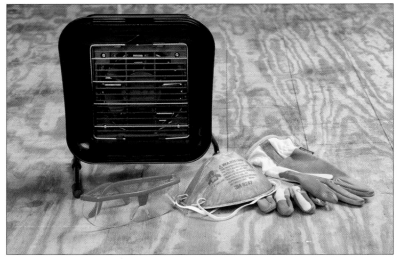

Figure 2-24:
Some common and necessary safety equipment.

Assembling Basic Drafting Supplies

Every stained-glass project starts with a design. Working from that design, you create templates that become the pattern pieces you use to cut out the individual glass pieces. Most of the supplies you need to move from the design stage to the pattern stage of your project are basic drawing and measuring tools, but you also need to purchase a few task-specific tools. I describe these supplies in more detail in the following sections.

Paper for patterns

I recommend you work with medium-weight, white craft paper. I buy my pattern paper on a 36-foot-wide roll because it allows me to cut the paper to any length I want.

You never ever want to piece together small 8-x-10-inch pieces of paper to create your designs. They'll cause you a plethora of problems down the road.

Rulers and triangles

It's important to work with a ruler that's as long as the panel you're building. After all, finished projects need to be just the right size, or else they won't fit into your doors and windows. I have a vast collection of metal rulers, ranging from 18 inches to 72 inches, in my studio so that I'm ready for whatever size project comes my way.

All the corners on all your panels have to be true right angles, which is why triangles are so important to all stained-glass design and fabrication work. Thus, I recommend that you have two clear plastic triangles — a 6-inch and a 12-inch — on hand at all times. (See Chapter 4 for more details about using this tool in your projects.)

Pattern shears

Pattern shears, which are three-bladed scissors, are another stained-glass tool you need to have in your studio. When you cut out your design templates, you have to make allowances for the strips of lead or copper foil that will be going between each piece of glass. Pattern shears are designed to remove just the right amount of material from each side of a pattern line as you cut (see Figure 2-25). Turn to Chapter 4 for more info on working with pattern shears.

The allowances for leaded projects are greater than those for copper-foil projects, so you need a pair of lead shears and a pair of copper-foil shears. Don't try to get by with only one if you plan on making both lead and copper-foil projects.

Adhesives

You need some kind of adhesive to temporarily attach pattern templates to glass surfaces for cutting. Rubber cement works really well for this task, but you can also use double-sided tape or spray adhesive (although I've found the spray to be really messy and not the best for the environment).

Figure 2-25:
Pattern
shears with
paper
templates.

Markers and knives

Each piece of glass in a particular project has a unique place in the project's pattern. Keep track of all your glass pieces by marking them with numbers and letters. Black permanent markers work great for writing on glass. The mark stays on the glass until you rinse it away with soap and water. When you're working with dark colors of glass, you may want to use a white grease pencil so you can see your marks.

When working with iridescent glass, test your marker before writing on the glass. Some iridescent surfaces are more porous than regular glass.

A simple craft knife is another handy tool to have in your toolbox for trimming pattern edges, working with foil, and doing other tasks around your studio.

Light box

Don't panic if you're not an artist — I couldn't draw a horse or a landscape to save my life, but I've designed thousands of stained-glass windows. You can find countless great patterns and designs in books and online. The secret is figuring out how to personalize that design or blend together multiple designs to render a custom look.

To help you personalize your design, you may want to use a *light box,* a wooden or metal frame or box that suspends a piece of glass over a light bulb or fluorescent light stick. A light box is perfect for copying designs and selecting the colors of glass you want to use. For example, I use a light box when cutting glass to help me identify the right shading on a piece of glass for each pattern template.

Chapter 3

Setting Up Your Glass-Working Studio

In This Chapter

▶ Finding an ideal place for your studio

▶ Establishing workstations in your studio and finding a place to store all your tools

*B*efore you can start your first stained-glass project, you have to find a studio location that can accommodate your new hobby. Good lighting, ventilation, and comfort are all important factors to consider during your search for a studio. In this chapter, I offer you some suggestions to keep in mind as you set up your stained-glass studio.

Because some of the materials and chemicals you use to create your stained-glass projects can be dangerous if they aren't used and stored properly, pay close attention to the guidelines I cover in this chapter regarding workstations and storage. To make sure your studio is the safest it can be, I recommend you read through the whole chapter before you finalize any of your studio plans.

Knowing What Makes for a Good Studio Space

Your new stained-glass hobby (and all the tools that go with it) needs a space to call its own. After all, creating beautiful projects involves working with several toxic products, such as lead, as well as broken, sharp pieces of glass, and you definitely don't want to risk letting those tools fall into the hands of someone who doesn't know how to use them. A spare room works well as a studio as long as you don't plan to also use it for an occasional guest room. Other great studio locations include garages, covered porches, and unfinished basements. Figure 3-1 shows an example of a good spot for a stained-glass studio.

The following sections focus on some key considerations to keep in mind when you're selecting your studio space.

Figure 3-1:
An ideal stained-glass studio.

Flooring

As far as flooring is concerned, a hard-surface floor is the best option for your studio because you want a surface that cleans up easily (in other words, one that you can sweep and mop easily). Tile, wood, and cement all work great. Carpet isn't a good idea because small chips of glass, fumes from chemicals, and dust can easily get trapped in it.

Lighting

Undoubtedly the most important feature of your studio is lighting. Stained glass requires lots of good lighting because the better you can see, the more accurate your work is, and the more accurate your work is, the easier it is to create professional-looking projects. If your studio has windows or skylights, great! Nothing lights up a piece of glass like sunlight. If it doesn't, make sure you position a few overhead lights over your work areas, which may or may not be in the center of the room.

To add lighting to your studio, I recommend installing 4-foot fluorescent shop lights, which can either be hardwired or plugged into an outlet. They're affordable and available at any home-improvement store, and most of them come with easy-to-install chains. Portable or clamp-on lights are also great for illuminating certain work areas in your studio.

When was the last time you had your vision checked? Believe it or not, your studio's lighting may not be the only thing inhibiting your stained-glass abilities. Making stained-glass projects requires a ton of detailed work, and new glasses may be just what you need to see your way to success.

Ventilation

Working with stained glass means dealing with dust, lead fumes, and potentially toxic chemicals, so you must make sure you have good ventilation in your studio before you start any of the projects in this book. Choose a studio space that has a few doors and windows that you can open while you work; they provide the best ventilation system you can have. If you don't have a space with open doors and windows, you need to install other ventilation in your studio. Here are a few of the best options:

- ✔ **Exhaust fan:** An exhaust fan mounted at work level and vented directly outside helps remove most of the fumes (which is especially important during the soldering and cementing processes; see Chapter 7 for more on soldering and Chapter 9 for more on cementing).

  Be sure to check with local codes regarding venting fumes before you install an exhaust fan or other ventilation device.

- ✔ **Fume extractor:** A *fume extractor* is a piece of equipment that draws in fumes, passes them through a filter, and exhales clean air, thus helping to ventilate the space around it. Be sure to do your research before you buy one, though, because some work better than others. I use a Weller Fume Extractor in my studio; it's available at glass shops and online.

- ✔ **Respirator:** Many stained-glass artists, myself included, use respirators in addition to venting systems. Respirators are designed to be used for a specific purpose. Make sure the one you select is specifically designed to remove particles smaller than ½ micron from the air; check the packaging to make sure it's OSHA (Occupational Safety and Health Administration) approved for that particular task.

  Don't forget to change the filter in your respirator as needed (see the instructions that come with it to find out how often you need to do so). If you're using a disposable mask, use it once and then pitch it; use a fresh one each time you work.

If you're pregnant or trying to get pregnant, stained glass isn't the hobby for you at this time. Nothing is as important as your health, and the chemicals and fumes involved in stained glass (even when you use a ventilator) are simply unsafe for you to be around. Also, always keep small children away from your stained-glass studio. They're much more susceptible to toxic chemicals and lead.

Storage spaces

Like my friend George used to say, "We all have our stuff, and we got to have a place to keep our stuff in case we need our stuff." The issue of space and storage is certainly something for stained-glass artists to consider as they choose their studios.

As you probably already know. this hobby involves quite a few bells and whistles, which means you need to find a way to store all your equipment in your studio in a safe and well-organized way. In other words, be sure your studio of choice has plenty of storage space available. Whether you have to build some storage units or they're already present, just be sure your studio has enough space to house everything you need to progress with your stained-glass projects.

Later in this chapter, I offer you some great DIY (do-it-yourself) projects that can help you get a handle on storing stained-glass-specific supplies. And in the next section, I tell you where and how to store all the different tools and supplies you'll need as you begin your stained-glass hobby.

Don't buy what you can't use right away unless you have plenty of storage space in your studio. After all, you certainly don't want to spend a small fortune on materials just to have them ruined because you didn't have the space to store them properly. Also, as you prepare to store your stuff, don't use cardboard boxes for storage; they soak up moisture and are hard to clean. In general, plastic containers are a much better solution.

Setting Up Workstations and Storage Areas within Your Studio

I tend to compartmentalize the stained-glass process because each step in the process leads to another step. Because you use different tools and materials for each step, establishing workstations within your studio makes a lot of sense. Although all artists have their own work styles and what's convenient for you may not be ideal for someone else, all glass studios — yes, I'm talking about yours, too — need to include a few basic elements.

The most important workspace to have in your glass studio is your worktable, but you also need to incorporate a workbench, a grinder station, plenty of good lighting, and ample, adequate storage for tools, glass, lead, and other glass-working items you're sure to need as you create your stained-glass projects.

The following sections provide you with all the details and guidance you need for setting up these various workstations and storage areas in your studio.

Workbench and worktable areas

If you're lucky and have plenty of space, consider having both a worktable and a workbench. The *worktable* is the center of your glass universe; it's the place where you do all your designing, cutting, and fabricating. If possible, place it in the center of your studio so you have walk-around access to all four sides of your projects. The *workbench* acts as a holding station for all the tools, grinders, saws, and other items you need while you work on your projects. It's also the place where you'll set up your light box (see the section "Building a Few Basic Support Tools for Your Studio" for more details on this particular piece of equipment).

With your worktable in the middle of your studio, the best place for your workbench is along one of the walls. That way, you can hang a piece of pegboard directly over your workbench to give you easy access to hand tools while you work on your projects. (See the section "Storage area for all your tools" for more info on storing your hand tools and other glass-working equipment.)

Try to keep the aisle between your worktable and workbench about 36 to 42 inches wide. You want the space to be close enough to reach across when you're working at the table but wide enough for someone to pass through without disturbing your artistic groove.

As you set up the main workstation in your studio, consider the height and size of your worktable carefully. How tall you are determines the height of your worktable. (I'm 5 feet 7 inches tall, and my worktable is just a little over 3 feet tall — 37 inches to be exact.) To determine the proper size for your table, consider these factors:

✔ Your worktable's height needs to be tall enough that you don't have to bend over while working.

✔ Your worktable needs to be low enough that when your arm is fully extended, the table is about 12 inches from your hand.

✔ The overall dimensions of your worktable depend on how much space you have in your studio.

My worktable, shown in Figure 3-1, is the perfect size for me — 4 x 8 feet. I have plenty of room to build large panels and still have ample space to lay out all my glass pieces and strips of lead came while I'm working.

You can't build a window that's bigger than your worktable. So when in doubt, bigger is better.

As I mention earlier in this chapter, lighting is an extremely important part of your studio. Be sure to consider lighting (and electrical outlets) when you configure your studio's layout, especially the placement and positioning of your worktable. In the past, I've put a four-outlet drop box right over the center of my worktable. If you want to try out this layout in your studio, find an electrician to help you set it up. You'll surely love the convenience of not having to step over cords while working on your stained-glass projects.

Be sure not to overload the electric circuits in your studio, and always use grounded, heavy-duty extension cords when needed.

Grinder station

A glass grinder is one of the greatest gifts a glass artist could ever receive. Trying to do a project without one is like building a house with a handsaw — possible but not practical. Although I worked without a glass grinder for two years before Santa Claus brought me one, now that I know how great it is, I don't know how I ever managed without it.

Like most gifts, glass grinders come with some baggage. In this case, the baggage — the water used to keep the glass cool during the grinding process — is a little messy. When you use your grinder, the water splatters and sprays a fine powdery mist in a 360-degree radius. The watery mist isn't a big problem, but you do need to contain it. I've created my own homemade grinder station system that does just that (see Figure 3-2).

Figure 3-2:
Effective
homemade
grinder
station.

To create your own grinder station, set your grinder in a plastic container or on a plastic food tray that extends 3 to 4 inches beyond the edges of the grinder. Then you just have to add a grinder shield (or *splash guard*) to minimize the mess of the misty spray. You can purchase a grinder shield or make one yourself out of lightweight plastic or even a cardboard box.

Although you can make your own grinder splash guard, you need to purchase and use the *grinder safety shield* recommended for your grinder. It protects your face from water and keeps small chips of glass from flying into your eyes. In addition, you need to wear safety glasses whenever you're working with glass, especially when you're cutting and grinding.

Wear a work apron when grinding to help keep you dry and clean. Keep a dry towel near your grinder station so you can dry off your glass pieces after grinding.

Storage area for all your tools

Keeping all your glass-working tools and supplies organized is the best way to make sure you have plenty of time to really enjoy your new hobby. After all, who wants to waste time looking around for patterns and glass cutters when they could be starting an awesome new art panel? This section offers you some basic tips for keeping your drafting supplies, patterns, and other tools organized in your studio.

Storing your drafting supplies and patterns

Every stained-glass project starts with a paper drawing. You make one or two copies of the drawing to use throughout the creation process, always keeping your original for your files — and out of harm's way — in case you want to repeat the design at a later time or, heaven forbid, if you need to repair the one you make.

If possible, store your drafting supplies and patterns away from your immediate work area (that is, your worktable). For example, I hang my rulers on the wall for easy storage and accessibility. As an added bonus, hanging up the rulers keeps them from bowing, and hanging them in descending order helps me stay organized (so I can tell right away if one is missing). You can hang the plastic triangles you use when designing and building panels in the same way. As for your drawing pencils, colored markers, and craft knives, keep them in an open jar or coffee cup for easy access.

Always keep the lids on your craft knives so you don't stab yourself when reaching for a pencil or pen.

As far as patterns are concerned, purchase pattern paper on a roll, and store it upright or on a roll cutter in your studio. That way, you can easily cut off just the right amount without wasting any. If you don't have a roll cutter, keep a pair of scissors nearby for cutting.

In a very short amount of time, you end up with lots of patterns. If they're small enough, you can store them in a large, flat, plastic storage container — you know, the kind you slide under your bed to store sweaters in during the summer. If your patterns are too large to lay flat in such a container, you can roll them up instead. If you have to roll a pattern, be sure you label it with the name of the design, the size, and perhaps the client or friend for whom the window was created; that way, you can identify each pattern without having to unroll it.

Storing all your other tools

As for your other stained-glass tools, like pliers and glass cutters, you can store some of them by hanging them up on a pegboard and others by laying them on a shelf. (For the record, I think pegboard is a great invention. It's cheap and easy to hang, and you can find numerous unique styles of hooks and hangers that can accommodate almost any tool shape.)

Arrange your tools together based on function. Put all your breaking pliers in one spot and your lead tools in another, for example. Doing so helps you work more efficiently and reduces cleanup time.

Never store you soldering equipment or chemicals on your workbench or on a shelf directly under your hand tools. I learned this the hard way when all my good hand tools ended up coated with rust. The fumes from the flux chemical you use when soldering filter right up from the flux bottles and your soldering tip cleaners through the air and deposit themselves onto your hand tools, making them rust. For this reason, keep your chemicals in airtight containers, and place your soldering equipment under your worktable or on a shelf away from all your other tools.

Store your glass cutters upright in a jar with a pad of paper towel or cloth saturated with cutting oil in the bottom of the jar. The cutting oil keeps rust away, and the paper towel protects the cutting wheel. Store your pistol-grip cutters on their sides in a small tray or box lid. They have a tendency to leak oil from time to time, so you don't want it to get all over your nice, clean shelves.

I don't recommend using a tool box to store your glass-working tools. I've seen far too many stained-glass students show up for class with a box full of rusted tools from spilled flux and other chemicals. If you're taking a class, I recommend using a plastic, open-topped storage caddy for transporting your tools. Carry your chemicals in a closed plastic storage bag, and don't forget to unpack them as soon as you get home from class.

Glass storage area

You have to store your glass standing up on its side. Stacking it up on the counter will lead to scratches and broken pieces. The following sections show you how to best store glass of various sizes.

Storing small pieces and scrap glass

A sturdy, upright rack, like a dish-drying rack or file holder, works well for storing 12-x-12-inch and smaller pieces of glass (see Figure 3-3 for an example of such a rack).

Figure 3-3:
A file rack
loaded with
small glass
squares.

Now, what about scrap pieces of glass? Over the years, I've come to accept that scrap glass often reproduces on its own; I never have enough storage space for it. To help keep your studio organized and clean (and your mind sane), you have to employ some tough love when it comes to your scrap glass: Never save any glass scraps smaller than 2 x 2 inches. You really can't do anything productive with them. But what about mosaics, you say . . . well, it's a possibility, but, believe me, it's better just to pitch the little guys before they take over your studio.

The glass scraps you do keep are best stored in clear, plastic shoe boxes, sorted by color. Label the boxes, and stack them in your studio. That way, when you need just a little piece of yellow glass for the center of that flower you're working on, you'll know exactly where to look.

Using glass racks for full sheets

Glass is less expensive if you purchase it by the full sheet, but doing so makes storing your extra glass a bit more challenging than simply standing it up in a dish-drying rack. Each glass manufacturer makes different sizes of glass sheets, but the average sheet measures 32 x 42 inches.

To store full sheets of glass, you need to set up a few glass racks in your studio. The wooden crates in which glass manufacturers ship their glass to local glass retailers work well as large-sheet glass racks. And because glass retailers cut the glass down into smaller sizes for sale to hobbyists, most of them are happy to sell the used crates to people like you. After purchasing the wooden crates, stand them upright, side by side in your studio. Be sure to secure them to each other and to the wall.

If you can't find wooden glass crates for sale, you can build your own. Don't worry — you don't need anything fancy here. A plywood box with wooden dividers does the trick. The ideal size for the box is 39 inches deep by 39 inches tall. Place the vertical wood dividers 6 to 8 inches apart.

Storing your glass projects properly

Most stained-glass artists work on several projects at one time. For example, you may have a window midprogress, a stained-glass lampshade half-completed, and a couple of sun catchers you're almost done with. Be sure to store all these projects flat and away from dust and humidity. You can slip flat-panel projects and lampshades into large, clear garbage bags; just be sure to seal them shut until you're ready to work on them again. Smaller projects can await your attention inside plastic shoe bins.

Storage area for lead and other metals

The lead cames you use to construct leaded stained-glass windows are very pliable, and they come in a variety of sizes. When it comes to storing them, I suggest organizing them by size and storing them carefully on a lead rack so they don't become damaged before you use them. (See the section "Building a Few Basic Support Tools for Your Studio" for details on how to build your own lead rack.)

When shopping for lead came, don't buy bent or twisted cames because they're almost impossible to straighten out. Instead, by straight cames, carefully loop them in half, carry them gently to your car, and lay them flat in the trunk. Transport the cames into your studio just as gently, and hang them on their storage rack. Always wash your hands with soap and water after you handle lead cames and solder.

You need to store your hard metals (metals like copper, brass, and zinc) flat, never standing on end, or they'll bow beyond use. I recommend keeping them on a shelf in your studio or under your worktable so they're out of your way. You also need to make sure to store them away from water or dampness. You'll surely have trouble soldering them together if they become corroded or discolored.

Part II

Easing Your Way into the Art: Basic Stained-Glass Techniques

The 5th Wave   By Rich Tennant

"I normally piece together stained glass, but I've got my soldering iron with me, and some 50/50 solder, so if you and the horses are done..."

In this part . . .

This part of the book focuses on the basic techniques you need to know before you can put together your first stained-glass project. I start by showing you how to use ready-made patterns to create some great projects. Don't worry — you don't have to be an artist to enjoy stained glass. I share some great resources that offer all kinds of project patterns. (I also include lots of my own patterns for you to enjoy later in Part III of this book.)

After you pick out a pattern, you're ready to cut some glass. Follow the tips and techniques I show you here, and you'll be on your way to becoming a proficient, effective cutter in no time. Then put your grinder and grozing pliers to the test as I show you how to fine-tune your glass shapes to fit your patterns. I finish the part with a quick look at how to solder the pieces of your project together.

Chapter 4

Designed to Succeed: Working with Patterns and Selecting Your Glass

In This Chapter

▶ Identifying the blueprints — or patterns — for your stained-glass projects

▶ Getting your pattern ready to work with

▶ Creating and organizing your pattern templates

▶ Selecting just the right glass for your projects

*T*he entire stained-glass process centers on the integrity of your original design, or *pattern,* as it's often called in the glass world. Your stained-glass pattern is your road map to successfully creating a functional object of beauty. Although stained-glass projects may look like paintings on the outside, they're actually the results of carefully designed structural interiors. Even a small sun catcher originates from a well-thought-out pattern.

In this chapter, you find out how to work with *ready-to-build patterns* (patterns that another artist has already created) and how to change those patterns to fit your projects. You discover how to mark, number, and cut up your patterns to create *templates* (the individual pattern pieces), which you then use to cut out each piece of glass for your projects (see Chapter 5 for more on cutting glass). Finally, you find out how to select just the right glass for your projects.

Patterns 101

The stained-glass process is a repeating succession — a piece of glass, a piece of lead or foil, a piece of glass, a piece of lead or foil, and so on and so forth — all of which you're putting together both horizontally and vertically at the same time. Because all the individual pieces of your stained-glass project must fit together perfectly and because your finished project needs to fit into the space you selected for it, whether it's a window, a door frame, or a skylight, creating a sound design plan from the get-go is extremely important. This sound design plan is where patterns — and this section — come in.

Patterns lay out the design for what you want the final glass project to look like (in other words, where you want each piece of glass to go); they also make accommodations for all the metals that surround and run throughout the project. Before you start designing your project, though, you need to determine what size you want the project to be. Based on that information, you can create a pattern that establishes all the framing requirements, design details, and lead or foil lines for your project. For example, your pattern tells you what size framing materials you'll use, thus establishing what size glass pieces you'll have to cut and, of course, how you'll assemble all these small individual glass pieces to create your final project.

Staying on pattern is your goal throughout the glass-cutting and fabrication stages. I discuss the idea of "staying on pattern" in much more detail in Chapters 6, 8, and 9, but, basically, it means making sure each piece of your stained-glass puzzle fits within your pattern's perimeters.

The following sections walk you through how to choose an already-existing pattern, why you need to have three copies of your project's pattern, and what you can do to change the size of your pattern to fit your space-specific needs.

Using ready-to-build patterns

Not an artist? Don't worry! The world of stained glass has millions of great patterns for you to choose from. Trust me, if I never created another original stained-glass design, I could still spend the rest of my life making hundreds of wonderful projects, thanks to the huge selection of ready-to-build stained-glass patterns available to artists today.

Even if you are an artist, be aware that designing your own stained-glass patterns is more complicated than you may think. You may be able to draw a great-looking flower or family crest, but transforming that artistic image into a workable stained-glass design requires a lot of experience and hard work. Take it from me, you need to work with ready-to-build patterns for a while before you dive into creating one of your own. After you have a better understanding of the way glass, metal, and gravity all work together, you'll be able to apply this knowledge to your own designs.

Working with ready-made designs helps cut down on the initial frustration you might experience trying to design your own patterns. Plus, using a ready-to-build pattern helps ensure that you can successfully cut out the individual glass pieces to fit the pattern. After all, you can't cut glass into just any shape. Certain shapes, such as deep interior curves, right angles, and long narrow strips, are practically impossible to cut without causing the glass to crack or break completely. Although you could use a power glass saw to cut out the more difficult shapes, the integrity of the glass piece would still be fragile and susceptible to breaking during the construction and soldering processes. (After you have a few projects under your belt, you'll know exactly what I'm talking about!)

To help you get started with a ready-to-build pattern, I include several such patterns throughout this book, particularly in Part III. If you work through all the projects in this book or if you're just looking for something a bit different, check out your local glass shop, bookstore, or even the Internet to find hundreds of ready-to-build stained-glass patterns. Generally, stained-glass books center around certain topics, such as nature, floral, animals, and geometrics. Some are organized according to project application, such as entry doorways, cabinet-door panels, windows, lamps, boxes, and gifts, while others focus on the different skill levels needed to build the projects, like beginner, intermediate, and advanced. Still others focus on the techniques used to make the projects (fused glass, copper foil, bevels, and lead, for example).

Having three copies of each pattern

After you find the pattern you want to use for your project, you need to make two photocopies of it. No, I'm not being wasteful — you'll need all three copies as you progress through the stained-glass process.

Save a fresh copy of any design you create so you can make it again if you choose and so you have it handy in case you ever need to make repairs. That fresh copy is called your *file copy*. (Keep in mind that after you start creating stained-glass projects, all your friends, family, and co-workers are going to ask you to make something for them. Trust me, already having a selection of design patterns in your files can save you a lot of time down the road.)

The second two copies of the pattern are your *working copies:*

   ✔ You cut apart the first copy to make templates for cutting out the individual glass pieces.

   ✔ You use the second copy as the answer sheet to your giant jigsaw puzzle. It's the overall pattern that tells you where all the individual glass pieces go.

You're probably wondering why you can't use the second copy as your file copy when you're finished with your project. Well, the reason is pretty basic: Your working pattern will get pretty trashed as you hammer nails into it, spill flux on it, and turn parts of it into ashes while soldering. Do yourself a favor — make that third copy.

Figure 4-1 shows three copies of a stained-glass pattern. Notice that each pattern piece has been numbered, color coded, and marked with an arrow. These markings help you make sure each glass piece ends up where it belongs in your finished project. Check out the section "Laying Out Your Pattern" for more details on what these markings mean and how to make them.

Enlarging designs with an opaque projector

Just because you've chosen a ready-to-build pattern that meets all your design needs doesn't mean you're ready to start cutting glass right away. Most of the time, you need to make adjustments to the size of your pattern based on where you plan to put the finished project.

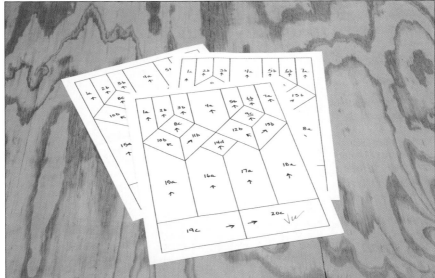

Figure 4-1:
Three copies of a numbered and labeled stained-glass pattern.

Depending on the size you're looking for, your local copy shop may be able to help you increase or decrease the size of your ready-to-build pattern. Just remember that a machine-made copy will be a little distorted from the original. Also keep in mind that the more you enlarge a design, the wider the pattern lines become and the more design issues you'll face.

A great solution for improving your pattern's size without sacrificing quality is the opaque projector, shown in Figure 4-2. Not only is it a useful tool for enlarging designs, but it's also a great tool for combining multiple designs and creating your own original designs.

An *opaque projector* works by projecting an image (either a black-and-white drawing or a colored photograph) onto a wall where you can trace it onto pattern paper. To adjust the size of the pattern, simply adjust the position of the projector. The closer it is to the wall, the smaller the design is. The farther you move the project away from the wall, the larger the design becomes.

Always position the projector on a flat, horizontal surface. If you accidentally prop up the front of the machine, the design will be distorted — wider at the top than the bottom. The opposite is true if you angle the front of the machine toward the floor — wider at the bottom than at the top.

The trick to getting a really clean image is to work in a darkened room. The darker the room, the better, especially when you're trying to trace a photograph. It's also easier to see your design when you work with white pattern paper for both the original design and the enlarged version. If necessary, darken the pattern lines on the original design so they project more clearly.

Figure 4-2:
An opaque
projector
and design
to be
enlarged.

When enlarging patterns, go ahead and draw in any straight lines that appear in the design, but be sure to double-check them with your ruler and triangle later to make sure they're straight and evenly spaced.

Laying Out Your Pattern

I'm sure you're thinking of lots of places around your home that you'd like to accent with a beautiful stained-glass panel . . . or two. Having an idea of where you want your finished project to go is great, but before you start making it, you need to make sure the panel you build will fit into the designated space. As long as you lay out your pattern correctly, your finished project will fit its new home like a dream come true.

Before you try to tackle a panel that has to fit into a specifically defined area (like a window), get some experience building *free-hanging panels,* which are panels that don't have to fit into a particular opening. You can frame free hangings in wood or metal and suspend them from chains or heavy-duty monofilament or fishing line. Note that you still need to determine what size you want your free-hanging panel to be before you can start your design.

The following sections take you through the process of laying out your pattern. With your finished pattern in hand, you can start cutting out your templates and selecting your glass. (I cover these topics later in this chapter.)

Determining your project's finished size

The first step in the process of laying out your pattern is to determine the *finished size* for your project (in other words, the size you want your panel to be when it's finished). If you want to install the finished panel into a specific opening, you need to determine what installation method you'll use. The two main installation methods are

- ✔ **Replacement method:** This method involves replacing the existing glass panel with your new stained-glass panel. To do so, you need to remove the wood molding that currently holds the existing glass in place. The molding consists of the thin wood strips that are tacked in place around the edge of the glass panel and is located on the interior side of the door or window you're replacing.

  The best way to remove window molding is to use your lead knife to carefully cut through the paint along the edge of the molding and then to gently pry the molding away from the frame.

  After you remove the molding, measure the width and height of the opening. Write down your measurements by recording the width first followed by the height. To give yourself a little wiggle room when installing the new panel, deduct ¼ inch from the width and ¼ inch from the height to determine your finished size.

  Tack the molding back in place after you finish measuring the opening so the glass doesn't fall out before you're ready to replace it.

- ✔ **Piggyback method:** This installation method is the most common and involves installing the new glass panel right over the top of the existing glass. You leave the clear glass and the molding in place (see Figure 4-3). To secure the stained-glass window in place, you use a seam of clear or color-matched silicone.

Figure 4-3: A beveled window that has been installed using the piggyback method.

To get the finished size measurement for this type of installation, measure the width and height from the inside edges of the moldings. Be sure to deduct ¼ inch from the width and ¼ inch from the height to allow space for the silicone.

Use duct tape to hold the panel in place while the silicone dries and cures. Make sure you use paintable silicone if you plan to paint over the seam.

Drawing the outside dimensions of your panel

After you determine your project's finished size, you're ready to start laying out your pattern. The first major step in the design process is drawing the outside dimensions of your panel, based on its finished size. To do so, you need the following tools and materials:

- A piece of pattern paper that's 2 inches wider and longer than the panel you're designing
- A metal ruler that's at least as long as your design
- A triangle
- A pencil
- An eraser

When you have everything you need, follow these instructions to draw the outside dimensions of your design with perfectly square corners:

1. **Place your metal ruler 1 inch from the edge of the pattern paper, and draw a line the length of your longest measurement of the panel (see Figure 4-4); make a mark at 0 (the beginning of the line), in the middle, and at the end.**

    If you're drawing a 12-x-24-inch rectangle, for example, you need to place a mark at the beginning of the 24-inch line, another mark at 12 inches, and the last mark at the end of the line.

    The line you establish in this step is the first side of your panel and is called your pattern's *base line*. You use this line in Step 2 to draw the perpendicular lines for the sides of the panel.

2. **Place your triangle along the base line you drew in Step 1 so that the right angle of the triangle is at the 0 mark on the line; draw a line up the side of the triangle, making sure the line is perpendicular to the base line (see Figure 4-5).**

    The intersection of these two lines establishes the bottom square corner of your design space.

Figure 4-4:
Establishing
your base
line on the
pattern
paper.

Figure 4-5:
Establishing
the bottom
square
corner of
your design
space.

3. **Slide the triangle down to the middle mark on the base line, and draw a light line across the middle of your design space (see Figure 4-6).**

   This line is called the *middle design line* and comes in handy when you're drawing geometric designs or centering free-formed designs.

4. **Flip the triangle over, and draw in the other bottom square corner for your design by following Step 2; this time, line up the right angle of the triangle with the mark at the end of the base line, making sure the bottom of the triangle is straight along the base line.**

Figure 4-6:
Establishing the middle design line.

5. **With your ruler, measure from your base line and mark the width of your panel at the top, middle, and end of the paper (see Figure 4-7).**

Figure 4-7:
Marking the width of your panel using a ruler.

6. **Use your triangle to complete the two square corners at the top of your design; draw a line connecting the three marks you made in Step 5 and the square corners, making sure the line is parallel to the base line (see Figure 4-8).**

This line establishes the other side of your panel. You now have the finished size of your design with perfectly square corners.

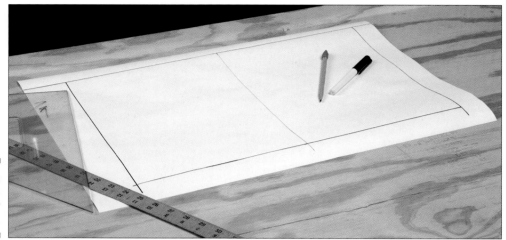

Figure 4-8:
Finished
rectangular
drawing.

Make sure your pattern's corners are perfectly square. If your panel's corners aren't perfectly square when it's finished, it won't fit in its opening. Even if your panel is free hanging, without square corners, it'll always look crooked when it's hanging in a window or on a wall.

Incorporating cut size into your pattern

If you're doing a leaded or large foil project, you'll support your glass panel using a metal *U-* or *H*-shaped frame made up of long strips of metal called *cames,* into which the glass pieces fit. Depending on the size and desired look of your panel, your cames can be made of lead, brass, zinc, or copper. (See Chapters 8 and 9 for a lot more about foil and leaded projects.)

Before you can start transferring your actual design to your pattern paper, you need to mark the *cut size,* or the line that indicates where to cut the exterior glass pieces, on your pattern. You determine the cut size by measuring the distance from where a piece of glass stops when inserted into the came to the backside of the came (see Figure 4-9).

Different styles and sizes of came have different cut-size measurements, so be sure to measure cut size for each project you do.

In my studio, I have a small sample of all the different sizes of came that I normally use for my projects. That way, I can do my design work without having to run to the store to purchase the exact came I want to use for a particular project.

When you know the cut size for your came, it's time to draw it on your pattern. Because the came goes around all four sides of your panel, you need to start from the finished-size pattern line and measure the amount of space you need to allow for the came you'll be using to connect your glass pieces. Draw a *cut-size line,* or a line that shows you how much space the cames will take up and how big your glass pieces need to be, around all four sides of your pattern (see Figure 4-10).

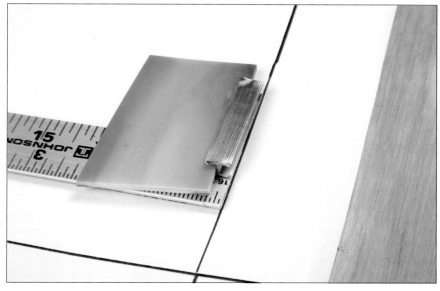

Figure 4-9:
Measuring
cut size by
inserting
glass into an
H-shaped
came.

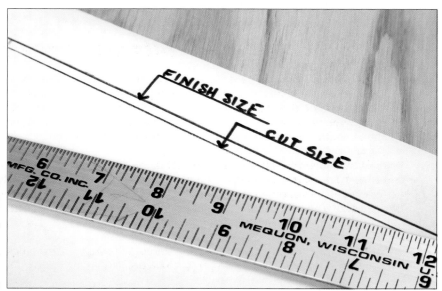

Figure 4-10:
Drawing
a cut size of
⅜ inch
on your
pattern.

Tracing your design onto your pattern

After you have your pattern's exterior dimensions marked, you're ready to trace your ready-to-build design onto your pattern paper. Use the center line you establish in the section "Drawing the outside dimensions of your panel" to center your design. You can use a light box or transfer paper to trace the design onto your pattern.

Always use a ruler to measure and draw the straight lines in your design. This is no time to go freestyle!

Numbering the pieces

Earlier in the chapter I tell you that you need three copies of every pattern. One is your file copy, one is the copy you'll cut into templates, and the third is the master copy you'll use to put all the pieces back together. Well, before you start cutting away at the template copy, you need to number each piece of your pattern — that is, if you want to know how to put the pieces back together again.

To number your pattern's pieces, lay out all three copies of your pattern, putting a piece of transfer or carbon paper between each of the layers, and number each piece of your pattern.

There's no real rule for how to number the pieces on a pattern as long as you make sure every individual piece has a number when you're done. I like to start at the top and move side to side, working my way to the bottom.

Color coding the pieces

In stained glass, *color coding* is the process of assigning an alphabet letter to each of the color groups represented in your pattern. For example, you may label all the leaves *A,* all the background pieces *B,* and so on. You may also choose to give each individual flower (or other shape in your pattern) its own color code. Although color coding your pieces isn't a necessary part of laying out your pattern, doing so can save you a lot of work down the road.

Color coding helps you determine how much glass you need in each color. It also helps you organize all the pattern pieces of one design element before you start cutting so you can select just the right shade and tone within each glass piece as you cut. For example, you may want to cut the center petals of a rose from a darker piece of red glass and the outside petals from a lighter glass to add a little dimension to the rose as a whole.

 Make yourself a little chart of the color-coding system you use for each project, especially when you're working on really large projects — you'll be glad you did as you get deeper into the stained-glass process. I once created a window that portrayed a peacock sitting on a fountain in a garden and contained over 2,000 pieces. On a project like that one, you really appreciate good numbering and color-coding systems — trust me!

Marking the grain of your glass

Woodworkers, stone masons, and quilters all seem to be pretty good glass artists, perhaps because they understand the *grain of the glass* concept. The *grain* is the arrangement, direction, or pattern of the fibers in wood, leather, stone, or glass. In art, the grain of the glass is critical to creating a fabulous, professional-looking stained-glass project. For example, if you're cutting out pieces for plant leaves, you want the grain of the glass to run from the center of each leaf toward its tip. Likewise, if you're cutting out border pieces, you want the grain of all the pieces to be going in the same clockwise direction around your project.

To help you better understand the grain concept, look closely at a piece of cathedral (or transparent) glass. You see a plethora of small air bubbles that are elongated and all heading in the same direction. The direction of the bubbles is your clue to the direction of the grain (they're the same!).

The grain in some glass is very obvious, but for others, especially opalescent glass, it's a little more obscure. The best way to determine the grain of a piece of glass is to place it over a light box or to hold it up to the sunlight. Although the grain generally runs from the top of a full sheet of glass to the bottom, always be sure to check smaller-size glass pieces individually.

After you number and color code your glass pieces, take a minute to mark the direction of the glass grain you're going to use for each piece in the pattern by drawing corresponding arrows (see Figure 4-11).

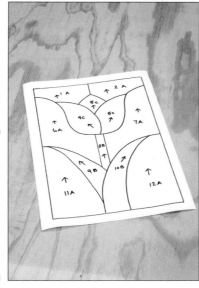

Figure 4-11: Numbered, color-coded, and grain-marked stained-glass pattern.

Cutting Out and Working with Templates

Stained glass is a process in which each step builds on the steps that come before it. Laying out your pattern provides a great foundation for your finished project. Now all you have to do is build on it.

When your pattern looks just the way you want it, you need to cut up one of the three copies you made earlier into the template pieces you'll use when you cut out your glass pieces. Before you start cutting the actual templates, use a ruler and craft knife to trim off the edges of your pattern along the cut size line; trim all four sides. When you're done, read on to find out everything you need to know about cutting and organizing your templates.

If you haven't decided which assembly technique you want to use for your project — lead came or copper foil — you need to do so now. Here are some things to consider when making your decision:

- Consider using lead came for projects that are

  - Larger than 12 x 12 inches

  - Architectural panels for doors, windows, sidelights, and cabinet inserts

  - Comprised of straight lines, borders, bevels, and large pieces of glass

- Consider using copper foil for projects that are

  - Smaller than 12 x 12 inches

  - Three-dimensional (like lampshades, boxes, and candle holders)

  - Intricate designs with small pattern pieces

Cutting templates

Stained-glass artists use specially designed pattern shears to cut out their glass templates. These shears have three blades, and they operate just like regular scissors except that they remove just the right amount of paper from your pattern during the cutting process to accommodate the lead came or copper foil that will run between each piece of glass when your project is assembled. Use *lead shears* for lead projects and *foil shears* for foil projects (see Figure 4-12 for a comparison).

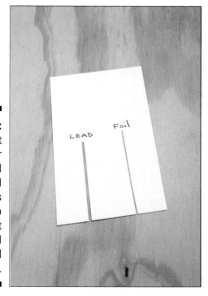

Figure 4-12:
The amount of paper removed using lead shears compared to the amount removed using foil shears.

Practice using the shears on a scrap piece of paper before you start cutting out your actual templates. The shears operate better when you make short, little strokes; if you make long strokes, you have to realign the shears after each stroke, which can be a pain.

Keeping track of your templates

Because replacing templates after you're knee-deep in a project is such a hassle, I like to store my templates in a clear plastic bin like the one shown in Figure 4-13. Bins like this one come in a variety of sizes and are available at your local craft store (probably in the scrapbooking section). If you don't have a plastic bin, you can use a shoe box or any other box with a lid.

Just make sure you don't mix templates from different projects together in the same box. Figuring out which templates go with which project can be a real challenge!

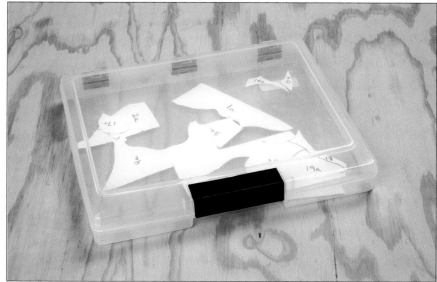

Figure 4-13:
Clear plastic storage bins work great for organizing and storing templates.

I don't recommend that you store your templates in an envelope because templates are much more difficult to use when they've been folded or crimped.

Selecting Glass for Various Projects

After you select your design and have a pattern ready to build on, it's time to select the glass you want to use. Walking into a glass shop for the first time is like being a kid in a candy store: You have thousands of different glass textures, colors, and varieties from which to choose. (If you don't have a stained-glass supply store near you, you can shop online. Advanced technology gives you a pretty good idea of what the glass will look like before you order it.)

The many glass varieties are basically divided into two major categories: *cathedral,* which refers to glass that you can see through, and *opalescent,* which refers to glass that's more difficult or impossible to see through, thanks to the dense, white base from which it's made. (Note that you'll find a lot of variances of transparency within each of these categories.)

The following sections tell you how to select the right cathedral or opalescent glass for your different projects. If you're curious about all the different types and colors of glass available in these two main categories, turn to Chapter 1.

If you're a bit overwhelmed by the huge number of glass choices out there, consider purchasing a glass sample set from your supplier or directly from a glass manufacturer. A sample set typically includes 2-x-3-inch samples of the most popular colors and textures of glass available from a particular manufacturer. Some sets are rather large, containing more than 100 pieces, while others contain only 30 to 40 pieces. You can expect to spend between $25 and $75 per sample set.

Don't stress too much about which glass to use for which project. After all, one of the best things about stained glass is that you can always cut a different colored or textured piece of glass if you don't like the way a particular piece looks in your project.

Keep a journal of the different types of glass you use in each project so you can use the ones you love again and avoid the ones you don't like. Glass manufacturers don't change their glass stock numbers often, so reordering a particular glass you loved is easy to do when you have the stock number handy in your journal.

Cathedral glass

Cathedral glass is the crown jewel of the stained-glass world. No matter what color you're looking for, you can find it in cathedral glass. From rich, blood red to pale amber, the range is incredibly vast and even includes a plethora of color mixtures that add characteristics like wispy, swirled, Baroque, and streaky to already-gorgeous glass pieces.

So when is it a good idea to use cathedral glass in your projects? Well, the final decision is up to you, but cathedral glass is a great choice for the backgrounds and borders of your window projects. However, you can also use cathedral glass for entire windows, if you want to, especially if you incorporate some of the streaky and wispy varieties.

Because cathedral glass allows light to pass directly through it, it's a less favorable choice for lampshades and windows where privacy is an issue. When used in the main portion of a lampshade, cathedral glass lets the light bulbs show through and creates hot spots that distract from the overall beauty of the lamp. When used in small pieces for borders and accents, though, cathedral glass works quite well for almost any project.

Don't forget to mix it up a little. When selecting glass for your project, use more than one shade of a certain color. For example, if your design features leaves, choose two, three, or even four varying shades of green to make your project more interesting. Think about the way leaves exist in nature: The shades of green vary depending on which side of the leaf you're looking at, how the sun is hitting it, and how new or old the leaf is.

Don't hesitate to buy scrap glass when you're first getting started, especially if you can hand select it. All retailers and online glass suppliers sell *scrap glass,* which is basically just smaller pieces of glass that may have broken off a larger sheet of glass when it was accidentally dropped or broken during its shipment. Scrap glass gives you a great opportunity to stock your studio with some different colors of glass without having to purchase large, more expensive stock sizes. Scrap glass is sold by the pound for $1 to $3 each.

Despite the clarity of cathedral glass, it still has a particular grain direction (see the section "Marking the grain of your glass" for more details on this glass characteristic). You need to determine which way the grain runs in the glass you select for your project so you can match up the grains of the glass with the arrows you drew on your pattern templates. Note that determining the grain in one-color glass pieces may be more difficult than doing so in multi-color glass pieces.

After you determine the direction of the grain in each piece of glass, use a permanent maker to mark the glass with arrows that correspond to that direction (see Figure 4-14). That way, you can match your glass's grain directions with the arrows on your pattern even when you're working with extra-small pieces.

Opalescent glass

Opalescent glass, which is also called *opal* or *opaque glass,* captures the light and illuminates itself from within because it's made from a white base to which one or more colors are added. Like cathedral glass, opalescent glass can be wispy, swirled, and streaky.

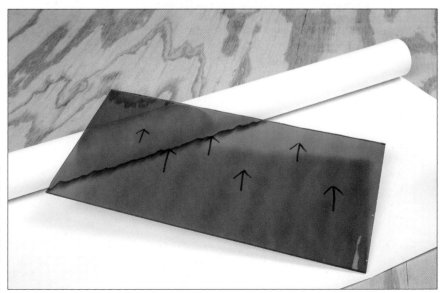

Figure 4-14:
Marking the grain direction on a piece of cathedral glass.

Any window you create out of cathedral glass can also be created out of opalescent glass. The decision of which type of glass to use is based on your interpretation of the design pattern you're working with. Opalescent glass is like paint that glows, making it a wonderful choice for flowers, landscapes, birds, people, clothing, architectural elements, and animals, as well as borders and backgrounds. Its density also makes it a perfect choice for lampshades and panels you make to create privacy.

Be careful when mixing cathedral and opalescent glass together in your project. Because their densities are so different, mixing them together in one area of a project can sometimes create a "visual hole" in the panel. For example, if the background of your window is opalescent glass and you add a cathedral accent piece within that background, it can allow in too much direct light and appear as a visual hole.

One of the best things about opalescent glass is that it provides you with numerous shades and densities of colors in one sheet of glass, so mixing up shades of color in your project is fairly easy and inexpensive to do. For example, if you're working with a two- or three-color-mixed sheet of green glass, you can find a variety of shades of green to achieve the look you want for all the leaves in your project from that one sheet of glass.

The grain direction in opalescent glass is much easier to detect than in cathedral glass, but it's a good idea to mark the grain direction on each piece of opalescent glass you select for your project, just as you do with cathedral glass (see the preceding section). Nothing is more heartbreaking than finishing a panel only to discover that the grain in one of your border pieces is running left to right while all the others are running up to down.

Textures and patterns

Both cathedral and opalescent glass come in a variety of textures and patterns. Generally, the texture is applied to the backside of the glass as it passes through rollers. (Check out Chapter 1 for more details on how glass is made and textures are created.)

When it comes to your projects, textured glass provides two functions:

- ✔ Because the glass isn't flat, it creates visual interest by giving the project a more complex surface.
- ✔ Because of the unique way the light bounces off the raised surface of textured glass, it heightens the luminescence of the glass's colors.

Don't overdo it with textured or patterned glass; in other words, don't use it just to use it. Select textured glass because it meets your needs as an artist. For example, making tree trunks out of rippled glass creates a much stronger impact than using flat cathedral or opalescent glass because rippled glass has a texture that resembles waves of ridges running across the surface of tree trunks.

Chapter 5

Making the Cut: Glass Cutting 101

In This Chapter

▶ Picking out your practice glass

▶ Getting ready to cut with your glass cutter

▶ Using your cutter to cut straight lines and curves

▶ Cutting out different shapes

After your work space is ready to go (refer to Chapter 3 for tips on how to set it up), you're ready to start cutting glass. Ironically, though, glass cutting doesn't involve cutting as much as it involves scoring and breaking. As the wheel of the glass cutter rolls over the surface of the glass, it leaves behind a white scratch mark on the glass; this line is called the *score line*. It tells the glass where you want it to break, and you use your hands or pliers — not the glass cutter — to do the rest.

Many people are hesitant to work with glass, but as long as you wear the right safety gear, which I describe in Chapter 2, and follow the guidelines that I provide in this chapter, you have little to worry about. With just a little practice — which you can start getting by working through this chapter — you'll be cutting glass successfully and having a great time doing so.

 A clean cutting surface is a must. Keep your bench brush handy to sweep up any small shards of glass you create as you work. A clean cutting surface not only protects you from cuts but also makes cutting glass easier. Always be sure to sweep up any glass that falls onto the floor. After all, a stray piece of glass on the floor can be just as slippery as ice.

Selecting Your Practice Glass

Glass is available in lots of different colors, textures, and sizes, but when you're first getting started, I suggest that you use clear glass to practice on. You can't master glass cutting without lots of practice, and clear glass is the cheapest and easiest-to-cut option available. You'll have plenty of time to work with colored glass after you start developing your skills. (Turn to Chapter 4 for tips on selecting glass for your actual projects.)

Note: Although I suggest using clear glass for your first few projects, I use colored glass in my projects throughout this book because it's easier to see in the photos.

Clear glass comes in several different thicknesses, the most common being single strength (1/16 inch thick) and double strength (1/8 inch thick). The most frequent use for single-strength clear glass is in picture frames because it's lightweight. However, because most art glass is generally 1/8 inch thick, choose double-strength clear glass for your practice glass-cutting sessions. That way, you'll get a truer feel for cutting art glass. All art glass supply stores sell clear glass in both sizes. Start out by buying three or four 1-square-foot pieces of clear glass. Then move up to working with colored glass. (If you don't have access to a local glass shop, an art framer or window repair shop may also be a good resource for clear glass.)

Glass shops often sell glass in 1-square-foot pieces, but they also carry scrap glass pieces, which are random pieces of glass ranging from 8 x 4 inches to 2 x 2 inches. When you're first getting started, buy the square-foot pieces because they're easier to transport, handle, and store.

Don't try to practice on old window panes. They may be made of tempered glass, which doesn't cut when scored but instead breaks into a thousand small pieces. Or they may be made of laminated glass — two pieces of glass with a sheet of clear plastic laminated between them. Neither option works for stained-glass projects.

Getting to Know Your Glass Cutter

Finding success in glass cutting takes practice and skill, but it also depends on the quality of the glass cutter you're using. Whether you choose to work with a barrel cutter or a pistol-grip cutter, I recommend buying one that's self-oiling and has a carbide cutting wheel (see Chapter 2 for more details about the various glass cutters).

In this section, I help you get your cutter's oil flowing and show you how to establish a proper grip on your barrel or pistol-grip cutter. (**Note:** If you're not using a self-oiling cutter, you need to manually apply oil to the cutting wheel between each score. The easiest way to do so is to place a square of paper towel in a shallow dish. Saturate the towel with cutting oil. Keep this dish handy while cutting, and remember to re-oil your cutter between cuts by passing the wheel over the saturated towel.)

Preparing the cutter

Before you start cutting your practice glass, you need to activate and test your self-oiling cutter. Lucky for you (and me) doing so is easy. Just follow these simple steps:

1. **Remove the screw cap on the end of your cutter, and fill the oil reservoir with the cutting oil recommended by your cutter's manufacturer.**

2. **Pump the cutter's** *head* **(the end with the cutting wheel) up and down against your palm until you see a small trace of oil coming from the wheel.**

   Don't worry: The cutting wheel only scores the glass. It won't cut your hand.

3. **Place a piece of cleaned, clear glass on top of your cutting surface.**

   Chapter 3 shows you how to set up your worktable for cutting glass.

   Before you start cutting any piece of glass, be sure to clean the glass surface using a good glass cleaner and a soft cloth. The manufacturing process used to create glass is very dusty and gritty, and you don't want that dust to get in the way of your project.

4. **Place the cutting wheel on the glass surface; apply a small amount of pressure and roll the cutter across the glass.**

   You should see a thin line of oil trailing behind the cutter.

   If you're using a pistol-grip cutter and it leaks or emits too much oil when you're cutting, try stuffing the reservoir barrel with cotton balls. Then saturate the cotton with cutting oil.

5. **If you don't see a line of oil on the glass surface, repeat Steps 2 and 4.**

If you're using an old or used glass cutter, you need to test it to make sure it doesn't have a damaged cutting wheel before you start cutting. To do so, roll the cutter across the glass, wipe the oil off the glass, and see if you can see a light white scratch line. If you see gaps in the line, you need to replace the cutting wheel or purchase a new cutter.

Getting a proper grip

The way you hold your glass cutter depends on the style of cutter you're using — barrel or pistol grip. I use a Toyo comfort-grip barrel cutter because its barrel is slim and long and fits in my hand comfortably, but you need to try out all the styles until you find your perfect fit. I've seen many successful glass artists in action, and all of them have their own styles and techniques when it comes to getting a good grip on glass cutters. (Check out the sidebar "Only in Vegas" to read about a unique style I recently encountered.)

If you're using a barrel cutter, I suggest you hold it like a pencil with your fingers extended down the full length of the barrel (see Figure 5-1). Because the heads on glass cutters swivel to help you score around curves, you need to find a way to control the swivel action as you score. This extended-finger position is perfect for doing just that.

If you're using a pistol-grip cutter, the grip is more standard because the cutter's shape is designed to fit into the palm of your hand (see Figure 5-2). Feel free to vary this grip to fit your own style.

Figure 5-1:
Holding a
barrel
cutter with
extended
fingers.

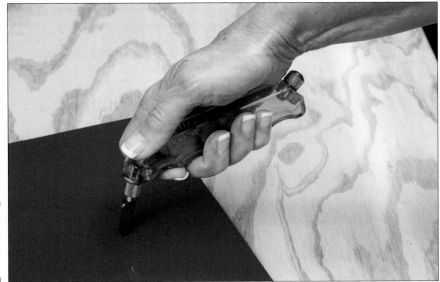

Figure 5-2:
Holding a
pistol-grip
cutter.

If you have trouble holding tension in your fingers for an extended period of time (because of arthritis, carpal tunnel syndrome, or weak wrists, for example), use the pistol-grip cutter because it'll be easier for you to grip.

If all these techniques are beginning to sound like your first golf lesson, relax! I also play golf, and, believe me, cutting glass is much easier to master. The key to remember is comfort. Find a cutter and a gripping style that you can comfortably maintain, and everything else will fall into place (after you read the rest of this chapter, of course!).

Only in Vegas

Every year the Vicki Payne International Glass Cutting Competition takes place at the International Glass Show in Las Vegas. The best glass cutters in the world compete to win the title and prizes. A few years ago, the winner actually steadied his cutter with his chin by resting his chin on the top of the barrel of the cutter while letting his hands guide the cutter around the glass. His technique certainly drew a crowd of onlookers. Now I'm not recommending this technique, but for this particular glass artist, it worked. The point is you need to find a comfortable grip that works for you; don't worry about what others do.

Cutting Straight Lines

The best way to start cutting glass is to figure out how to cut a straight line; then you can move on to more complex curves and shapes. Your goal here is to make a good score line that's easy to break.

Before you start to make your first score, take the time to limber up with a few circular arm rotations. Being loose and relaxed helps you concentrate on your technique and makes the entire process more fun and successful.

I always cut glass standing up because applying even pressure and maintaining the flexibility and mobility of movement you need when cutting is difficult to do while sitting down. In fact, you won't find many steps in the stained-glass process you can do while sitting. This art is more active than you may have thought!

First things first: Making the score line

The true secret to being able to cut out various glass shapes lies in your ability to apply an even, steady pressure on the glass surface as you score the glass. Notice that I don't say anything about speed. Steady as you go is the mantra to keep in mind when you're cutting glass. But, like any skill, the more you practice, the faster you'll get.

Maintaining even, steady pressure on the glass as you score it ensures that your score line will be even and unbroken, which is important because although glass is very pretty, it isn't very smart. It can't figure out what you want it to do without a road map — which is where the score line comes into play. If there's a gap in the score line or if the line stops in the middle of the glass piece, the glass can't figure out where to break. Imagine that the gap in the score line is a bridge that's been washed out; it's up to the glass to create its own detour. As a general glass-working rule, you never want to let glass forge its own trail — the outcome is never good.

Wear your safety glasses at all times when working in your glass studio. (Check out Chapter 2 for more information on choosing safety glasses and other important stained-glass equipment.)

Follow these steps to score a straight line. For this practice exercise, use a piece of clear, 6-x-6-inch glass, and try to cut it into two approximately even 3-x-6-inch pieces.

1. **Place a clean piece of clear glass on your prepared cutting surface.**

   See Chapter 3 for details on how to get your worktable ready for cutting glass.

2. **Use a black permanent marker to draw a line down the middle of the glass, end to end (see Figure 5-3).**

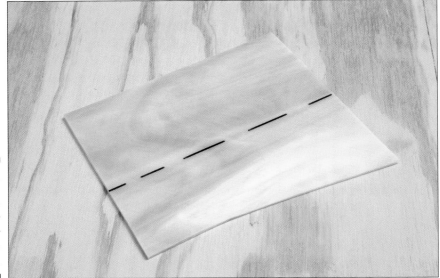

Figure 5-3: Marking your glass piece for your practice score.

It's not necessary to use a straight edge when drawing the line or during the cutting process. The goal here is to feel relaxed throughout the cutting process, not to achieve perfection.

3. **Check your glass cutter to make sure the oil is flowing to the cutting wheel.**

   Check out the section "Preparing the cutter" earlier in this chapter for complete instructions.

4. **Using the line you drew in Step 2 as your guide, place your cutting wheel on the surface of the glass about $\frac{1}{16}$ inch away from the edge of the glass; hold the cutter at a 45-degree angle to the glass surface (see Figure 5-4).**

   Starting with your cutter already on the glass surface is easier than trying to roll up onto the edge of the glass and helps you get your score line off to a successful start.

5. **Push down on the cutter, applying even, steady pressure, and roll the cutting wheel across the glass following the black line (see Figure 5-5).**

   Make sure the cutting action comes from your shoulder and not your wrist.

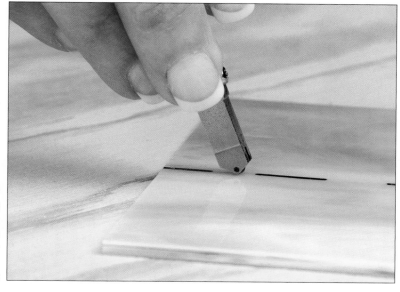

Figure 5-4:
Positioning
your glass
cutter for
the score.

You should be able to hear a soft scratching sound as the cutting wheel
rolls over the glass surface. If you can see small chips of glass jumping
from the score line, you're scoring too hard. If you can't see your score
line, you aren't applying enough pressure.

Figure 5-5:
Applying
even, steady
pressure to
make the
score line.

6. **Stop when you're about ¹⁄₁₆ inch away from the opposite edge of the
   glass (see Figure 5-6).**

   Stopping before you run off the edge of the glass protects your cutting
   wheel from chipping.

Always start scoring at one edge of the glass and continue to the other end. Remember that you're the tour guide; don't leave it up to the glass to figure out where you want it to break.

Figure 5-6:
Ending
the score
before you
come to the
edge of the
glass.

Practice making score lines until you can make a smooth, even, white scratch on the glass surface.

Letting it all fall apart: Breaking scored glass

When it comes to breaking your scored glass pieces, you have a few options for how to do so. The most basic method is to use your hands for leverage; however, because art glass projects normally contain many pieces of glass in various shapes and sizes, using your hands isn't always practical. Some pieces are just too small to be broken by hand. Another good option, particularly for small pieces, is to use breaking pliers. When you're working only with straight lines, you can also use running pliers.

In the beginning, you may choose to use pliers most of the time because they give you more confidence and make you feel more in control, but you need to work toward using your hands whenever possible because your hands allow you to be more successful and work faster.

Always break art glass with the scored side of the glass facing up. If you try to break the glass with the score line facing down toward the table, the glass won't break.

Breaking glass by hand

Follow these steps to break glass by hand along a straight line. Use the glass you scored in the earlier section "First things first: Making the score line" as you move through these steps.

1. **Grip the scored glass with both hands, with your thumbs on top of the glass on either side of the score line, keeping the edges away from and off of your hands (see Figure 5-7).**

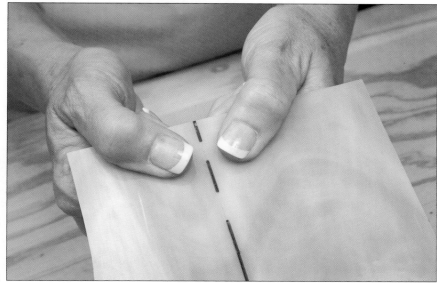

Figure 5-7:
Getting your
hands in
the right
position to
break the
glass.

2. **Maintaining a firm grip on the glass, rotate your hands by snapping your wrists (see Figure 5-8).**

   Doing so causes the glass to break in an upward motion.

3. **If the glass doesn't break, reposition your hands closer to the score line and repeat Steps 1 and 2.**

4. **If the glass still doesn't break, rotate the glass clockwise, and repeat Steps 1 and 2 at the other end of the score line.**

Using breaking pliers

When breaking small pieces of glass, you need more leverage than your hands can provide. Here's where pliers come into play. The most common pliers used for breaking glass are *breaking pliers*. They have flat, square jaws with smooth edges, and you use them like an extension of your hand when you break glass.

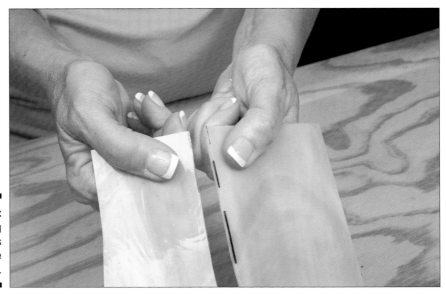

Figure 5-8:
Rotating
your hands
to break the
glass.

Follow these steps to make a break using breaking pliers (follow the steps in the earlier section "First things first: Making the score line" to create the scored glass for this exercise):

1. **With one hand, place the flat edge of the breaking pliers ¼ inch away from the score line.**

2. **Align the jaws of the pliers so that they're perpendicular to the score line (see Figure 5-9).**

3. **Use your free hand to hold the edge of the glass opposite your pliers, and follow Steps 2 through 4 from the section "Breaking glass by hand" (see Figure 5-10).**

Figure 5-9:
Positioning
breaking
pliers to
break the
glass.

Figure 5-10:
Breaking
the glass
with break-
ing pliers.

When cutting really thin strips of glass, you may need to use two pairs of pliers, one on each side of the score line. If you don't have a second pair of breaking pliers, use a pair of household pliers. Just make sure you wrap the jaws in duct tape to protect the glass.

Using running pliers

As long as you're only breaking glass along a straight line, you can use a special type of pliers called *running pliers.* Running pliers have adjustable jaws and can be a great tool when you're separating large sheets of glass or when you're working in combination with a strip-and-circle cutter.

A *strip-and-circle cutter* is a great tool for cutting multiple strips of glass to a designated width. The cutting wheel is mounted onto a bar that rides along a straight wooden rail. I show you how to use this special cutter in Chapter 11 when I explain how to make a stained-glass box.

Never use running pliers on curved cuts. Because the pressure exerted by these pliers forces the score line to separate very fast, the glass can't break along a curved score line.

Take a piece of scored glass (which you can create by following the steps in the earlier section "First things first: Making the score line"), and follow these simple steps to make the best use of running pliers:

1. **Adjust the jaws on your running pliers by turning the set screw until the opening is just slightly bigger than the thickness of the glass you're breaking.**

2. **Supporting the glass with one hand, place the pliers on the glass ½ inch from the edge with the score line positioned in the center of the pliers (see Figure 5-11).**

3. **Gently squeeze down on the pliers until the glass breaks along the score line (see Figure 5-12).**

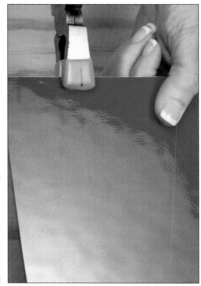

Figure 5-11:
Positioning
running
pliers for
breaking the
score.

Figure 5-12:
Completing
the break
with running
pliers.

Working with Curves

Not all projects are created using straight strips of glass, so you also need to be able to cut along curved lines. The scoring technique doesn't change whether you're cutting along a straight line or a curved one. You always want to apply steady, even pressure when you lay down your score lines. The only major difference here is that the line is curved. To help you score good curved lines, try to keep your cutter perpendicular to the glass surface.

Don't tilt your cutter to the left or right as you score around a curve. Doing so causes the glass to break at an angle, resulting in a sharper glass edge on which you can easily cut yourself.

Cutting curves

Follow these steps to cut a gentle curved line:

1. **Place a clean piece of clear glass on your prepared cutting surface.**

   See Chapter 3 for details on how to get your worktable ready for cutting glass.

2. **Draw a gentle curved line across the glass surface with a permanent marker.**

   Make sure the line starts at one edge of the glass and continues to the other edge (see Figure 5-13).

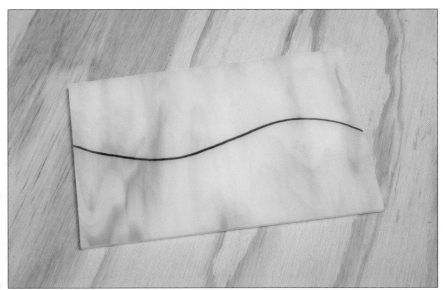

Figure 5-13:
Drawing a curved line with your marker.

3. **Before you put your cutter on the glass, do a practice score by moving your cutter ¼ inch above the glass surface.**

4. **Reposition your glass piece so your movement is more fluid and easier to execute; then take another practice score.**

   See if you can comfortably make the complete score; if you can't, reposition the glass, not your body.

5. **Follow Steps 4 through 6 in the section "First things first: Making the score line."**

   Make sure you start and complete the score line without shifting your weight from one foot to the other or letting your arm feel confined and hard to control.

6. **Use your hands or a pair of breaking pliers to gently break the glass by pressing down a little more firmly on one side than the other (see Figure 5-14).**

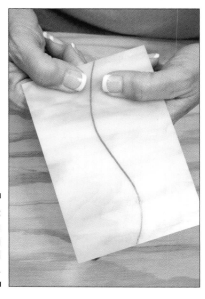

Figure 5-14:
Breaking
glass along
a curved
score line.

Curved lines are harder to break than straight lines. Don't rush the breaking process when you're working with curved lines. Trust me, you'll have a lot more success if you take the time to finesse the break than if you try to force it quickly.

Controlling the break and run

Stained-glass artists have come up with lots of little sayings to capture the essence of the different tasks they perform during the creation process. When it comes to glass cutting, the one you need to remember is "Control the break, control the glass." Essentially, what this mantra means is that after you figure out how to lay down a nice, smooth, evenly pressured score line, the real skill comes in breaking the glass. When glass starts to break along a score line, the action that occurs within the glass is called a *run*. You probably recognize the run as the crack that works its way through the glass before the two sides start to separate. Have you ever seen a chipped windshield? When that chip starts to spread, you can see the crack in the glass — that's the run.

As you develop your glass-cutting skills, you figure out how to control the speed of the run as it travels through the glass. You begin to "feel" the run, so to speak. The more pressure you apply when breaking the glass, the faster the glass separates and the less control you have over the break. But when you focus on the feel of the glass and the speed of the run, you start to control the glass — and that's what glass cutting is all about.

If you get in a hurry and try to push a break on the glass, you'll end up with a bad break and run. In other words, the glass will break where it wants to break, not where you want it to break (see Figure 5-15).

Glass particles are always in motion; a piece of glass never becomes completely solid. Creating a score line relieves the tension off the surface of the glass and allows it to break along a designated path. If your score line has a gap in it, the glass will break along the path of least resistance, which generally isn't the line you want it to follow. The same is true when you try to break a curved line too fast. The glass runs down the score line until it reaches a curve, at which point it loses control and continues to travel in a straight line away from the curved score line — just like when you drive a car too fast into a curve (and end up crashing straight ahead).

Figure 5-15:
A bad break and run.

Controlling the break and run in a piece of glass is especially important when you're cutting curved lines. Lucky for you, doing so isn't too difficult if you follow these steps:

1. **Score a piece of clear glass by following Steps 1 through 5 in the section "Cutting curves."**

2. **With one hand, place the jaws of your breaking pliers on the glass so that they're on one side of and parallel to the score line; with your free hand, hold the glass on the other side of the score line (see Figure 5-16).**

3. **Start pulling gently away and down with the pliers.**

   Go really slow! You'll hear a small crack first and then see the run start to appear.

4. **After the run gets ⅓ of the way across the score line, follow Steps 2 and 3 on the opposite end of the score line.**

Figure 5-16:
Holding the glass and pliers in position for breaking the glass.

5. **When you a have a short run at both ends of the score line, put down your pliers and use your hands to gently work the run from one end and then the other until the two runs meet in the middle and the glass breaks apart (see Figure 5-17).**

After you master this technique, you're well on your way to being a great glass cutter.

Figure 5-17:
Use your hands to finish the run and break the glass.

Cutting Out Shapes around Your Templates

Most stained-glass projects incorporate various sizes and shapes of glass. You start by drawing a design on paper; then you number all the pieces, choose the glass colors you want to use for them, and use special pattern shears to cut up a copy of the design into the paper templates you'll use to cut out the glass shapes (see Chapter 4 for all the details you need to know about working with patterns and templates).

Templates in hand, you're ready to start positioning them on your glass and then to cut out the shapes for your design. I explain how to do each of these tasks in the following sections.

Positioning templates for cutting

Before you can start cutting out glass shapes, you need to position the paper templates on your glass so you know exactly how big and what size each piece needs to be. Where you place the pattern pieces directly affects the amount of glass you need to complete your project and, more important, the success or lack of success you have when cutting out your shapes — because the largest mass controls the glass. It's important that you let this bit of physics work for you and not against you. To do so, try to eliminate as much excess glass as you can when laying out your templates.

Lay out all your pattern templates on top of the glass, moving them around to determine the best layout. Keep in mind the grain and color of the glass (check out Chapter 4 for more on glass grain). Make sure you can separate the larger pieces of glass without cutting through sections that you need for other pattern pieces. See Figure 5-18 for an example of how to lay out your pattern templates. After you achieve the layout you want, use rubber cement or spray adhesive to adhere the pattern pieces to the glass surface.

Figure 5-18:
Laying out your pattern templates.

Cutting the right way: Inside curve, outside curve, straight line

After you adhere all your pattern templates to the glass, you're ready to start cutting. Before you jump in, though, you need to know which shapes and which lines to cut first.

As for which pieces to start with, I suggest you always cut out the largest pattern pieces first in case you have to recut a piece. (Don't worry if you have to recut a piece or two; you can use the discarded glass pieces for your smaller pattern templates.)

When deciding which lines to cut first, follow this unbreakable glass-cutting rule: Cut inside curved lines first, then outside curved lines, followed by any straight lines. (In case you're wondering, *inside* curves are the concave template edges; *outside* curves are the template edges that bow or arch outward.) If you approach every pattern template with this cutting order in mind, you'll find plenty of success as a glass cutter because all glass shapes consist of at least one of these types of cuts. It's important to start with inside cuts because they're the most difficult to control and are perfect examples of how the mass controls the glass.

Follow these steps to see this glass-cutting rule in action:

1. **Score an inside curve line by placing your cutter as close as possible to the pattern template, pushing down on the cutter, applying even, steady pressure, and rolling the cutting wheel across the glass following the outside of the pattern.**

2. **Without trying to break the cut you made in Step 1, move your cutter over ¼ inch, and score another cut line parallel to the line you made in Step 1.**

   This extra cut is called a *relief cut.* Relief cuts help you support any small tips or sharp points on your glass pieces during the cutting and breaking processes.

   Deep inside cuts may require you to make two or more relief cuts. To do so, simply move the cutter ¼ inch away from the last relief cut you made to make another one. Figure 5-19 shows a pattern piece with four relief cuts (drawn with a marker so you can see them more clearly); to cut this particular piece, you'd start by making a score line right next to the pattern. Next you'd make the score line marked 1 in the figure and break away that portion of the glass. Then you'd score and break the lines marked 2 through 4. Your final break would be at the first score line you made next to the pattern edge.

3. **Using your breaking pliers, gently start breaking the last score line you made and then the next until you reach your desired score line.**

   This breaking process may seem painfully slow, but the time you spend on this step will undoubtedly save you dollars in broken glass and hours of cutting frustration.

Figure 5-19:
Making
relief cuts
when
cutting
curves.

4. **After you successfully cut out the inside curves, move on to the outside curves and then the straight lines; follow Step 1 to cut out these lines.**

   You can usually make these last two types of cuts using just one score each; you don't need to make any relief cuts.

Many glass shapes contain a combination of these three types of cuts, but don't worry. The cutting order is still the same: Inside curve, outside curve, straight line.

Cutting colored glass

When you're ready to make your first stained-glass project, you'll find thousands of beautiful colors and textures of art glass available. Unlike clear glass, colored glass has a right side and a wrong side on which to score the glass. The right side is the smoothest side. If you're working with textured glass, determining the smoothest side is easy, but for beginners, some types of art glass look the same on both sides.

The best way to determine the right side is to hold the glass piece in your hands and rock it back and forth, allowing the light to bounce off its surface. Then turn it over and do the same to the other side of the glass. One side will always look smoother than the other (that's the right side to score).

Don't worry if this process seems a little like guesswork. With a little practice, you'll become a real pro at determining which side of the glass to score. Even if you're just starting out, always select glass based on the way it affects your project, not based on how easy it is to cut. You'll be glad you did when you see your finished project!

When you purchase your glass, ask the retailer to help you out by marking which side of the glass is the right side to score. Before you start cutting, mark that side with a big X. Doing so keeps you from flipping a piece over backward while cutting out your pattern pieces.

When cutting templates, your goal is to cut as close to the pattern's edge as possible without running onto the paper. Because glass doesn't break right along a score line when the line has a gap in it, you should stop scoring as soon as you run over the paper. Take a second to realign your cutter at the point where you ran over the paper, and then start scoring again. You don't want to go over a score line more than once, though, so make sure you don't backtrack too far. (Check out the section "First things first: Making the score line" for more details on scoring glass.)

Cutting out circles

The circle is a very common shape in stained-glass projects. Although circles may seem more complex, they're really just a series of outside cuts. The main difference is that you need to leave at least ½ inch around all the sides of each circle pattern when you glue the paper template to the glass.

Follow these steps to cut out a circular piece of glass:

1. **Start at the edge of the glass, and make a score line up to the pattern edge.**

2. **Make a curved score line along ¼ to ⅓ of the circle, and continue your score line to the opposite side of the glass (see Figure 5-20).**

3. **Continue making a series of these curved score lines until you've scored completely around the circle.**

4. **Using your breaking pliers, start breaking off the unwanted glass pieces, beginning at the score line you made in Step 1.**

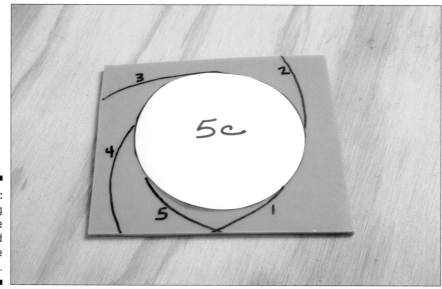

Figure 5-20:
Making relief score lines around a circle pattern.

Chapter 6

Grozing and Grinding Glass for a Perfect Fit

In This Chapter

▶ Filing away the rough edges on your glass pieces with grozing pliers

▶ Using a glass grinder to file faster and make more adjustments to your already-cut pieces

---

Stained glass is a very precise, step-by-step craft that builds on the quality of each task you complete. If you don't lay out your pattern correctly, for example, cutting out accurate glass shapes will be quite difficult. And if those shapes have excess glass and rough edges on them, it'll be next to impossible to finish your project.

Are you starting to worry about how you can make all your newly cut glass pieces just the right size and shape to fit your pattern? Never fear — I'm here to offer you an easy solution that'll fix all your cutting errors. In this chapter, I show you how to fit all your glass pieces to your pattern by making simple (or major) adjustments using your grozing pliers and glass grinder. I can already hear you giving a sigh of relief.

If, at any stage of a stained-glass project, you find yourself saying, "I wonder if I can get away with this . . ." the answer is *no*. Letting a mistake go unfixed at any point will only make your work harder down the road, and you won't be happy with the results.

Working with Grozing Pliers

After you cut out your glass pieces according to your paper templates, you have to tweak the edges a bit to make the pieces fit your pattern perfectly (see Chapter 5 for everything you need to know about cutting glass). To smooth the edges of your glass pieces so they match your templates, you need to recruit the help of your grozing pliers, or what I like to call filing-nipping-and-prying pliers.

Don't worry, you didn't do anything wrong. All glass artists, regardless of how experienced they are, have to fine-tune the edges of the glass shapes they cut out. It's just the way glass breaks. Take a look at the circle-shaped glass piece in Figure 6-1; you can easily see the excess glass around the pattern template. The following sections show you how to remove this extra glass and how to smooth out the edges so they match your template perfectly.

Figure 6-1:
A circle-shaped glass piece after you cut it but before you file it.

Always wear your safety glasses when cutting, grozing, or grinding glass. In fact, it's good practice to keep your safety glasses on at all times when you're in your studio. If you don't, you risk injuring your eyes from flying pieces of glass and dust.

Filing

Grozing pliers have small ridges or teeth on the interior sides of their jaws that act like a file against your glass's edges. File each of your cut glass pieces by rubbing it up and down against the pliers until it looks exactly like the template and has relatively smooth edges (see Figure 6-2).

Don't take the paper template off your glass piece until the glass matches the shape on your pattern exactly. The template gives you a guideline to follow when filing away extra ridges. When you're happy with the glass's shape, you can remove the template. Just don't forget to transfer the pattern number to the glass piece using a permanent marker or other glass-marking pen.

Nipping and prying

In addition to filing, you can use your grozing pliers to nip or bite at your cut glass pieces to remove larger *flanges,* or sections of excess glass. You need to use great care when doing so because you don't want to create a *fisheye,* or round chip along the edge of your glass shape. (Depending on the size of the fisheye, you may need to cut out a replacement piece.)

Always save any leftover glass pieces you have after you finish cutting just in case you have to recut a shape or two.

When nipping away bits of glass, use just the corners of your pliers. Close down on the unwanted glass with the pliers, and apply a small amount of pressure as you pry the pliers up and away, removing small bits of glass each time (see Figure 6-3). Don't try to hurry during the nipping process; if you do, you risk taking too big a bite of glass, resulting in large chips and broken pieces. Be patient and take small bites of glass until you've removed all the excess glass and your glass shape matches your template.

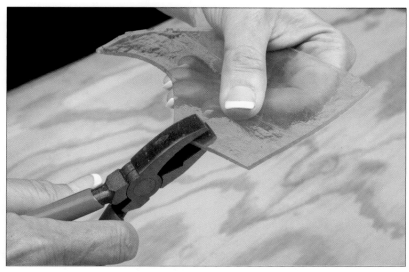

Figure 6-2: Grozing a piece of glass.

Figure 6-3: Using grozing pliers to nip at excess glass edges.

Powering Up for Faster Results: Glass Grinders

If you're wondering whether there's a faster way to file and nip your glass pieces to make them match your pattern templates, you'll be happy to meet the glass grinder, a tool that really speeds up the grozing process. Keep in mind, however, that it isn't the tool of choice for every project. For leaded projects, you want your glass pieces to have a few little ridges because they help the glass "sit" better in the lead-came channels. (I explain this concept in more detail in Chapter 9.) But you can use your glass grinder to remove excess glass if you don't feel confident in using your grozing pliers to fine-tune your pieces. For copper-foil projects, on the other hand, you want to grind every edge on your glass pieces to obtain a smooth surface that allows your foil to adhere to the glass. So if you plan to do any copper-foil projects, you need to purchase a glass grinder.

The following sections show you how to use your grinder effectively to create smooth edges on all your glass pieces.

Make sure you use the grinder safety shield recommended by the manufacturer whenever you're grinding, and wear your safety glasses at all times.

Using your grinder

Here's how to work with a grinder:

1. **Check the water level on your grinder before you use it, and make sure the sponge is clean and wet.**

   You never want to grind glass with a dry bit. Doing so wears out the bit too quickly; plus, the heat of the friction can easily break your glass piece.

2. **Turn your grinder on and place your glass piece on the grinder's work surface; using the paper template as your guide, firmly push the glass up against the grinder bit (see Figure 6-4).**

   Keep a firm grip on the glass at all times.

3. **Rotate the glass piece along the grinder to remove all the excess glass showing around the outside edges of your pattern template.**

   If you're having trouble fitting a standard-size grinder bit into the small, inside curves and shapes of some of your glass pieces, you may want to purchase a ¼-inch bit that attaches to the top of your standard grinder bit. All manufacturers offer a variety of bit sizes and styles, so you shouldn't have trouble finding just what you need for any task.

4. **After you finish grinding the piece, dry the glass, keeping the pattern template in place, and fit it to your master pattern.**

   You may need to make a few last-minute adjustments to your pieces when fitting your pieces together on your pattern, and you'll want to use the pattern templates as guidelines.

Protecting your pattern

During the grinding process, you want to make sure you keep the master copy of your pattern dry. The best way to do so is to cover the pattern in plastic wrap or, if it's small enough, slip it into a plastic sheet protector (which you can find at your local office-supply store).

Warped patterns are a nightmare when you're trying to fit your glass shapes together and when you're constructing your project. Always wipe each piece of glass after you grind it to make sure it's perfectly dry before you place it on your master pattern.

Making sure your glass selection fits your project

Seeing all your colorful glass pieces laid out on the pattern is an exciting part of the stained-glass process. It's the perfect time to get a sneak peak of what the finished project will look like, especially if you have a light box.

Take a few minutes to make sure you're happy with all your color selections and to double-check that all the glass grains are going in the right direction. For example, if the yellow glass you've chosen for the center of your flower is too bright for the project, take the time to recut this piece using a different color of glass.

To create a new pattern template, trace around the original piece and cut inside the traced line. Then fit the new piece to your project. Recutting one or two pieces for your project takes only a few minutes but can make a big difference in the final outcome. Keep in mind that now is likely the last chance you'll have to make these kinds of changes to your project.

Figure 6-4: Using a grinder to shape a glass piece.

After you finish grinding all your glass pieces and fit them to your master pattern, you can remove your pattern templates. Just don't forget to use a permanent marker or other glass-marking pen to transfer the template number and any arrows onto the glass. Be sure to keep each piece numbered until the project is fully constructed. If a number gets wiped away during handling, just remark it.

Marking your pieces before making adjustments

When you cut out your paper pattern templates, you use pattern shears that leave just enough room for the lead came or copper foil that will fit between each of the individual glass pieces when you assemble your project (see Chapter 4 for details). After you finish cutting out and filing or grinding your glass pieces, you need to make sure none of the glass shapes extend over your pattern lines (see Figure 6-5).

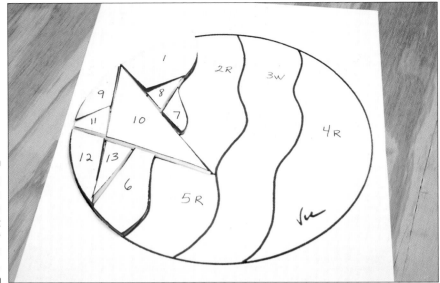

Figure 6-5:
Making sure your glass pieces fit inside your pattern lines.

If any of the glass shapes do extend over the pattern lines, use your grinder to reshape just that section of the glass. If you overgrind your glass pieces, your finished project will be sloppy and difficult to build and solder.

When you're using the grinder to make adjustments to the shapes of your glass pieces, the easiest way to prevent overgrinding is to mark your glass before you start using the grinder. Using a permanent marker, draw a line perpendicular to the glass edge where you want to start grinding and another line where you want to stop. Also draw a line that runs parallel to the glass edge to indicate the amount of glass you want to remove between your two perpendicular marks (see Figure 6-6). These lines help guide your grinding so that you don't accidentally remove half the glass's shape!

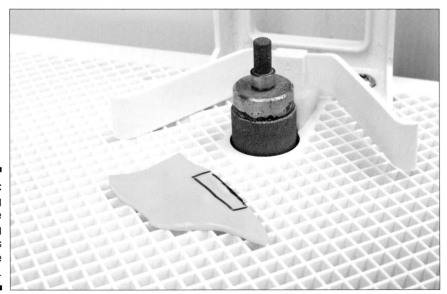

Figure 6-6:
Marking glass before making adjustments with the grinder.

Chapter 7

Soldering Your Way to Well-Jointed Projects

....

In This Chapter

▶ Understanding the basics of solder

▶ Getting your soldering iron ready to work

▶ Using the right soldering techniques for copper-foil projects

▶ Creating the perfect joints on lead-came projects

▶ Developing safe and healthy soldering practices

....

The purpose of soldering in stained glass is to keep all the pieces of glass and metal together — yep, it's like glue in other crafts. How well you solder your projects together is one of the most important aspects of your stained-glass work; it's the standard by which you and other glass artisans judge the quality of your work.

Not to worry. Through my television show, instructional DVDs, and hands-on workshops, I've taught tons of people how to solder, and I have confidence that I can turn you into a great master of the "silver-tongued devil" — also known as soldering — in no time.

In this chapter, I share all my soldering techniques with you so you, too, can develop great skills for both copper-foil and lead-came projects. Soldering is all about understanding how to use your equipment and how the metals, flux, and heat react to one another. Beyond that, all you need to master the art of soldering is practice, practice, and more practice. So get ready to heat up those irons and start soldering!

If you need more information about soldering equipment, flip to Chapter 2, and turn to Chapter 17 for ten strategies that'll help you master the art of soldering.

Solder 101: What It Is and How It Works

Solder is a fusible metal *alloy,* or mixture, made up of two or more metals (tin and lead make up the solder you use for stained-glass projects). When heated, the metal becomes a liquid that flows onto the copper foil or lead came you used to construct your project. When the solder cools, it becomes a hard metal again, creating a permanent bond that holds the project together.

Solder starts out as a solid. As it starts to melt (when you touch it with your heated soldering iron), it goes through the following three stages. You control these stages by changing the temperature on your soldering iron (see the section "Setting your iron to the correct temperature" for more details):

- **Paste stage:** In the first stage, the solder is thick, and you can push it around with your soldering tip.

- **Ideal liquid stage:** The next stage is a liquid; it runs, drips, and flows. This stage is the perfect working temperature for creating smooth copper-foil soldering seams and lead-came joints.

- **Too-hot liquid stage:** In the final stage, the solder gets so hot that it actually starts to heat up the glass. When the glass gets too hot, the metal runs through the spaces between the glass pieces. This too-hot solder doesn't allow you to create the smooth seams and joints you're looking for.

Prepping and Using Your Soldering Iron

Starting off with a clean soldering iron that's set to the right temperature is key to successfully soldering both copper-foil and leaded projects. Read on to find out how to hold your iron for maximum effectiveness and how to make sure your iron is always clean and ready to go.

Setting your iron to the correct temperature

Controlling the temperature of your soldering iron is paramount in stained glass because you want your solder to be at the perfect working temperature (see the section "Solder 101: What It Is and How It Works" for the lowdown on the different heating stages of solder). If you don't control the temperature of your iron, it can reach temperatures of 900 to 1,100 degrees, which are way hotter than you need because solder melts at much lower temperatures (around 360 to 400 degrees). Excess heat not only shortens the life of your soldering iron, but can also melt some of the other metals in your projects, such as lead, zinc, and copper.

When it comes to soldering irons, you can use either a *thermostatically controlled iron,* which has a thermostat built into the soldering tip to maintain a set temperature, or an *iron-rheostat combination,* which relies on a separate rheostat to control the temperature. (For more info on these two irons, turn to Chapter 2.)

The perfect temperature you want to set your iron to varies depending on the type of iron you're using, the solder you're working with, whether the project is copper foil or lead came, and how fast you work. If you're a speedy, confident artist, you'll demand more heat from your iron. If you work more slowly, you'll need a cooler iron tip.

If you're using a thermostatically controlled soldering iron, like the Weller SP100, the tip temperature is preset at the factory. On the back of each tip, you find the number 6 (600 degrees), 7 (700 degrees), or 8 (800 degrees). The standard tip is a 7 tip; it offers a great working temperature for most stained-glass projects. If you want a hotter or cooler working temperature, all you have to do is change your iron's tip. The tip's thermostat works just like the heating and cooling thermostat in your house. When the iron starts to cool down, the thermostat turns the iron back on and the tip heats back up to the predetermined setting.

If you're using an iron-rheostat-combination iron, you need to plug your iron into a rheostat to regulate the temperature. Note that the control dials on a rheostat don't display actual temperature readings; instead, they have high-to-low operating controls and display indicator numbers — generally 1 through 5. For copper-foil projects, I work at a setting between 3 and 5. For lead-came projects, I use a setting between 2 and 3. As you experiment with your own soldering iron and rheostat, you'll be able to determine the perfect settings for any soldering task. Figure 7-1 shows a rheostat that's been set for soldering a copper-foil project.

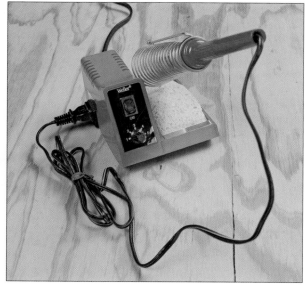

Figure 7-1: Setting up a rheostat-controlled iron for a copper-foil project.

Always use a soldering iron stand when working with a hot iron, and keep the electric cord away from the iron tip.

Getting a good grip on your iron

I recommend that you hold your iron like a club rather than a pencil. Irons are designed to distribute their weight evenly from end to end, and as long as you hold the iron handle as shown in Figure 7-2, you should be able to solder a smooth, even bead or an even joint (depending on whether you're working on a copper-foil or lead-came project). Holding the iron like a pencil transfers even the least amount of shakiness down the barrel of the iron, creating lumpy solder seams.

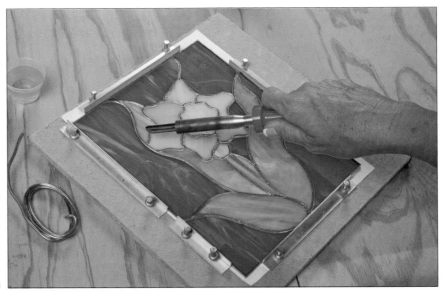

Figure 7-2:
Holding your
soldering
iron the
right way.

Keeping your tip clean

One of the most important tools in your soldering toolbox is a simple little
sponge called a *tip cleaner*. Having a clean and natural tip cleaner ready at
all times is super important because you need to clean your iron's tip as you
solder (and the tip cleaner is the only thing you should use to clean your
soldering iron tip). As you solder your projects together, flux, corrosion, dirt,
and oxidation build up on your iron tip, making it difficult to solder the perfect beads or joints for your projects. A wipe across your tip cleaner clears
all the gunk away and keeps your iron's tip nice and shiny.

While soldering, make it a habit to wipe off all four sides of your tip every few
minutes. Your tip will last longer and your projects will look better if you do.

Soldering Copper-Foil Projects

Soldering copper-foil projects is a lot like painting except, of course, that you
use hot, molten metal rather than paint. Each line of solder you create with your
iron is called a *bead* or *seam,* and it becomes the glue that holds your project
together. Similarly, the copper foil that surrounds each piece of glass provides
the conduit or base for the solder beams; solder doesn't stick to the glass.

The following sections go through the process of soldering copper-foil
projects, including selecting the right solder, using flux, tack soldering, and
removing extra solder.

Note: After you solder one side of your project panel, you have to flip it over and
repeat the same process on the reverse side of the project. You aren't finished
soldering until you've coated all the copper foil throughout the entire project.

Don't forget to wear your safety glasses at all times while soldering to protect your eyes from popping solder. You may want to wear gloves and long sleeves, as well.

Selecting the right solder for copper-foil projects

For all your stained-glass projects, you'll work primarily with solders that are composites of tin and lead. The top of each spool of solder indicates how much of these two metals are in the solder (see Figure 7-3). The first number always indicates the amount of tin; the second number indicates the amount of lead. For copper-foil projects, you need to use 60/40 solder. (You use 50/50 solder for lead projects; see the later section "Soldering Lead-Came Projects" for more details.)

Figure 7-3:
Spools of stained-glass solder.

The higher the tin content, the faster the solder melts and the faster it cools, which is why you need to have more tin when you're working on copper-foil projects. You want the bead of solder to cool quickly so it maintains a nice, high, round seam. (Because 50/50 solder takes longer to cool, it stays molten longer, allowing it to flatten out and blend into the face of the lead came.)

A number of specialty solders are available specifically for lamp making, box making, and decorative soldering. In general, if you need your solder to set up extra quickly, choose a solder with a higher tin count.

Applying flux to your project

The *flux* you have to use before you solder any stained-glass project is a chemical cleaning agent that removes any oxidation from the surface of metals, allowing the hot molten solder to bond to that surface. The primary ingredients in flux are ammonium chloride and zinc chloride, both of which are pretty nasty chemicals. Over the years, milder fluxes, including new organic fluxes, have been developed.

In my experience, some fluxes definitely work better than others, but they all perform a little differently. Try out several different types of flux until you find the perfect one for you. I prefer using a liquid flux because it's easier to clean up than a paste flux. I also try to work with the least-toxic flux I can find.

To apply flux to your stained-glass project, use a disposable flux brush to brush it across the surface of the metal (in copper-foil projects, that metal is the foil itself; in lead projects, that metal is the lead came); see Figure 7-4. You can't overflux because metals oxidize each time you heat them up. Reapplying flux before you try to re-solder an area will help the solder flow more evenly, resulting in smoother solder seams.

Always solder in a well-ventilated area, and don't forget to wear your respirator and safety glasses. Hot solder often pops and sends small specs of solder flying.

Don't be fooled by the fact that flux is a cleaner. It, too, can rust and corrode anything it comes in contain with — like your glass cutters, pliers, and other metal tools. Always store flux in a clearly labeled, resealable plastic container. Never store it in your toolbox or near your glass-working tools. Clean up any spills immediately with soap and water, and spray your metal tools with W-D 40 after they come in contact with flux to prevent rusting.

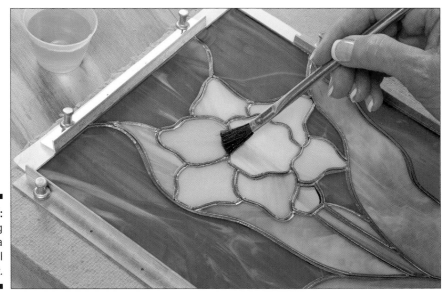

Figure 7-4:
Applying flux to a copper-foil project.

A word about lead-free solders

If you're concerned about working with lead, especially if you have young children who may be interested in working in your studio, consider creating only copper-foil projects and working with lead-free solder. *Lead-free solder* is an alloy comprised of tin, silver, and copper, and it's available at glass shops and online. Lead-free solder is more expensive and a little more challenging to work with, but if you're creating a lead-free studio zone, it's worth the effort and the price.

Tackling tack soldering

Tack soldering is the process of applying small dots of melted solder to various parts of your project. The purpose of tack soldering is to stabilize the individual glass pieces so they won't shift or move during the solder-beading process. You primarily use tack soldering on copper-foil projects, but sometimes you may use it on leaded projects, as well.

This technique is as important to stained-glass artists as pins are to a seamstress and nails are to a carpenter, so be sure to always tack solder before you start running a bead (see the next section for details on running a bead).

To tack solder, follow these steps:

1. **Set your iron to the perfect working temperature, and make sure the tip is clean.**

   The perfect working temperature is hot enough to melt the solder into a liquid but not so hot that the solder runs through the project to the other side each time you try to move the iron along your seams. (See the section "Setting your iron to the correct temperature" for details on how to achieve this temperature.)

2. **Apply a small amount of flux to the area you're going to tack solder.**

3. **Lay ¼ inch of the solder across a seam where two copper-foiled glass pieces meet; apply the flat face of your hot iron over the solder.**

4. **Hold the iron against the solder until the solder melts and flows into the seam (see Figure 7-5).**

   The solder that flows into the seam is your *tack*. Be sure to keep your tacks flat. If they look like buttons on top of your seams, you're using too much solder and not holding the iron on the tack until it melts completely.

If you have gaps smaller than ³⁄₁₆ inch between any of your glass pieces, now's the time to fill them in with melted solder. Use the same technique you use for tacking except apply more solder. Continue to feed solder into the gap until it's completely filled in. If your gaps are larger than ³⁄₁₆ inch, consider recutting the glass pieces to reduce the size of the gaps. (Turn to Chapter 8 for more details about tack soldering and filling in gaps.)

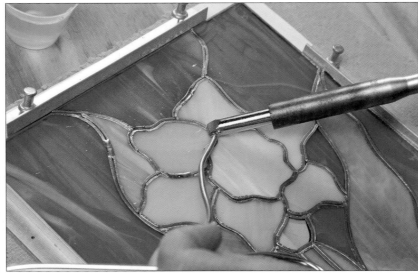

Figure 7-5:
Tack
soldering a
copper-foil
project.

Running the perfect bead

Ready to start running? No, I don't mean taking a lap around the block. In stained glass, *running* describes the motion you use when soldering copper foil. You can literally run your hot iron tip along the surface of the copper foil. The *bead,* or rounded seam, you create behind the soldering iron as the solder cools is what holds together your glass panel (see Figure 7-6).

A perfect seam is smooth, never ending, consistent in size, and free of any ridges, lumps, bumps, and holes. Because solder is liquid only until it cools, at which time it turns to a hard finish, you need to master the art of soldering fast. After all, your total working time is very short. Don't worry, though. The more you practice, the quicker you'll be at soldering.

Figure 7-6:
Running
a bead of
solder on a
copper-foil
project.

In general, I start soldering a project from the top and work my way down to the bottom of the panel. Doing so keeps the flux off my sleeves and allows me to focus on one area at a time. I work on one area until I'm happy with the way the bead looks; then I move on to the next part.

To run a bead of solder, follow these steps:

1. **Set your soldering iron to the perfect working temperature.**

   If the copper foil gets hot along with the solder, it's almost impossible to create the perfect bead of solder you're looking for. So if your soldering iron gets so hot that it heats your foil, use the wet sponge on your iron stand to quickly cool your iron tip, and then adjust the temperature setting on your rheostat. (See the section "Setting your iron to the correct temperature" for more details on setting the right temperature.)

2. **Brush a liberal amount of flux onto the surface of the copper foil in the area where you're working.**

3. **Position your solder against the tip of your soldering iron (see Figure 7-7).**

   Notice that your iron tip is up on its edge. You don't want to use the larger flat edge when you're trying to create a nice rounded solder bead because doing so overheats the seam and results in a flat bead.

4. **Gently push the solder into the hot iron tip; at the same time, move the iron along the seam.**

   The solder will melt and run down around the tip, forming a small pool of melted solder (see Figure 7-8).Your goal is to keep this molten ball of solder consistent in size as you move the soldering iron down along the foil seam. When the ball gets smaller, slow down and push more solder to the tip of your iron.

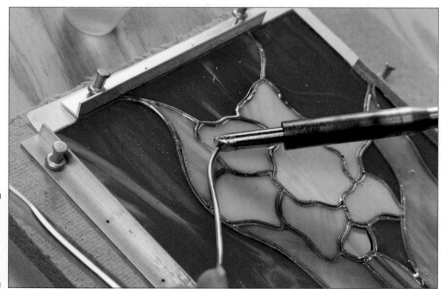

Figure 7-7:
Positioning
the iron and
solder to run
a bead.

5. **Continue to move the iron down the seam, applying an even amount of solder as you go.**

   Don't worry if your solder bead is a little lumpy and bumpy. You can go over your solder seams a second (or third, fourth, fifth . . .) time to smooth everything out (see the next section for details).

Entrance and exit strategies for repairs

Even the best soldering professionals have to go over their solder seams two or three times to get them smooth and perfect. Don't despair if you have to go over your seams 10 or 12 times on your first few projects. You need lots of practice to master the art of soldering. Just be careful not to overheat one area by working it too much at one time. Let the project cool for a few minutes, reflux the area you're working on, and try it again.

The objective of touching up your seams is to eliminate ridges and bumps — not to create more of them. When touching up a seam that has already been soldered, be sure to keep your iron tip on its side. Start by placing the hot tip down on top of the seam. Wait until you see the solder melt around all sides of the iron before you start moving along the seam again (see Figure 7-9).

How you exit the seam is equally as important as you how you enter it. Whenever you remove your iron from the seam, pause and let the solder melt all around the tip; then slowly and smoothly slide your tip out the side of the molten seam (see Figure 7-10). Never lift your iron straight up from a seam because doing so causes waves, which result in ridges.

Heat cracks are the most heartbreaking sound a glass artist can hear. These small hairline cracks in the glass occur when you overheat the glass during the soldering process. To prevent heat cracks from invading your panels, always allow the glass to cool completely before you re-flux and try to re-solder a seam.

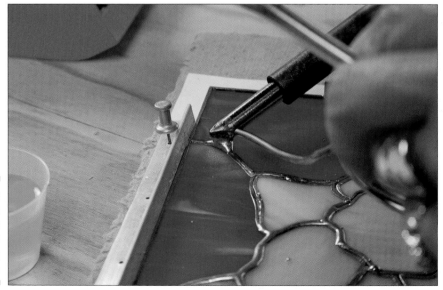

Figure 7-8: Molten solder ball under the soldering tip.

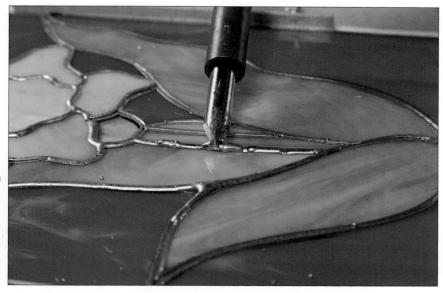

Figure 7-9:
Reintro-
ducing the
iron to a
seam for
repairs.

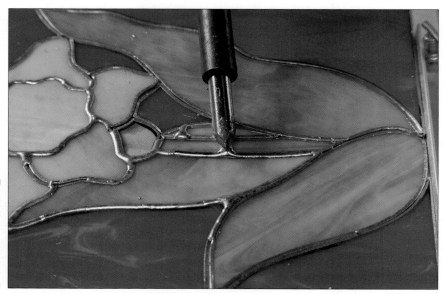

Figure 7-10:
Removing
the iron tip
from a
finished
seam.

Soldering intersections

The point at which two or more pieces of glass meet is called an *intersection.*
When approaching an intersection while soldering, make sure the entire area
has been fluxed, and then move the molten solder up and down each branch
of the intersection, keeping all the seams molten at one time (see Figure 7-11).
Doing so eliminates large, bulky intersections.

Never stop and start in an intersection. Instead, introduce your iron down
the line from one of the seams and work your way into the intersection.
Remember to use the entrance and exit strategies I describe in the preceding
section as you go.

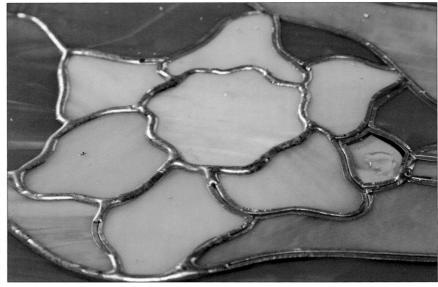

Figure 7-11:
Soldered
intersec-
tions with
multiple
seams.

Dealing with holes, craters, and pops

Don't panic if your solder seams look more like the surface of the moon than nice, rounded beads. Flux has a tendency to overreact to heat. Think of your solder seams, especially the wider gaps between glass pieces, like volcanoes. Flux gets trapped inside these spaces, and, as the solder starts to cool, the flux starts to boil. As it boils, the oxygen pops through the solder, leaving a hole or crater on the solder seam (see Figure 7-12). If your seams are full of holes or craters, let them cool off and then re-flux and re-run the seams.

If you experience excessive popping, you may want to change fluxes. After all, some brands are better than others; you just have to find which one is right for you. The good news is that flux is cheap, so you don't have to pay a fortune to try out several different fluxes until you find the one that works best.

Removing excess solder

If you overdo it with the solder during any of your passes across the seams, you'll have to remove some of it. The easiest way to do so is to flux the area, place the flat side of your soldering iron on top of the excess solder, and remelt it. Then lift the iron straight up from the project. Lucky for you, solder will travel up with the iron so that all you have to do is wipe off your iron tip with a wet sponge to remove the extra solder. Repeat this process until you have removed all the excess solder from your panel.

Don't forget about those heat cracks. It's easy to create one during this process, so be sure to take your time and let the glass cool off from time to time as you remove excess solder.

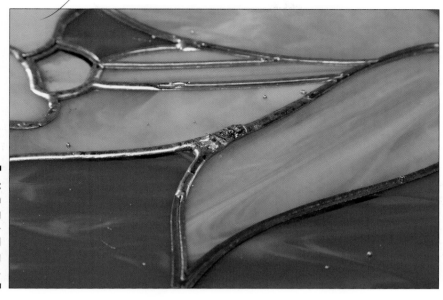

Figure 7-12:
Common
soldering
imperfec-
tions caused
by popping
flux.

Soldering Lead-Came Projects

Many of the soldering principles you use for copper-foil projects also apply to lead-came projects. In case you're wondering, *lead cames* are *H-* or *U-*shaped strips of lead that connect all the individual pieces of glass together in a leaded project (in other words, they take the place of the copper foil). Because of their shape, you don't have to do as much soldering for lead-came projects as you do for copper-foil ones. You solder only the intersections, or *joints,* where two pieces of lead meet.

Although many of the techniques are similar for both lead-came and copper-foil projects, you will find some differences between them. The following sections focus on the ins and outs of lead-came soldering.

Selecting the right solder for lead-came projects

You can use the same soldering iron and equipment for both copper-foil and lead-came projects; just make sure you use 50/50 solder rather than 60/40 (which is what you use for copper-foil projects). Like the name implies, 50/50 solder has equal amounts of tin and lead; it also has a higher melting point than 60/40 solder and takes longer to cool. The fact that the 50/50 solder stays molten longer allows you to flatten out each solder joint and track it across the face of the lead (see the section "Soldering the perfect joint" for details on how to do so). Your goal here is to make the intersections blend in or disappear, creating a seamless flow of metal throughout your panel.

Testing your iron's temperature

Unlike copper foil, lead came can melt very quickly if your soldering iron is too hot. For this reason, you need to get in the habit of testing the heat of your soldering iron on a scrap piece of lead before soldering any lead-came project. Lucky for you, testing your iron's temperature is easy to do. After your iron has heated up, test the temperature by pushing solder into the tip. If it melts quickly, you know your iron is hot enough.

How do you know if the iron's too hot? Using a scrap piece of lead came, place the flat side of your soldering iron directly on the came (see Figure 7-13a). You should be able to hold your iron on the face of the came for a full slow count to ten without the iron melting through the lead. If the iron does melt through the lead, as shown in Figure 7-13b, you need to turn down your soldering iron. After doing so, wait three to five minutes and then retest the iron.

Be sure to wipe your soldering iron across your tip cleaner after your first test, but remember that doing so quickly lowers the temperature of your iron. Wait a couple of minutes before conducting your next test to get accurate results.

I like to use the same size and profile of lead for testing as I use in my project. That way, I can eliminate any disappointing surprises when I start soldering my real project.

Soldering the perfect joint

In lead-came projects, the main focus of your soldering efforts is on the *joints,* or intersections where two or more pieces of lead come together. Your goal when soldering is to achieve a *perfect joint.* The first aspect of a perfect joint is that all its branches are equal in length. More specifically, you want your soldered joints to extend the same size as the width of the lead you're soldering in all directions (see Figure 7-14). You don't have to mark how far down the lead your joints need to extend like I do in the figure; just eyeball it and try to keep all your joints consistent.

You can use the same type of flux for lead-came projects that you use for copper-foil projects (see the section "Applying flux to your project" for details). When applying flux to a lead-came joint, don't brush it all over the face of the came. Using a disposable flux brush, paint a ½-inch strip of flux over the intersection where two strips of lead meet. If you have to go over the joint a second or third time, don't forget to re-flux between each try.

Figure 7-13:
Use some scrap lead came to see if your iron is too hot.

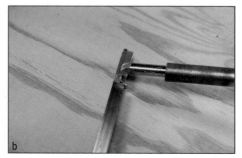

When soldering lead came, use a straight down-and-up hand motion. You don't run a bead or paint with your soldering iron tip (as you do with copper foil). You simply let the heat move the solder evenly around the joints. Remember that melted solder is a liquid; it will flow evenly in all directions as long as your worktable is level.

Your grip on the soldering iron is the same here as it is with copper-foil soldering. You hold the handle like a club, not a pencil (refer to Figure 7-2). The weight of the iron's tip helps level your motions and yields a better solder joint.

The second aspect of a perfect joint is that it's low and flat to the lead face. It should blend into the lead perfectly. If your solder is raised up and looks more like a button, you're doing one of two things:

✔ Using too much solder

✔ Not leaving your soldering iron on the joint long enough for the solder to become completely molten and bond with the lead came

Both errors are easy to fix. For your next joint, simply use less solder or leave your soldering iron on the joint longer so that the solder has time to bond with the lead. Check out the next section for tips on how to smooth out your already-soldered joints.

To help you determine whether your soldered joint is the right height, pass your fingernail across the edge of the joint. If it makes a clicking sound, your joint is too high. The edge should be completely flush with the came face and, therefore, not make any sound when you pass over it with your nail.

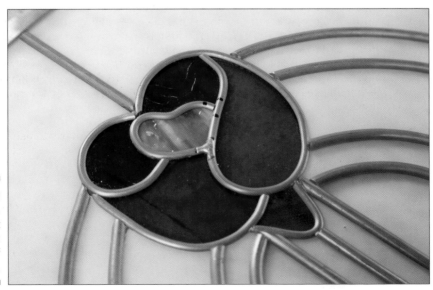

Figure 7-14: The size of a perfect joint marked on the face of the lead.

Removing excess solder

You remove excess solder from lead-came projects the same way you do for copper-foil projects. Here are the basics you need to know:

1. Flux the excess solder.

2. Place the flat side of your soldering iron over the solder you want to remove, and heat it until it becomes molten.

3. Lift your soldering iron straight up from the area.

4. Wipe the tip of your iron on your wet tip cleaner.

5. Repeat Steps 1 through 4 until you have removed all the excess solder.

Soldering Safety

When soldering, keep in mind that you're working with a tool that can reach temperatures of 1,000 degrees, strong chemicals, and lead. Naturally, you need to follow a few simple but important guidelines to keep you and your studio safe.

Keeping your studio clean is one of the best safety tips I can give you, so get in the habit of cleaning up after you complete each step in the stained-glass process. Put away your tools after you finish working with them to keep them from being contaminated by flux spills, lead fumes, and dust.

Here are some important tips to help keep you safe while soldering (see Chapter 2 for more details on what safety equipment to have in your studio):

- ✔ **Vacuum and damp mop your studio floors and wipe down all your counters with a wet cloth on a weekly, if not daily, basis.** Exactly how often you need to do so depends on how much time you spend in your studio.

- ✔ **Dress for safety.** Wear your safety glasses and an apron or smock to protect your eyes and your clothing. I have a pair of closed-toe shoes that I keep in my studio so that my feet are always protected while I work. I change out of those shoes before I walk into other areas of my home so that I don't track small chips of glass, lead dust, and other possible contaminates throughout my house. Changing shoes is especially important if you have children or pets who spend most of their time on the floor and then put their hands and paws in their mouths.

- ✔ **Invest in a good ventilation system.** In addition to turning on your fume extractors, open the doors and windows in your studio when possible; doing so lets the fresh air in and the bad air out. Wear your respirator when soldering. After you do one or two projects, using the right safety equipment will become second nature to you.

- ✔ **Don't throw glass chips in your regular trash.** Not only are they harmful to the environment, but glass chips can also cause a nasty cut to anyone handling your trash. Instead, keep your glass chips and scraps in a small cardboard box. When the box is full, tape it shut and put it into the trash or recycle bin.

- ✔ **Check with your local waste management department regarding how to dispose of scraps of lead, solder, and chemicals.** Many stained-glass shops have recycling programs that can take your scraps and dispose of them properly.

Part III
Practice Makes Perfect: Stained-Glass Projects Aplenty

The 5th Wave   By Rich Tennant

"Beautiful. This is the finest stained glass work I've ever seen done on a peephole."

In this part . . .

This part is filled with dozens of great ideas, step-by-step instructions, and patterns to help you create just about any project you can think of. I start with copper-foil projects, showing you how to wrap each glass piece in copper tape and how to create beautiful solder lines to join them all together. Then I cover lead-came projects, focusing on how to use lead came to unite the pieces of your project, how to solder perfect joints, and how to make them airtight and waterproof.

Want to make a stained-glass box or lampshade? Great! I offer you simple instructions for creating both projects in this part. And, in case you want to create a different style or size project than the ones I include here, I show you a few ways to customize my patterns and designs to make them your own.

As an added bonus, I include a few of my favorite stained-glass designs so you can get some more independent practice. So grab your glass cutter, grinder, and soldering iron, and get ready to have some glass-making fun!

Chapter 8

Creating Copper-Foil Projects

Copper-foil projects are comprised of individual pieces of glass, each wrapped in a copper-foil band. These pieces can contour to any surface — which is why one of the most well-known glass artists of all time used this technique to build his fabulous lampshades. (I'm talking about Tiffany, of course!)

So you have your eye on a particular copper-foil project and are ready to get started. Great! In this chapter, I provide all the information you need to succeed on just about any copper-foil project. Plus, I provide you with several great project patterns that are ready to go, in case you don't know exactly where to start.

Now is not the time to try your hand at designing your own pattern. Practice on a couple of ready-to-make patterns to get comfortable with the steps and techniques of copper-foil glass making first. If you haven't found the perfect design for you yet, spend some time flipping through a few stained-glass pattern books and perusing a few Web sites. You'll find so many wonderful patterns that you'll surely run out of places to put your windows and other projects long before you run out of designs.

Cutting and Foiling Your Glass Pieces

No matter what copper-foil project you're working on, you need to follow some basic steps and master a few important techniques if you want to end up with a well-constructed, beautiful panel. In this section, I walk you through the steps and techniques involved in prepping and using a pattern, cutting and shaping your glass pieces, and foiling them. You can apply these steps to any of the projects and patterns provided in this chapter, as well as any other copper-foil patterns you work with.

I suggest that you start out by selecting a pattern that's a manageable size. Try to keep it smaller than 12 x 18 inches. You'll have plenty of time to build the really big ones later.

Make sure you wear your safety glasses at all times in your glass studio to keep your eyes safe from flying glass chips, dust, chemicals, and everything else you work with as you create your copper-foil project.

Prepping the pattern and cutting your glass

Prepping your pattern and cutting your glass pieces to fit it are the first steps of any copper-foil project. Here's what you need to do:

1. **Use a permanent marker to label each pattern piece with a different number; make three copies of the pattern.**

   One copy is your master, which you use to help you put your project together, one you cut up to make the templates for your glass pieces, and one you file away in case you need to make repairs later. Check out Chapter 4 for more details on working with patterns.

2. **Use an art knife to trim off the exterior of the pattern, and use foil shears to cut out each pattern piece.**

   It's important that you use foil shears and not lead shears here because foil shears leave just the right amount of space between the pattern pieces for the copper foil and solder that you'll apply later in the process.

3. **Separate all your pattern pieces based on color codes.**

   Doing so gives you a good idea of how much glass you need in each color. (See Chapter 4 for details on adding color codes to your pattern pieces.)

4. **Purchase your glass, and attach your pattern templates to the appropriate glass sheets.**

   I suggest that you buy 25 percent more glass than you think you need just in case. After all, running short on glass and not being able to match one piece up to your other pieces is a real heartbreaker.

5. **Cut out all your glass shapes according to your templates.**

   Turn to Chapter 5 for everything you need to know about how to cut glass.

6. **Use a glass grinder (or grozing pliers) to edge and fit each piece to the pattern.**

   See Chapter 6 for details on how to use grozing pliers and grinders.

7. **Remove the patterns from the glass pieces, clean the glass using a damp cloth, and use a permanent marker to relabel each glass piece with its pattern number.**

8. **Check to see that your glass pieces fit properly to the pattern by placing each piece on top of its matching number on the pattern, as shown in Figure 8-1.**

   You want some space between the glass pieces to allow for the copper foil. If they seem to be fitting too snuggly to your pattern, use your grinder to make any final adjustments. Remember to mark your pieces before you take them to the grinder so you know exactly where you need to grind. You don't want to grind off too much glass and end up with big gaps, so just take a little glass off at a time.

Figure 8-1:
A copper-foil project that's fitted to the pattern and ready for foil.

Setting up your work board

Before you can start putting your glass pieces together for your copper-foil project, you need to set up your work board. In terms of size, your work board needs to be at least 2 inches larger than your project on all sides. In terms of material, Homasote works best for building copper-foil projects. (An 18-x-24-inch board works well for most projects, but if your project is larger, you may need a bigger board.) *Homasote* is a material made of compressed newspaper, and it's available at your local home-improvement store. Although it's lightweight, it doesn't warp like ceiling tile or cardboard, making it the perfect surface on which to build a flat and level project.

You may want to keep a variety of sizes of Homasote boards on hand in your studio so you always have one ready to fit your project.

To set up your work board for your copper-foil project, place a copy of your pattern in the center of the work board. Use metal push pins to anchor your *layout blocks* (metal strips you use to keep the glass pieces lined up straight) around your project's *frame,* or the outside line of your pattern (refer to Figure 8-1).

Always check the frame to make sure you've set it up square. *Square* means that all four of the corners are perfect 90-degree angles. If your frame isn't square, your project panel won't fit the space where you plan to put it.

Selecting your foil

Foil is what gives your project strength; it provides the base for the solder. Plus, it adds a little splash of color to your project. The following sections take a closer look at the different widths and colors of foil you can choose from.

Sizing up the foil

Choosing just the right size of foil is important because using foil that's too small will cause your panel to fall apart from sheer weight. After all, glass and metal are a heavy combination. But using foil that's too large will require too much solder, making the panel bulky and overweight from the excess solder.

The most common widths of foil used for stained-glass projects are $\frac{7}{32}$ inch, $\frac{3}{16}$ inch, and $\frac{1}{4}$ inch. The thickness of the glass you're working with determines the foil size you need to use. In general, you want more of the foil to overlap the glass edges if the glass piece is both thick and large in volume and less if the glass is both thin and small. But no matter how big or little your glass is, you want the foil to be large enough for it to overlap the edges of the glass pieces by at least $\frac{1}{16}$ inch.

Figure 8-2 shows you a $\frac{1}{8}$-inch-thick piece of glass foiled in $\frac{3}{16}$-inch foil and then the same-sized glass foiled in $\frac{1}{4}$-inch foil. Can you tell which one is the right size? (Hint: Smaller is better here.)

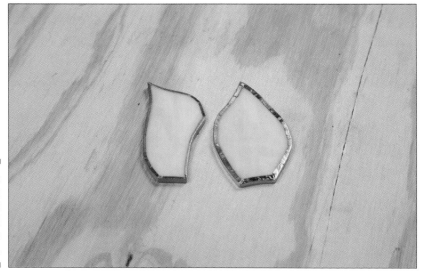

Figure 8-2:
Comparing
proper-sized
foil (left) and
too-large
foil (right).

Choosing the right color

Copper foil comes with a variety of colors for its adhesive backing and just as many metal finishes on the face of the foil. The sole purpose of the different colors is to help you blend all the metal finishes and glass colors together throughout your project.

One color of foil is as easy to work with as any other, so when you're choosing which color foil to use, consider the subject matter and the colors of glass and metal you're using in your project. Figure 8-3 shows you three different metal finishes — silver, black, and copper — you can add to your project's solder to give it a particular color. For each metal color, you want to use the same color of foil backing so that any of the foil you see through the glass matches the color of the metal finish. In general:

✔ If you're using silver-finished solder, use silver-backed foil.

✔ If you're using black-finished solder, use black-backed foil.

✔ If you're using copper-finished solder, use standard copper-backed foil.

Figure 8-3:
Considering three different metal finishes when choosing foil colors.

If you're using all opalescent glass (glass you can't see through), you don't need to worry about the different colors of foil backing because you won't be able to see the foil's backing through the glass. But if you're working with clear glass or cathedral glass, you need to choose your foil color carefully because you'll be able to see the foil's backing through the glass surface (see Figure 8-4). Notice how the foil lines in the figure are copper but the solder isn't; if you want to see a band of copper throughout your project, you have to add a copper finish to the solder (see the later section "Applying metal patina" for details).

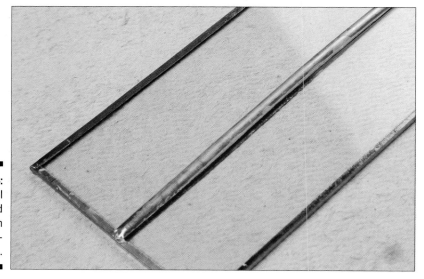

Figure 8-4:
Cathedral glass foiled with copper-backed foil.

As for the face or front side of foil, copper is the standard color, but you can find silver and brass, too. The only reason why you'd want to use these different colors is if you don't want to coat all the foil surfaces with solder. In that case, the foil serves a more decorative function. Keep in mind, though, that you still have to use solder to hold your project together, so you will see the different colors of foil and solder in your finished project unless you apply a metal finish to your solder that matches the foil color.

Keep your foils in a handy foil dispenser so that you have easy access to any size or color of foil and so that the foil doesn't get bent or crimped (see Figure 8-5). Then store your dispenser in a plastic, airtight bag to keep the copper from oxidizing and the adhesive from failing.

Figure 8-5:
Foil
dispenser
loaded with
various
types of foil.

Applying the foil

Applying copper foil to your glass pieces is one of the easiest processes in stained glass. Even so, you need to take your time as you apply the foil to your glass because you want your foil lines to be as even and consistent as possible so that your solder appears even, too.

Before you start applying foil to your glass, make sure you have the following tools handy (see Chapter 2 for more details on each one):

   ✔ Foilmate roller (or craft stick) to burnish down the foil

   ✔ Utility knife to trim the foil

   ✔ Clean cloth to wipe away any dust or oil on the glass

   ✔ Foil (of course!)

After you have all your cut glass pieces fitted together on top of your pattern and secured on your work board (see the sections "Prepping the pattern and cutting your glass" and "Setting up your work board" for details), follow these steps to apply foil to each piece of glass:

1. **Wash your hands to remove any oil or dust, and then remove one piece of glass from your pattern.**

2. **Peel back the protective coating on the back of the foil, trying to keep your fingers off the sticky side of the foil.**

3. **Center the edge of the glass piece on the sticky side of the foil, and gently rotate the glass piece, keeping it centered on the foil (see Figure 8-6).**

Figure 8-6:
Centering a glass piece on the foil.

4. **Wrap the foil around the entire piece of glass; when you get to the end of the piece, overlap the foil about ⅛ inch and then cut it with a craft knife.**

   Always use a new, sharp blade in your craft knife when trimming foil. A dull blade will tear at the foil and leave a ragged edge.

5. **Use your Foilmate roller to tightly burnish the foil to the glass by rubbing the roller along the glass's edge (see Figure 8-7).**

   If you don't have a Foilmate roller, you can use the edge of a craft stick to burnish the foil to the glass.

6. **Use the crimper on the Foilmate or your fingers to gently crimp the foil over the edges of the glass (see Figure 8-8).**

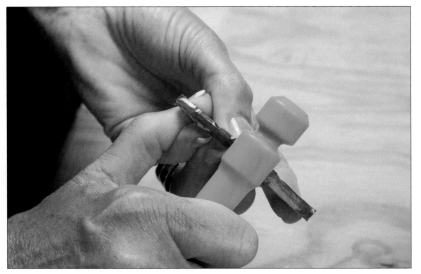

Figure 8-7:
Burnishing
the foil to
the glass's
edge.

Figure 8-8:
Crimping
the foil over
the glass's
edges.

7. **Lay the foiled glass piece on a clean, flat surface, and use the Foilmate roller to burnish the foil to the top side of the glass (see Figure 8-9).**

8. **Turn the glass over and repeat Step 7 for the bottom side of the glass.**

9. **Place the foiled glass piece back into the design.**

10. **Remove the next glass piece from your pattern, and repeat Steps 2 through 9 to apply foil to it.**

Remove only one piece of glass at a time from your pattern when foiling. If you lift out several pieces and then try to refit them to your pattern, they'll never fit back together the same way. When I owned Cutters Art Glass studio in Detroit, Michigan, we were commissioned to do a huge project for a new home. We were making ten windows with 300 pieces of glass per window. After we cut and fit all the pieces to the pattern, I left the studio. When I returned, I found three studio apprentices trying in vain to piece back together all the panels. They thought it would be faster to foil all the pieces if they removed dozens of pieces at a time. Needless to say, it took them hours to get the windows put back together. So learn from their lesson: Keep those pieces in place and work on one piece at a time.

Figure 8-9:
Burnishing
the foil
tightly to
the glass's
sides.

Soldering Copper-Foil Projects

After all your glass pieces are cut, fit to the pattern, and foiled, you're ready to start soldering. Don't panic. Although soldering is the most difficult stained-glass skill to master, with a little time and practice (and help from me, of course!), you'll see your skills and techniques start to improve quite nicely. Before you get going, though, take one last look at your neat and orderly, well-put-together pattern pieces because all that clean, shiny glass and metal is about to become pretty messy!

In this section, I focus on the soldering techniques you need to use to complete your copper-foil project. For a complete explanation of what soldering is and how to do it, turn to Chapter 7, and for details on how to solder lead-came projects, turn to Chapter 9.

Framing and tack soldering for stability

Securing your foiled glass pieces involves two separate steps. The first is creating a frame for your project using layout blocks; I show you how to do so in the earlier section "Setting up your work board." Essentially, all you have to do is pin down the layout blocks along the pattern line on your work board. The glass pieces are all contained inside this frame until you finish soldering your project.

After your frame is ready to go and all your glass pieces are set up inside the frame on the pattern, you're ready to start the second step — soldering.

Note: After you foil all your glass pieces and fit them on the pattern, notice that there's a little wiggle room (less than $\frac{1}{16}$ inch) around some of the glass pieces. That's a good thing because glass expands when it gets hot. You also want the molten solder to flow down between the glass pieces, surrounding them with metal to support the project.

To keep all the glass pieces in place during the soldering process, you have to use a technique called *tacking* (or *tack soldering*). Tacking is simply the process of melting a small amount of solder at various seams throughout the project before you start the beading process (I cover beading later in the section "Running a bead to connect the pieces").

Here's how to tack solder your project together:

1. **Plug in your soldering iron, and let it heat up to the perfect working temperature.**

   The *perfect working temperature* is the temperature at which the tip of the iron melts the solder as soon as it touches it but doesn't heat up the glass itself. See Chapter 7 for more on setting and testing your iron's temperature.

2. **Check your project to make sure all the glass pieces are properly placed on the pattern and the pieces fit within the project's finished size and pattern lines; secure them with metal push pins.**

   See Chapter 4 for more on working with patterns and finished sizes.

3. **Uncoil about 2 feet of 60/40 solder from the roll, and wind it around your hand to form an easy-to-hold coil (see Figure 8-10).**

   Working with a coil of solder rather than a full roll is easier because it's lighter weight. You definitely don't want to drop a ton of solder onto your glass project during the soldering process. Uncoiling the solder from a handheld coil is also much easier to do as you solder your project than uncoiling it from a roll.

4. **Using a flux brush, apply a ½-inch-wide strip of flux to each corner of your project and to any points where two or more glass pieces intersect.**

Figure 8-10:
Stained-glass project, soldering iron, brush, flux, and coiled solder ready to use.

In case you're wondering, *flux* is a cleaner that removes oxidation from the foil. It allows the solder and foil to bond together. Without flux, the solder won't stick, so be sure to add flux to any area you want to solder.

5. **Place the end of the solder over the spot where you want to create a tack; place the flat side of the soldering iron over the solder to melt it into the space between the glass pieces, thus bonding them together (see Figure 8-11).**

    If the tack isn't flush with the glass surface, re-flux and reheat the solder tack until it lays flat.

6. **Repeat Step 5 until all the pieces in your project are secure.**

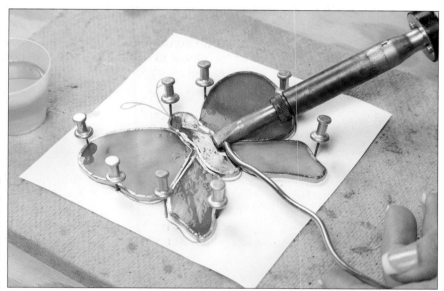

Figure 8-11:
Position
of solder
and iron
when tack
soldering.

Filling in the gaps

If you have visible gaps between your glass pieces (gaps that are bigger than ¹⁄₁₆ inch), you may want to fill them in with solder before you start the beading process (which I cover in the next section). To do so, flux the area of the gap, and then melt solder into the gap using the flat side of your soldering tip. Keep the solder height low like you did when you were tack soldering. All you want to do here is fill in the gaps so that the molten solder doesn't run down into these gaps when you're running a bead. Think of this process as filling in a hole with dirt before you level the ground.

Running a bead to connect the pieces

When you're working with copper foil, your goal is to create a smooth *bead,* or *seam,* of solder that coats all the exposed copper foil on your project (you run beads on both the front and the back of your project). This process is called *running* because it involves using a hot iron to move (or *run*) a molten liquid (the hot solder) over the copper-foil surface. I explain how to run the perfect bead in the following sections.

Note: I use the terms *bead* and *seam* interchangeably to describe this aspect of copper-foil soldering.

Holding your iron correctly

Before you start running beads throughout your project, you need to make sure you hold the iron correctly. The best way to hold your iron is to hold it like a club or bat — not like a pencil (see Figure 8-12). While beading, keep your iron's tip on its narrow side. The flat side heats up too much of the glass surface, making the bead flat rather than raised and rounded.

Figure 8-12: Correct way to hold your soldering iron.

Creating the right size bead

In general, the perfect soldering bead on copper-foil projects is as tall as it is wide. However, if you have really large gaps between your glass pieces, your soldering bead may be slightly wider than it is tall because you never want your bead to be taller than ⅛ inch.

To run a smooth bead, heat your soldering iron as you do before you tack solder (see the section "Framing and tack soldering for stability") and follow these steps:

1. **Use a flux brush to apply flux to the top portion of your project.**

   If any of the foil is dull and shows signs of oxidation, rub the flux brush gently back and forth over the foil until it's shiny.

2. **Wipe the tip of your hot soldering iron on the wet tip cleaner.**

3. **Holding your iron like a bat with the small side of your tip touching a foil seam, gently push the end of the solder coil into the side of the iron.**

4. **After a small pool of molten solder (about ¼ inch in diameter) forms around the soldering iron tip, start to slowly pull the soldering iron tip down the foil seam, dragging the solder pool with you (see Figure 8-13).**

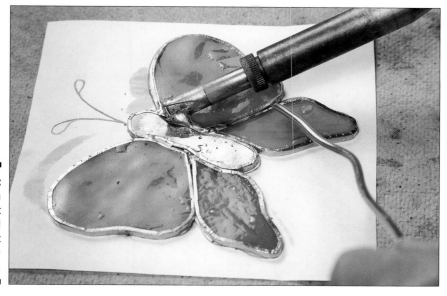

Figure 8-13: Creating a pool of hot solder and dragging it down the foil seam.

5. **As you move along the foil seam, feed more solder into the side of the tip to keep the molten pool of solder the same size as it was when you started.**

The secret to keeping your beads consistent in size is to apply only small, even amounts of solder to the seams the first time you attempt to run a bead. You then go over the seams a second time to refine your soldering. The second time around, you may or may not need to add more solder. Just focus on keeping the seams round and even.

If you have a hard time keeping your beads from becoming too tall and wide in the intersections where two or more seams meet, read on to find out how to eliminate this problem.

Soldering intersections

In stained glass, *intersections* are the points where two or more pieces of glass come together. They can be as simple as two pieces meeting at a right angle or as complex as multiple pieces coming together to form the center of a flower. The more pieces you have in an intersection, the more foil you have, and the more foil you have, the more likely it is that solder will start to pool in the center of the intersection, creating a large, raised lump or button on your project.

To keep your project's intersections small and smooth, I use what I call the *branching-out technique,* which I describe in the following section. The key to this technique is reducing the amount of solder you bring into each intersection.

Branching out

Follow these steps to branch out your solder at complex intersections:

1. **Starting at the top of a seam, apply flux down the seam and 1 inch out onto any branches that lead away from the main seam.**

2. **Begin soldering the seam from the top and move down; as you pass through an intersection, branch out about ½ to 1 inch onto the other seam with your solder bead.**

   See the section "Running a bead to connect the pieces" for details on how to run the perfect bead down your foil seam.

3. **Keeping your iron on the seam, back up into the hot solder and branch out about ½ to 1 inch onto the next seam in the intersection.**

4. **Back up again and return to the main seam; pause with your iron on the intersection for a couple of seconds to make sure all the solder is liquid, and then proceed down the main seam.**

Throughout this process, watch where you're going, not where you've been! You can't do anything about what's behind you, but knowing what's up ahead allows you to make adjustments to the angle of your soldering iron tip and the amount of solder you use.

Figure 8-14 shows a couple of solder seams created using the branching-out technique.

The secret to mastering the branching-out technique is the zigzag motion: Down, past the branch, back up and out the branch, back down the branch, pause, up the seam again, and back down the seam past the branch. This movement may sound complicated, but it isn't. It's well worth your time to give it a try; your smooth, small intersections will thank you.

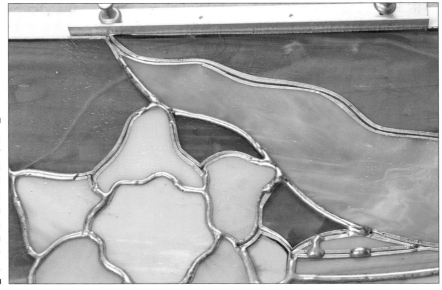

Figure 8-14: Solder seams that have several branches leading away from the inter-sections.

Keeping intersections small

Because solder doesn't stick to glass (it sticks only to the foil), you can help keep your soldered intersections small by keeping your foil intersections small when you're applying the foil to the glass (see the section "Applying the foil" for details). Before you start soldering, use your craft knife to trim away small amounts of foil from the intersection seams to expose more glass and eliminate solder build up.

Removing excess solder from seams

If you end up with too much solder on your seams or intersections, you can remove it a couple of different ways. The easiest is to let gravity do the work. If your panel is small and strong enough, you can lift one side of the panel, flux the excess solder, and melt it using the flat side of your iron tip. Because melted solder is a liquid, it runs off the seam and across the glass. It also cools quickly and doesn't stick to the other solder seams. Wait until the solder drips have cooled before you lift them from the glass.

If your project is large or if you haven't soldered enough of the project to make it strong enough to move, you have to use heat to remove the excess solder. Flux the area, melt the solder using the flat side of your soldering iron, and then quickly lift your soldering iron straight up from the seam and sling the hot solder off the iron onto a scrap piece of Homasote. Continue to repeat this technique until you've removed all the excess solder.

Don't go crazy with the slinging of hot solder. It's more of a snap of your wrist than an all-out swing. Make sure no one is close to you or your work space, and always wear your safety glasses.

Creating a solder frame for smaller projects

As you may have already guessed, copper foil isn't really that strong. Its strength comes from being coated in solder. The adhesive backing is there only to help you during the foiling process. In fact, it melts away as soon as you apply heat to the seam. For this reason, you have to provide some type of support for the outside foiled edges of your project.

For larger copper-foil projects, you need to use hard-metal cames, such as brass or zinc, to support the weight of your project. For smaller projects, you can create a simple frame by building up the outside edges with solder. Most artists use this technique for finishing off sun catchers, boxes, lamp edges, and small panel edges.

To create a simple frame, you use a process called *tinning* to coat the face of the foil with a thin coating of solder. After you've beaded your project on the front and back, keep your panel laying flat on your work board, put on a pair of garden gloves, and follow these steps to tin the flat edges:

1. **Reduce the temperature of your iron.**

   The iron should be hot enough to melt the solder but not so hot that you can keep a drip of solder on the tip of your iron. See Figure 8-15 for an example of an iron that's too hot.

   If you're using a thermostatically controlled iron, you can cool it down by wiping it on a wet tip cleaner before each application.

2. **Flux the surface of the foil surrounding the outside edges of the project.**

3. **Coat the tip of your iron with solder by touching the hot tip to the solder.**

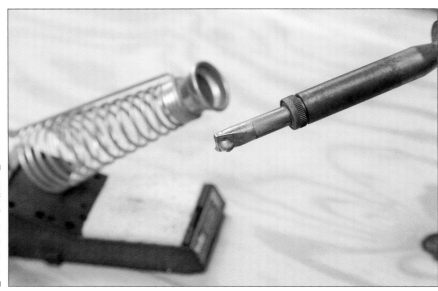

Figure 8-15:
A drip of solder clinging to an iron tip that's too hot.

4. **Using the flat side of your iron tip, run the iron along the foiled edge of your project.**

   Your goal is to coat the foil with a thin layer of solder — not to build up a bead along the edge.

5. **Repeat Steps 2 through 4 on the other side of the project.**

6. **Holding the project steady, apply a small amount of solder to the foil edging the outside glass pieces (see Figure 8-16).**

   At this stage, you need to coat anything that's still copper with a thin layer of solder.

7. **Hold the panel steady until the solder cools.**

8. **Repeat Steps 6 and 7 until you've gone completely around the exterior edge of the project.**

   If the project is round or free form, you need to be patient and make sure the solder has cooled completely before you rotate the piece or else the solder will just roll off the edge. Don't forget to flux the edges as you go.

Figure 8-16:
Holding the project while creating a frame with solder.

Abracadabra: The Magic of Wire

When it comes to creating stained-glass projects, wire can be both structural and decorative. Wire is inexpensive and easy to work with, and it's available in a variety of sizes and metals, including brass, copper, and *pre-tinned* (wire that has been coated with a thin layer of solder). The different wire sizes are called *gauges,* and the larger the gauge number, the smaller the diameter of the wire. Gauges 14 through 20 are the most common sizes used in glass work, so having these sizes on hand in your studio is a good idea.

The following sections cover the basics of using wire to add a decorative zing to your projects as well as to provide structural strength.

Decorative accents

Wire can be an important decorative tool in some stained-glass projects, particularly jewelry, edging treatments, centers of flowers, butterfly antennas, and wire *filigrees* (or decorative openworks made from metal). You'd be surprised by the many ways you can improve a project simply by introducing wire accents into it (see Figure 8-17).

Structural applications

If you need to, you can use wire to add strength to your stained-glass projects. Sun catchers with wings or other extending glass pieces need additional support. To add that support, you can wrap wire around the outside edges of the project and secure it with solder. You can also use wire to create hooks for hanging small projects (wire's most common use in glass art) or to reinforce the top and bottom of stained-glass lamps. (Turn to Chapter 11 for more on working with lamps.) Check out the projects at the end of this chapter for more information on working with wire.

Figure 8-17:
Adding
brass wire
to add visual
appeal to
this golf-
inspired
project.

Before you can use wire for anything, though, you must stretch it. Stretching wire is easier to do when you have a friend to help you. To stretch your wire, cut a 36-inch-long piece of wire, have each person hold onto an end using pliers, and then stretch the wire until you remove all the kinks and the wire becomes rigid. You can prestretch wire and keep it ready in your studio for upcoming projects.

To add wire to your project, you have to embed it either into a solder seam or around the outside edges of the project where more strength is required (see Figure 8-18).

Figure 8-18:
Applying
wire to the
outside
of a small
stained-
glass
project.

Tinning the wire gives it additional strength. Pre-tinned wire is available and saves time, but you can easily tin your own. Just follow these steps:

1. **Cut the wire into 18-inch-long pieces after you stretch it.**

2. **Hold one end of the wire with needle-nose pliers, and coat the wire with flux.**

3. **Melt a small amount of 60/40 solder with your iron tip.**

4. **Place the iron and solder onto the top of the wire (see Figure 8-19); slowly move the iron and solder down the length of the wire, allowing the solder to blanket the entire wire surface.**

5. **Add more solder if necessary.**

   Your goal is to coat the entire piece of wire with a very thin coat of solder.

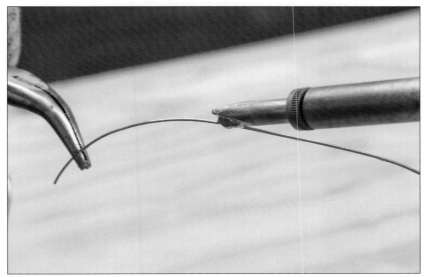

Figure 8-19:
Tinning wire
with 60/40
solder.

Cleaning Up and Adding Finishing Touches

Cleaning up your latest project is always exciting because it means you're almost done! For some projects, though, you may want to add one more step to the project before you're completely finished. That is, you may want to use a chemical compound called *patina* to change the color of your project's solder if the shiny, silver-colored solder isn't quite what you were looking for.

The following sections show you how to clean up your project and add patina to achieve the look you envisioned when you first saw your design pattern.

How to make your projects shine

A simple soap and water bath is all most projects need to shimmer and shine in the sunlight. However, to help the metals retain their shine, you can apply a simple coat of car wax. Any wax that contains Carnauba wax will work.

I prefer the clear waxes to the white liquids because they're easier to buff off when you're done. Follow the wax manufacturer's instructions and shine away.

Cleaning your project

The best way to clean a copper-foil project is to use soapy water and a sponge. If the project is small enough, you can wash it in the sink or in a dish pan. You can clean larger projects by laying them flat on your worktable and scrubbing them there. After you remove all the flux and dirt, rinse your project with clean water and dry it with a soft cloth.

Always test any new cleaning product before you use it on your stained-glass project. Be careful about using products that are sold specifically as stained-glass flux removers and finishing compounds. I've been very disappointed with the long-term results of some of these products. After a few months, a dull, white film begins to appear on the finished metal surface of projects.

Never put your stained-glass projects in the dishwasher. The heat is too intense for the foil and may even crack your glass.

Applying metal patina

Patina is a coating that occurs over time on most unfinished metal surfaces thanks to *oxidation* (a process that occurs when metal combines with oxygen). The most common example of patina is the blue-green coating that appears on copper surfaces when they're exposed to weather and time. If you like this kind of effect and want to incorporate it into your project, you can speed up the oxidation process by applying metal patinas to the solder in your project.

The color of patina you choose to add to your project depends on the project you're making and the color of foils you're using. Black patina turns your solder lines (which are naturally silver) to black, copper patina turns them to rosy copper, and brass patina gives solder seams a warm gold glow (refer to Figure 8-3 for some examples).

You can apply patina with a cotton swab or paint brush, but make sure you wear rubber gloves to protect your hands from staining. Also be sure to always apply patina in a well-ventilated area; if your studio isn't well-ventilated, remember to wear your respirator.

It's best to apply patina right after you clean the project with soap and water and dry it completely with a soft cloth. Just be sure you don't use Windex or any other product that contains ammonia to clean your project before you add patina; ammonia affects the way patina works on the solder.

To apply patina to your project, follow these steps:

1. **Pour a small amount of patina into a plastic container.**

   Never dip your paint brush or cotton swab into and out of the bottle of patina. Dirt dilutes its effectiveness.

2. **Using a cotton swab or paint brush, apply the patina only to the solder seams, being careful not to get it on the glass.**

   Some patinas stain certain colors of glass. If you get patina on the glass, remove it quickly with a clean cotton swab or cloth.

3. **Allow the patina to dry completely.**

4. **If needed, apply one or two additional coats, allowing the patina to dry between each application.**

5. **Let the project dry overnight.**

6. **Use Carnauba wax to buff the patina the next day.**

   See the nearby sidebar "How to make your projects shine" for more details about making your stained glass shine.

When you're finished applying the patina to your project, be sure to properly dispose of any remaining liquid.

Project: Butterfly Sun Catcher

Ready to get started with your very own copper-foil project? Great! This section shows you how to apply all the techniques I describe in this chapter to make a lovely butterfly sun catcher. For this project, you need one piece of colored glass for the wings and another smaller piece for the body. After you choose your glass, make three copies of the pattern I provide here, set up your work board using one copy of the pattern (see the section "Setting up your work board" for details), and follow these steps:

1. **On the second copy of the pattern, number and color code the pattern pieces and mark the direction of the glass grain.**

   The *grain direction* is the general direction of the air bubbles or color streaks you see in a piece of glass (see Chapter 4 for more details). Pay close attention to the grain of the glass you select so you can match the grain direction of the glass to your pattern.

2. **Use foil shears to cut out the pattern templates.**

3. **Glue the pattern templates to the glass sheets using rubber cement or double-sided tape.**

4. **Cut out each piece of glass along the pattern lines.**

   Check out Chapter 5 for everything you need to know about cutting glass.

5. **Use your grinder to fine-tune the glass shapes and to smooth out any rough edges; then remove the paper templates from the glass, remembering to transfer the pattern numbers to the glass using a permanent marker.**

   See Chapter 6 for all the details on grinding glass.

6. **Place the glass pieces on the pattern on your work board.**

   Use metal push pins to hold the pieces in place. Make sure all the glass pieces fit your pattern; if any of them don't fit, continue grinding them until they do.

7. **Remove one piece of glass from the pattern at a time, apply $\frac{7}{32}$-inch copper foil around the edges of each piece, and return it to the pattern (see Figure 8-20).**

   See the section "Applying the foil" for more details.

8. **Flux the project's corners and intersections, and tack solder the project pieces together; then remove the push pins.**

   See the section "Framing and tack soldering for stability" for more details.

Figure 8-20:
Sun catcher
project
ready for
soldering.

9. **Flux all the visible copper foil, and then run a bead of solder along all the project's seams.**

   Use the branching-out technique for best results. See the sections "Running a bead to connect the pieces" and "Soldering intersections" for more details.

10. **Use a small amount of solder to tin the foil around the outside edges of the project.**

11. **Turn the project over, and repeat Steps 9 and 10 on the back.**

   To keep melted solder from dripping through to the other side, place a damp towel under the project when you turn it over. Doing so cools the solder quickly and keeps it from melting through to the other side.

12. **Using solder, build up a frame around the outside edges of the butterfly (see Figure 8-21).**

   See the section "Creating a solder frame for smaller projects" for more details.

13. **Use one piece of pre-tinned copper wire to shape the antennas for the butterfly; flux the wire and fill the loops at the top of the antennas with melted solder (see Figure 8-22).**

   See the section "Abracadabra: The Magic of Wire" for details.

14. **Wrap another piece of wire around a pencil to form a hook for hanging the sun catcher (see Figure 8-23).**

15. **Solder the antennas and the hook to the back of the butterfly.**

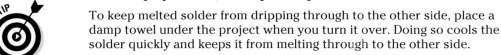

   Always use needle-nose pliers to hold your wire when soldering. Wire is a great conductor of heat, and you'll burn your fingers really quickly if you aren't careful.

Figure 8-21:
Butterfly
project
with solder
frame.

Figure 8-22:
Shaping the
antennas.

Figure 8-23:
Antenna
and hook
ready to be
attached to
the butterfly.

16. **After the project has cooled, clean it up with soap and water; apply patina if you want to.**

See the section "Cleaning Up and Adding Finishing Touches" for more details. Figure 8-24 shows what the finished butterfly looks like.

Figure 8-24:
Finished
butterfly sun
catcher.

Project: Sunflower Panel with Metal Frame

I bet you can guess the most popular subjects in stained glass. Yep, you're right — flowers. The wide variety of colors and design possibilities makes flowers the perfect inspiration for beautiful stained-glass projects. So how could I not include a flower-based panel in this book?

I've based this project on an 8-x-10-inch pattern, but you can use a copy machine to enlarge the pattern to any size that fits the space where you want to put it. To make an 8-x-10-inch panel, you need one 12-x-12-inch piece of glass for the background and another 12-x-12-inch piece for the flower. You need a 6-x-6-inch piece of glass for the center of the flower and another 6-x-6-inch piece for the leaves. After you choose your glass, enlarge the pattern shown here to be 8 x 10 inches, make three copies of it, set up your work board using one copy of the pattern (see the section "Setting up your work board" for details), and follow these steps:

1. On the second copy of the pattern, number and color code the pattern pieces and mark the grain direction on each one.

Check out Chapter 4 for more info on working with patterns and marking glass grains.

2. **Use foil shears to cut out the pattern templates.**

3. **Lay out the pattern templates on the glass, making sure to follow the grain arrows you drew on each pattern piece (see Figure 8-25).**

   See the section "Prepping the pattern and cutting your glass" for more details.

4. **Glue the pattern templates to the glass, and cut them out.**

   Turn to Chapter 5 for more details on cutting glass.

5. **Use your glass grinder to smooth out the edges of the glass pieces and make them fit your pattern; then remove the paper templates, remembering to transfer the numbers from the templates to the glass using a permanent marker.**

   See Chapter 6 for more details on grinding glass.

6. **Place the glass pieces on the pattern on your work board.**

   Use metal push pins to hold the pieces in place. Make sure all the glass pieces fit your pattern; continue grinding them until they all fit.

   All the pattern pieces need to fit within the outside pattern lines (called the *finished size*) of your pattern. You want a little space in between the pieces so that you have enough room for the foil.

7. **Remove one piece of glass at a time for foiling; apply ³⁄₁₆-inch foil by following the steps I provide in the section "Applying the foil."**

   Remember to return each glass piece to the pattern before removing another piece to foil.

8. **Flux the project's corners and intersections, tack solder the pieces together, and remove the push pins.**

   See the section "Framing and tack soldering for stability" for more details.

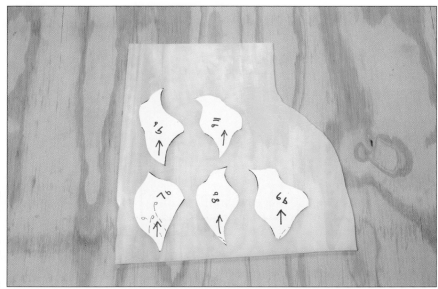

Figure 8-25: Pattern templates laid out for gluing.

9. **Flux all the visible copper foil, and then run a bead of solder along all the project's seams and intersections using the branching-out technique I describe in the section "Soldering intersections."**

10. **Use a pair of lead nippers to cut four pieces of *U*-shaped came to fit around the outside of the project.**

    This panel is too large to use just foil around the outside edges, so to strengthen the panel, you need to use ⅛-inch *U*-shaped zinc came to create a frame for it.

    Chapter 9 shows you how to work with lead nippers.

11. **Slip the metal cames onto the edges of the panel, and secure them with push pins (see Figure 8-26).**

    If you have trouble fitting the zinc came over the edges of your panel, check to make sure your solder seams aren't too tall. If they are, use the tip of your iron to melt the seams back ⅛ inch from the edge. Doing so should allow the frame to slip easily onto the panel.

12. **Flux the frame and the outside edges of the panel's seams on one side.**

13. **Tack solder the corners of the frame; then secure the frame to the panel by tack soldering it where each seam meets the frame.**

14. **Repeat Steps 12 and 13 on the other side of the panel.**

Figure 8-26: Panel with zinc frame ready for soldering.

15. **Attach wire hanging rings to the vertical edges of the zinc frame by applying flux to the frame and wire rings and then soldering the rings to the frame (see Figure 8-27).**

    Be sure to measure and mark the location so the rings are even.

    Apply your flux with a small paint brush to keep the solder from flowing off the edges and onto your frame. Be sure to use pliers to hold the rings while soldering, and don't let go until the solder has cooled.

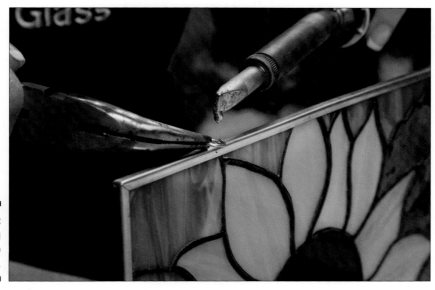

Figure 8-27:
Attaching
wire rings to
the frame.

16. **Clean the project with soap and water, and apply patina if desired.**

    See the section "Cleaning Up and Adding Finishing Touches" for details.
    Figure 8-28 shows what the finished sunflower panel looks like.

Figure 8-28:
Finished
sunflower
panel.

Project: Round Rose Window

Although finished round windows look like they take a lot of work to create, they aren't too difficult to build, especially when you use copper foil. The round rose window I include here is framed in a ladder-back chain, and the steps for how to create it are based on a 10-inch window. (Note that you can use a copy machine to enlarge or reduce the pattern's size to fit your space needs.) To create a 10-inch circle, you need 1 square foot of glass for the background and 1 square foot of glass for the rose. For the leaves, you need an 8-x-8-inch piece of glass.

TIP

To add more interest to your finished project, try mixing several shades of glass for the rose. I use two different shades of pink iridized glass for my sample here.

After you choose your glass, enlarge the pattern shown here to be 10 inches across, make three copies of it, set up your work board using one copy of the pattern (see the section "Setting up your work board" for details), and follow these steps:

1. **On the second copy of your pattern, number and color code your pattern templates, mark the direction of the glass grain, and cut out the pieces using foil shears.**

   See Chapter 4 for more on working with patterns and marking glass grain.

2. **Lay out the pattern templates on the glass, and glue them in place using rubber cement.**

3. **Cut out the glass shapes.**

   See Chapter 5 for everything you need to know when cutting glass.

4. **Use a grinder to smooth out the edges of the glass shapes and to make them fit your pattern.**

   See Chapter 6 for more details on grinding glass.

5. **Remove the paper templates from the glass pieces, transfer the pattern numbers to the glass using a permanent marker, and lay out your glass pieces on your work board, using push pins to keep the pieces in place while you're fitting and foiling them.**

6. **Remove one glass piece from your pattern at a time, and apply ³⁄₁₆-inch foil to its edges.**

   See the section "Applying the foil" for more details.

   If you're using cathedral glass for any of the pieces in this project, be sure to match the color of the foil to the color of patina you plan to use on the project. See the sections "Choosing the right color" and "Applying metal patina" for more details.

7. **Flux the project's corners and intersections, and tack solder the pieces together; then remove the push pins.**

8. **Flux all the visible copper foil, and then run a bead of solder along all the project's seams and intersections using the branching-out technique I describe in the section "Soldering intersections."**

9. **Tin the outside edges of the project using the technique I describe in the section "Creating a solder frame for smaller projects."**

10. **Clean up the project with soap and water, let it dry completely, and then apply patina if desired.**

11. **Measure the circumference of the finished panel, and cut a piece of ladder-back chain one link longer than the measurement.**

    Ladder-back chain comes in silver, brass, and copper. It's easy to work with and contours nicely around the edges of round panels.

12. **Using needle-nose pliers, open up the last link in the chain; then wrap the chain around the perimeter of the panel, using the opened link to attach the chain together (see Figure 8-29).**

13. **On the back side of the panel, tack solder the ladder-back chain to several intersections around the perimeter of the panel to hold it in place.**

Figure 8-29:
Framing
the window
with ladder-
back chain.

14. Solder two wire hanging hooks to the two top seams in the design.

See the section "Abracadabra: The Magic of Wire" for details. Figure 8-30 shows what the finished rose window looks like.

Figure 8-30:
Finished
round rose
window.

Chapter 9

Building Leaded-Glass Projects

*L*eaded glass is the most traditional technique used for creating stained-glass windows. In fact, most residential entryways and church windows are created using strips of lead came to link the glass pieces together. Because of the real-life architectural aspect involved, building leaded-glass windows is one of the most rewarding aspects of working with glass. After all, you're actually building a panel you can use to complete the architecture of a specific space.

The leaded-glass process is a very physical activity that requires the use of hammers, nails, boards, and cement — it just screams construction, doesn't it? Afraid of wearing a hard hat and hammering nails? Don't panic. This chapter walks you through the general steps and components of creating a leaded-glass project. You can choose one of the projects at the end of the chapter, or you can select one from another source if you've already found a design you really like.

Selecting and Working with Lead Came

In leaded projects, lead cames take the place of copper foil in holding the glass pieces together. *Lead cames* are 6-foot strips of lead that have been formed into channels of different shapes so they can cradle the edges of different glass pieces. Lead cames come in a variety of sizes, but the standard channel height is 3⁄16 inch to accommodate 1⁄8-inch-thick art glass.

Good-quality lead came is manufactured from 100-percent pure lead. Exacting quantities of tin, antimony, copper, and bismuth are added to give it strength. The lead is pliable enough to bend and form around all sizes and shapes of glass pieces, but it's also strong enough to support giant cathedral windows — pretty cool, right?

When you're working with lead came, always make sure you work in a well-ventilated area, wash your hands after handling lead strips, keep small children and pets out of your studio, and don't eat or drink while handling lead.

Choosing the right size and profile of lead came

Lead came comes in two profiles: *H*-shaped and *U*-shaped. In general, you use the *U*-shaped profile to create the perimeter of your leaded panel; you use the *H*-shaped profile to piece together the individual pieces of glass on the interior of your project. Occasionally, you may need to use *U*-shaped cames internally and *H*-shaped cames on the perimeter.

Both came profiles come in a variety of sizes. The width of the came's *face* (the part of the lead you see when viewing a leaded-glass window) determines the came's size. Sizes range between $3/32$ inch to $1/2$ inch wide. The size of the came's *channel* (the space that holds the glass piece) is usually the same no matter which size came you use — $3/16$ inch wide. Although this size accommodates most glass thicknesses, you can special order cames with wider channels for specialty glasses. The standard width of the *heart of the lead* (the lead strip that separates the two glass channels) is $1/32$ inch, but some *U*-shaped profiles may be slightly thicker. Figure 9-1 shows several different sizes of both *U*- and *H*-shaped lead came.

You'll work with various sizes of lead came even in the same project. If you're building a window with lots of small pieces, for example, you need to use a came with a smaller face width for those small pieces so you don't hide the glass. On the other hand, if you're working with the larger background or border glass pieces on that same window, you may select came with a wider face to lend support and visual impact to your project. Choosing which lead came to use for a particular project is a lot like selecting wood molding or trim for a woodworking project: big profiles for crown and door casings; smaller profiles for cabinet trim and details.

Figure 9-1: Different came profiles and sizes.

Every manufacturer's lead came varies to some degree. After you find a brand of came that you like to work with, stick with it. Don't mix different brands of lead within the same project.

Stretching lead came

Before you can use lead came in a project, you have to stretch it to give it strength. As an added bonus, the stretching process I describe in this section also removes kinks and makes the lead easier to work with.

Inserting came into a vise

To stretch a lead came, you need to use a lead vise, which you can mount to the end of your worktable. The vise works like a sailing jip: The more you pull or stretch the lead, the tighter the vise grips onto the came.

Insert the lead came into the vise (see Figure 9-2). Then grip the other end of the came with a pair of household pliers, and pull away from the vise in one continuous motion.

Be careful not to use little jerky pulls to stretch the came. Doing so stresses the metal, weakens its strength, and causes it to be more brittle.

Knowing how far to stretch the came

When it comes to stretching came, the real trick is knowing how far to stretch it. The larger the came, the more difficult it is to stretch. Your goal is to stretch it 2 to 4 inches, depending on the size of the came. You may be able to stretch ⅜-inch lead only 1 to 2 inches because it takes a lot of strength to stretch it. That's fine. Smaller-profile lead cames stretch more easily, but you don't want to go overboard. Try not to stretch any profile more than 4 inches. You know you've stretched the came enough when it's perfectly straight. After you stretch the came straight, trim away the damaged lead (the ends you gripped with the vise and the pliers).

Be careful not to overstretch the came. Doing so narrows down the channel, making it impossible to fit the glass into the channel. You also run the risk of overstressing the metal, causing it to become brittle and weak.

Stretch only as much lead as you can use in one day. Lead starts to oxidize after being stretched, making it more difficult to solder over time.

Cutting lead came

After you stretch your lead came, you're ready to cut it. To do so, you can use either a lead knife or a pair of lead nippers. Which tool you use depends on the look you want to create. You can make cuts with your nippers much faster than you can with a lead knife, but if you want to make long, sweeping cuts, the lead knife is the better option.

Figure 9-2:
Inserting lead came into the lead vise.

When you're trying to decide which tool to use, keep these tips in mind:

- ✔ Nippers work great when you're working with smaller profiles of lead came and when you want to speed up the process.

- ✔ Lead knives work great when you're working with larger-faced cames and flowing lead intersections.

Using a lead knife

The secret to working with a lead knife is keeping it sharp. A dull knife will crush the lead rather than cut it. When you're cutting lead came with a lead knife, keep a wet stone handy so you can resharpen your knife when it starts to dull. (You know it's time to resharpen when you have to exert more and more pressure to make a cut.)

When using a lead knife, never cut down on the face of the came because doing so crushes the heart of the came, making it difficult to fit the glass into the channel (see Figure 9-3a). Instead, turn the came onto its side, and place the lead knife on the edges of the came (see Figure 9-3b). Gently rock the knife left to right as you push it into the came. You can increase the length of the cut by adjusting the angle of the knife. Using a lead knife allows you to cut long, sweeping angles that can really make your projects stand out.

Using lead nippers

Lead nippers are the fastest way to cut almost any lead-came angle. Although they can't yield you the long, sweeping angles you get with a lead knife, they make up for it in the speed they offer. Because most lead cuts are simple straight lines or easy angles, you can use nippers in most of your projects. And, unlike lead knives, lead nippers rarely need to be sharpened.

Figure 9-3:
Incorrect versus correct cutting positions when using the lead knife.

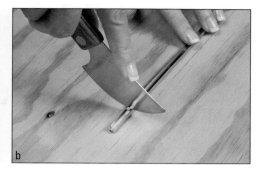

Lead nippers make two different angles each time they cut through the lead. One side of the cut is flat, and the other is pointed. The shape of the nippers' blades creates these angles naturally.

As when using the lead knife, never cut down on the face of the came with the nippers because doing so crushes the heart of the lead. Instead, turn the lead onto its side, and cut through the came by placing the nippers around the came so they're parallel to the heart of the lead. Squeeze the handles on the nippers to make a straight cut (see Figure 9-4).

To cut an angle using the nippers, make a straight cut first and then rotate the nippers toward the left (see Figure 9-5). For a longer angle, you can cut the top face of the lead first and then cut the bottom face.

Don't worry if these techniques sound difficult. With a little practice, you'll easily master the art of making straight cuts and angles with lead nippers.

Figure 9-4:
The proper position for cutting lead came with lead nippers.

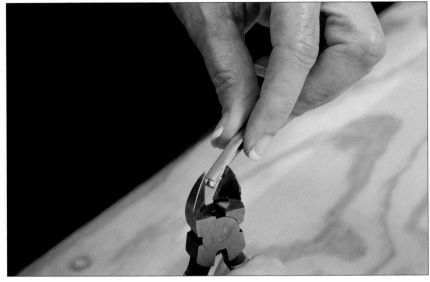

Figure 9-5:
Proper
position for
cutting a
slight angle
with lead
nippers.

Preparing Your Work Board and Laying Out Your Pattern

To build lead-came projects, you first need to set up a wooden work board (as opposed to the Homasote board you use for copper-foil projects) on which you'll construct your glass panel. Your work board needs to be a minimum of 2 inches larger on all sides than the size of the project you're building.

After you determine how big your board needs to be, create the table part of the board using a ½- to ⅜-inch-thick piece of plywood and two 1-x-2-inch boards that are as long as the work board you're building. (These boards are called *squaring bars,* which are any glass or wooden strips you use to keep your project square as you build it. See the section "Squaring it up" for details on the glass version of squaring bars.) Using wood screws, attach the squaring bars so that they make a right angle at one of the corners of the board.

Take care when attaching the squaring bars to create a perfect right angle. Use a ruler and carpenter's square to get it right on the money. If your work board isn't square, you won't be able to build a square window, not to mention whatever shaped window you do create won't fit in the space you picked for it.

After you start building a leaded project, your work board has to remain flat and stationary. If you're taking a class or working at a friend's studio, think about how you'll transport your work board before you build it. For example, if you drive a sports car, don't plan to transport a French door panel (and the work board big enough to accommodate it!).

When you're ready to attach your pattern to your work board, use a ruler and craft knife to trim the left side and bottom edge of your pattern along the *finished line* (the line that indicates the size of the finished project). This corner fits into the right angle you created on your work board using the squaring bars. Use masking tape to attach the pattern to your work board. If you built your work board correctly and cut your pattern out right, the pattern should match the corner of your board perfectly (see Figure 9-6).

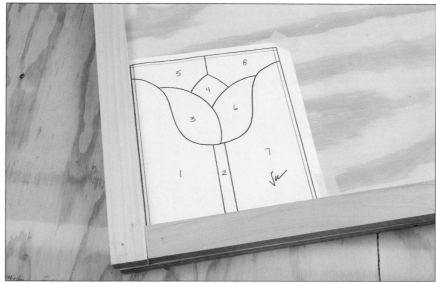

Figure 9-6:
Laying out your trimmed pattern on the work board.

Constructing Your Lead Project

Up to the point of assembly, you don't see many differences between making copper-foil projects and making leaded-glass projects. After all, you set up the pattern, cut out the glass, and grind the pieces to match your templates and pattern using the same techniques you use for copper-foil projects. (Turn to Chapter 4 for details on how to work with patterns, Chapter 5 for how to cut glass, and Chapter 6 for how to grind your glass pieces.) The construction process — the focus of this section — is where lead projects take on lives of their own.

Note: For leaded projects, you need to use horseshoe nails to hold the glass pieces in place (rather than the push pins you use for copper-foil projects). The nails are flat on two sides so they're easy to hammer into the wooden work board and just as easy to remove. Plus, the flat sides of the nail hold the glass pieces in place without turning.

Never put a nail directly against a piece of glass. If you do, the nail will chip the glass — and you definitely don't want that! Instead, put scraps of lead came (called *spacers*) in between the nails and the glass to protect the glass's edge.

Framing it up

The first step in constructing a leaded-glass project is creating a frame for it. To do so, follow these steps:

1. **Stretch and cut two strips of *U*-shaped, ¼-inch lead came; cut each strip 1 inch longer than the width and height of your project.**

   For example, if you're building a 10-x-12-inch panel, you need to cut one 11-inch-long came and one 13-inch-long came.

2. **Place the longer strip of lead, face up, on top of your pattern, along the longer squaring bar; place the other strip of lead along the other squaring bar.**

   The two lead cames should fit together in the right angle of your work board.

3. **Hammer a horseshoe nail at the end of each lead strip to keep it from slipping (see Figure 9-7).**

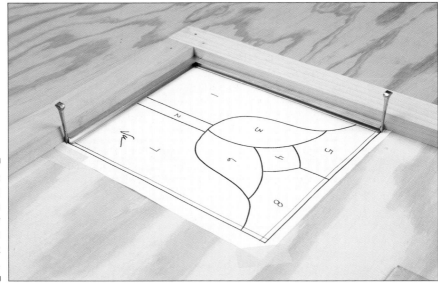

Figure 9-7: Securing lead cames around your pattern on the work board.

I like to use ⅜-inch *H*-shaped lead came for the perimeter of some of my projects because it gives them a little more support and looks less clumsy than large *U*-shaped came. After years of trying to install thousands of windows into openings that aren't perfectly square, I've come to appreciate the extra space that *H*-shaped lead came allows (compared to *U*-shaped came). You can easily use a lead knife to trim away the extra lead after you solder the panel together.

Putting the project together piece by piece

Lay out all your glass pieces on your worktable (the same table on which you place your work board). If your project has quite a few pieces, group them in numerical order for quick access. Don't put them on top of your pattern because they'll end up getting in your way during the construction process — or worse, they may get broken.

When you prepared your glass pieces to fit your pattern, you numbered each one to match the corresponding number on your pattern. Keep track of those numbers, and, as you construct your window, never substitute one piece for another even if they look the same. They're not!

The key to the leaded-glass construction process is remembering this sequence: a piece of lead, a piece of glass, a piece of lead, a piece of glass, and on and on, until the window has been completely constructed. This process starts in the right angle of your work board and builds out in all directions. Start with the glass piece that goes into the right-angled corner of your work board and then follow these steps:

1. **Insert the first piece of glass (the corner piece) into the lead came channels on the perimeter of your work board so that it fits in its place on the pattern.**

2. **Secure the glass piece by holding a lead spacer next to the glass piece and tapping a horseshoe nail into the work board so that it's flush to the spacer; add two spacers and nails if necessary (see Figure 9-8).**

Before you secure your first piece of glass (and all subsequent pieces), make sure you can see the black pattern line around the edges of the glass. This process is called *staying on pattern,* and it's important because the window has to end up a certain size when built. After all, you can't trim the glass after you build it into a project without removing that piece from the panel completely (and to remove it, you have to remove all the pieces you built in around it).

If a piece of glass extends beyond the pattern line, mark where the excess glass needs to be removed, and use your glass grinder to remove the glass. Dry the glass piece, and refit it back into the window.

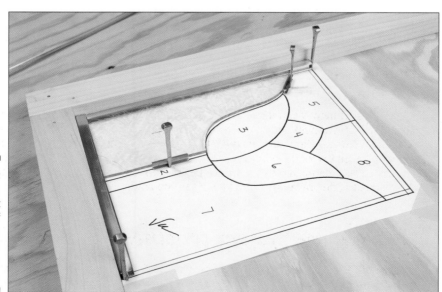

Figure 9-8: Securing the first piece of glass with spacers and horseshoe nails.

3. **Cut a piece of ⅜-inch *H*-shaped lead came to fit onto the other side of the piece of glass you secured to the board in Step 2.**

   See the section "Achieving the perfect lead fit" for details on how to cut the lead came to fit the glass just right.

4. **Gently remove any nails that are in the path of the lead came, and fit the interior edge of the secured glass piece into the came.**

5. **Insert the next piece of glass into the other side of the piece of lead came you used in Step 4.**

   Which glass piece goes in next depends on your project. You determine your next piece by trial and error. Like with a jigsaw puzzle, if you put in the wrong piece, you'll know right away because the next piece won't fit. If the piece you try doesn't work, simply remove it and try another piece in another location. The most important thing to remember is to always build out from the squared corner of your project.

6. **Follow Steps 2 through 5 to insert the rest of your glass pieces.**

Achieving the perfect lead fit

When connecting your glass pieces in a lead project, you need to custom cut each lead came so that you leave enough space for the next intersecting piece of lead. The easiest way to determine how much space you need to leave is to use a scrap piece of the same kind of lead you're using for your project as a gauge. Slip the scrap lead onto the glass and mark where you need to cut your piece of came so that you have just enough space for the next piece of lead came to pass by the lead and create an intersection (see Figure 9-9).

If you cut the came too short, replace the lead and try again. No matter how many lead replacements you have to make, you never end up wasting much lead because you can always use scrap pieces for shorter came cuts or spacers.

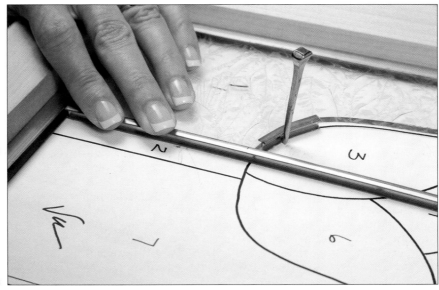

Figure 9-9:
Using a scrap piece of lead to mark where to cut an intersecting lead came.

If you have a circle- or oval-shaped piece of glass, you want the lead to take the exact shape of the glass's edge. To make the lead fit the glass's shape, I suggest that you wrap your lead came around the complete circumference of the glass piece by rolling the glass down the strip of came (see Figure 9-10). Cut the lead came so that it fits all the way around the circle. You can then slip this glass-lead unit into place in your project design just as you do a piece of lead came by fitting the next glass edge into the outside perimeter of the unit.

Figure 9-10: Wrapping a circle-shaped piece of glass in lead came.

Squaring it up

After you slip the last piece of glass into the lead channel, double-check that you can see the black pattern line that indicates the cut size of the glass (see Chapter 4 for more on cut sizes and finished sizes). If all your glass is inside the cut-size line, you won't have a problem squaring up your panel.

To square up your project, slip two strips of came (use the same size and type of came that's on the already-squared perimeter of your project) on the last two sides of the panel (the sides you didn't cover in the section "Framing it up"). Use your triangle or carpenter square to make sure the sides are perfectly square, and then secure the complete panel by hammering in horseshoe nails along the sides of the last two strips of came.

Use your strip cutter or hand-held glass cutter and a ruler to cut two 1- to 2-inch-wide strips of double-strength clear glass the same length as the panel you're building; these glass strips are another version of squaring bars (see the section "Preparing Your Work Board and Laying Out Your Pattern" for info on the wood version). Protect the edges of these strips by wrapping them in masking tape. Slip the bars into the perimeter or up against the outside edges of the last two cames you added to the outside of your project (remove the nails you used to secure them while you cut out the glass squaring bars); use horseshoe nails to hold the bars in place (see Figure 9-11).

Figure 9-11:
Checking
a leaded
panel for
square
corners.

Note: You can also make minor adjustments to the panel by gently tapping on the edge of the glass squaring bars. The bars move the glass and lead all in one direction, keeping the panel from bowing or the lead from being damaged.

Soldering Lead-Came Projects

Most stained-glass artists agree that soldering leaded projects is a snap compared to soldering copper-foil projects — probably because running a bead of solder along all the edges of a copper-foil project is much more time-consuming than simply soldering the intersections of a leaded project (refer to Chapter 8 for details on copper-foil projects). In this section, I show you all the ins and outs of soldering lead-came projects, including how to get your iron ready and how to solder perfect joints.

Setting your iron's temperature

Because you use 50/50 solder for lead soldering, you need to set your solder-ing iron at a lower temperature than you do for copper-foil soldering. The 50/50 solder melts quicker and stays molten longer so that you have time to flatten out the solder joints and blend them into the came face. You know your iron's at the right temperature if you can hold the iron on the joint for a minimum of ten seconds without melting the lead came.

Because lead came is easy to melt during the soldering process, be sure to test your iron before you solder a lead joint. Check out Chapter 7 for basic tips on testing your iron's temperature and soldering.

Soldering joints and intersections

The places where two or more lead cames meet are called *intersections* or *joints*. The goal when soldering is keeping these joints low and smooth — I show you how to do so in this section.

The better you fit the lead cames together during the construction process, the easier soldering the joints will be, and the nicer your finished project will look. Gaps in the intersections are difficult to fill in with solder; not to mention, it's almost impossible to make big, solder-filled gaps look like the rest of the lead in the project. Figure 9-12 shows a comparison of a joint with too big of a gap (Figure 9-12a) and a perfectly sized joint (Figure 9-12b). See the difference?

Figure 9-12:
A joint with too big of a gap and a perfectly sized joint.

Soldering the first joint

When you're ready to start soldering, start with the four outside corners of your panel to help stabilize the project. After finishing those four joints, try to solder the joints that are at the top of the panel and work your way down to the bottom. This technique keeps you from missing any joints as you go.

As you get started, keep in mind that you want to use an up-and-down motion as you solder; then follow these steps:

1. **Flux the intersections of the project; you can flux just a few intersections at a time or do them all at once.**

   Flux is a chemical that acts as a cleaner to remove oxidation from the face of the soldering surface, allowing the solder and metal to bond. See Chapter 7 for more details.

2. **Lay the end of the solder across the joint; place the flat side of the soldering iron tip directly on top of the solder and the joint.**

   The solder melts instantly and blends into the came.

3. **When the solder joint has flattened out, lift your iron straight up off the joint.**

   If you're trying to melt a larger area, continue placing your iron down on top of the solder, melting the area completely. Then lift the iron straight up and away as you move across a joint.

4. **If the joint looks raised and lumpy, re-flux and reheat it.**

   If you can still see the seam where the strips of lead meet, add more solder.

   Don't let your solder joints get too wide, and don't use the iron tip to spread or paint the solder onto the joints. Let the heat do the work.

When you finish soldering the first joint, follow Steps 1 through 4 to solder all the other joints on one side of your panel. Then flip the panel over, and do the same on the other side.

Keeping joints small

The perfectly sized lead joint is one that extends in each direction the same width as the face of the lead came (see Figure 9-13). The smaller the came width, the smaller the joints need to be.

To help you create the right-size joints, use a pencil to mark the came face where you want your solder joint to stop.

Removing excess solder

To remove excess solder from a joint, re-flux it and melt the extra solder again. As soon as it's melted, lift the iron straight up from the joint and flick the excess solder off the tip onto your work board. If necessary, repeat this process until you've removed most of the excess solder.

Be careful when flicking hot excess solder off the tip of your iron. You definitely don't want to burn yourself or anyone else, so make sure no one is near you in your studio and always wear your safety glasses.

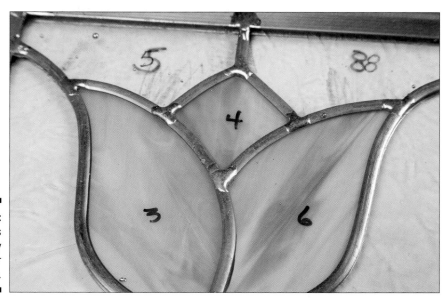

Figure 9-13:
Examples of perfectly sized solder joints.

Don't stress if your panel still has a little excess solder on it. You can't completely remove all traces of excess solder, but over time the solder will darken and blend with the came's patina, making it much less noticeable (see the section "Polishing the glass and adding patina" for more details).

Finishing Up and Cleaning Up

You can turn an ordinary stained-glass project into a real beauty if you know how to make a big finish. For lead projects, making a big finish means cementing the project to give it strength and shine and cleaning it so the glass really sparkles. The following sections show you how to do just that.

Making a panel airtight and waterproof

Lead came is a soft metal; its strength comes from being stretched, soldered, and cemented. (I cover stretching and soldering in the earlier sections "Stretching lead came" and "Soldering Lead-Came Projects.") *Cementing* is the process that fills in all the gaps around the glass pieces, making the panel airtight and waterproof and giving it beauty and appeal. It's a messy process that you should do outside if you can.

Gathering the right supplies

You can buy already-mixed cement, or you can mix up your own using the recipe I include in this section. I prefer to mix my own because it's easier to work with, it blends the patinas of the lead and solder beautifully, and, most important, it makes the panel strong and weatherproof.

To make cement, simply mix the following ingredients (which you can find at any home-improvement store) in a large disposable container until all the powder is dissolved and small air bubbles disappear from the surface of the mixture:

- ✔ 4 cups of whiting (chalk dust)
- ✔ 2 cups of plaster of Paris
- ✔ 1½ cups of turpentine
- ✔ 1 cup of boiled linseed oil
- ✔ 1 cup of Portland cement
- ✔ Optional: Powdered lamp black or grout colorant (to color)

Note: These ingredients make enough cement for a 12-x-18-inch panel.

Before you can start cementing, you need to gather the following additional supplies:

- ✔ 1 cup of whiting (chalk dust)
- ✔ 2 natural bristle brushes
- ✔ Old newspapers or craft paper (enough to cover your work space)

✔ Wooden craft sticks sharpened to a point

✔ Respirator (see Chapter 3 for details)

✔ A bench brush and dust pan for clean up

Cementing your soldered panel

Because the cementing process fills the air with lead dust, I recommend doing it outside if possible. But if you must work indoors, make sure you have plenty of good ventilation, and don't forget to wear your respirator. Damp mop the floors and dust all surfaces with a damp rag to keep lead dust from becoming air born.

No matter where you end up cementing, find a flat, level work surface, and follow these steps:

1. **Cover your work surface with newspapers or craft paper, and lay your panel on the paper.**

2. **Pour ⅓ of the cement mixture over the panel.**

3. **Use a natural brush to gently work the cement around the surface of the panel and into all the edges of the lead came (see Figure 9-14); add more cement if needed.**

   Working the brush in a circular motion helps force the cement under the face of the came. Your goal is to fill in any gaps between the glass and the lead.

4. **After you fill in all the gaps, use your brush to remove any excess cement from the surface of the glass by scooping it off the glass surface (see Figure 9-15); clean off your brush along the edge of the cement container as you do so.**

Figure 9-14:
Using a natural brush to spread cement over the panel's surface.

Figure 9-15:
Using the
brush to
remove
excess
cement from
the panel.

5. **Sprinkle the surface of the panel with a sprinkling of whiting (think powdered donuts here).**

6. **Using a clean brush, work the whiting around the panel in a circular motion (see Figure 9-16).**

   The whiting dries up the excess moisture in the cement and polishes the glass and lead cames.

7. **Use a sharpened wooden craft stick to scrape any remaining cement from the edges of the came faces (see Figure 9-17); then brush off any remaining cement residue.**

Figure 9-16:
Working
the whiting
around the
panel's sur-
face with a
clean brush.

Figure 9-17:
Removing any remaining cement with a craft stick.

8. **Repeat Steps 5 and 6; then brush away any remaining cement residue.**

   This time really put some elbow grease into the process! The friction from the whiting, the brush, and your energy make your panel shine and give the lead a beautiful look.

   Don't apply too much downward pressure as you brush around the whiting. You don't want to risk breaking a piece of glass after all your hard work!

9. **Flip the panel over, and repeat the same process on the back of the panel.**

10. **Dust off the panel, throw away the dirty newspapers, and replace them with clean ones.**

11. **Lay the panel on the clean newspapers to dry.**

    Let the panel lay perfectly flat for a minimum of 24 hours to allow the concrete to *cure* (or harden), longer if it's a larger panel. Figure 9-18 shows what a dried, finished panel looks like.

Polishing the glass and adding patina

After the panel has dried and the concrete has hardened completely, use a glass cleaner to polish the glass and remove any remaining residue. Just be sure to apply the window cleaner to a soft cloth — not directly to the window.

If the solder joints don't blend completely with the lead came, you can use some black patina to help darken the joints. *Patina* is a chemical that's designed to copy the look of the natural color change that happens to metals as they age and are exposed to air and water. Over time, the joints will darken naturally, but patina speeds up the process by 10 to 20 years.

To apply patina to the joints, use a cotton swab or small paint brush to paint the patina over the solder joints. Don't apply it to the lead came face or the glass because it will stain their surfaces and leave an unnatural appearance.

Figure 9-18:
Example of a finished, dry, shiny panel.

Framing your project

Before you can hang your project, you need to put it in a proper frame so that the lead doesn't stretch over time and pull apart your project. As far as what kind of frame to use, you can use either wood or metal as long as it fits the size of your glass project. Check out your local framing shop for help choosing the right frame.

You can save some money by building panels that fit standard-size picture frames, such as 9-x-12-inch and 14-x-16-inch frames, so think about what kind of frame you want to use for your project before you choose the size for your panel. Many times I find a frame that I just love and then build a window to fit that frame.

If you aren't installing a leaded panel in an actual window or door frame and you don't want to invest in a custom-made frame, you can substitute zinc, brass, or copper metal came in place of the lead came for the perimeter of your project.

Project: Geometric Leaded Panel

Lead came is a natural medium for geometric-designed windows, so, naturally, I include one here. Although this first project is a relatively simple panel, it has a lot of style.

I base this project on an 8½-x-12½-inch panel, but you can use a copy machine to enlarge the following pattern to fit any space. (For more details on working with patterns, turn to Chapter 4.)

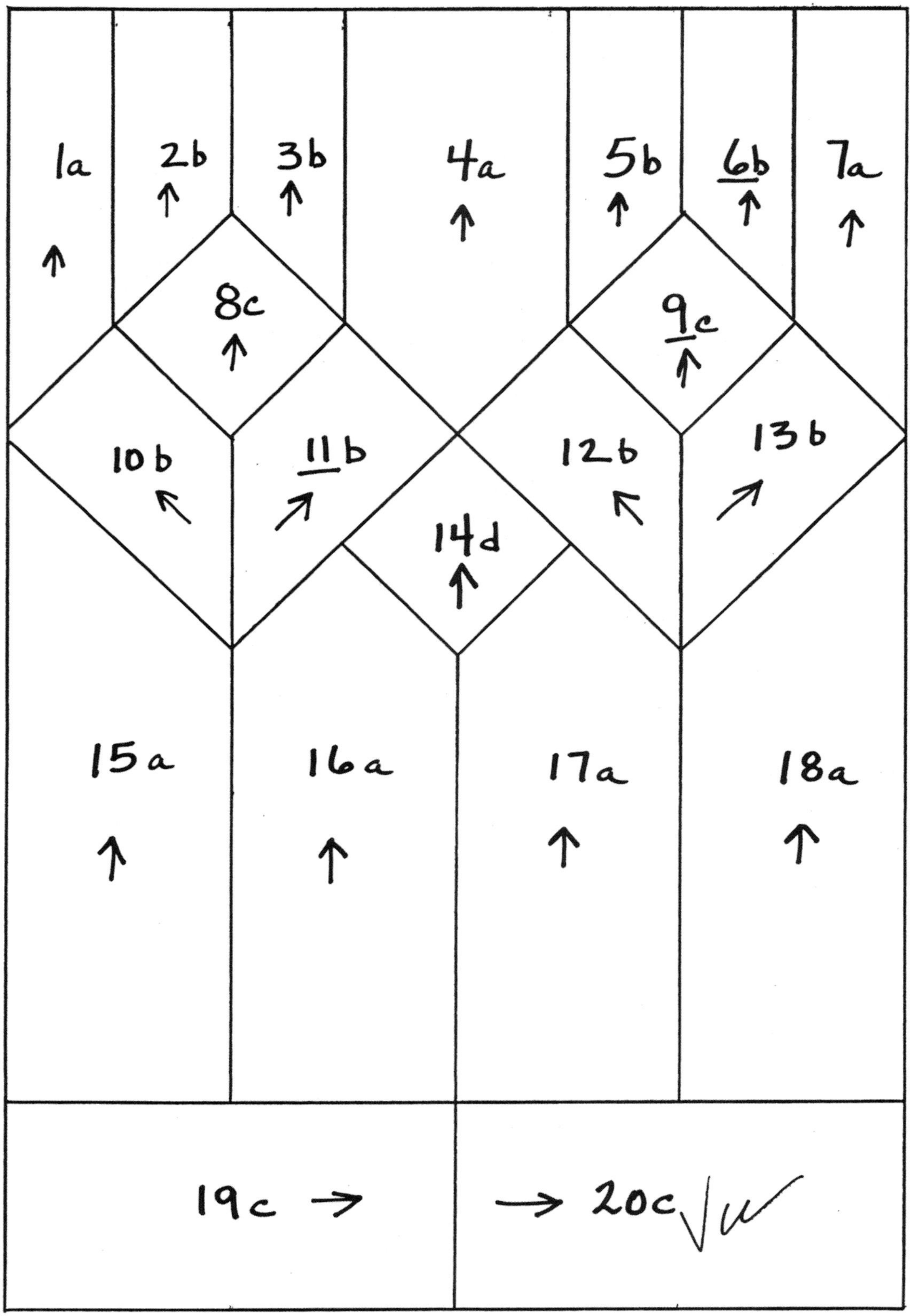

1a ↑

2b ↑

3b ↑

4a ↑

5b ↑

6b ↑

7a ↑

8c ↑

9c ↑

10b ↖

11b ↗

12b ↖

13b ↗

14d ↑

15a ↑

16a ↑

17a ↑

18a ↑

19c →

→ 20c ✓w

To make the 8½-x-12½-inch panel, you need one strip of ⅜-inch *H*-shaped lead came for the perimeter of the project and two strips of ³⁄₁₆-inch *H*-shaped lead for the interior lead work. In terms of glass, you can use either cathedral or opalescent (I use opalescent); you need 2 square feet of one color for the background and 1 square foot each of three to five additional colors.

After you have all your lead and glass handy, enlarge the pattern to be 8½ x 12½ inches, make three copies of it, set up your work board using one copy of the pattern (see the section "Preparing Your Work Board and Laying Out Your Pattern"), and follow these steps.

Note: To make this project easier to construct, I've numbered the pattern pieces in the order you will use them in leading up this window (1 through 20).

1. **Using a lead vise and a pair of pliers, stretch the lead came you plan to use for this project.**

   See the section "Stretching lead came" for details.

2. **Mark the cut and finished sizes around all four edges of your pattern (see Figure 9-19).**

   Note that ⅜-inch *H*-shaped lead came has a cut size of ³⁄₁₆ inch. Turn to Chapter 4 for more details about establishing the cut size and finished size for your pattern.

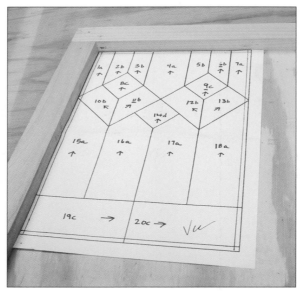

Figure 9-19:
Marking the cut and finished sizes on the pattern.

3. **Number and color code the pattern pieces, and indicate the grain direction for each piece (refer to Figure 9-19).**

   The *grain direction* is the direction of the color streaks or air bubbles in the glass (see Chapter 4 for more details).

4. **Cut out the pattern pieces using lead shears, and glue them to the glass, making sure you match the grain direction on the template to that of the glass.**

   Don't use foil shears to cut out your pattern templates; if you do, you won't have enough space between the glass pieces for the lead came.

5. **Cut out all the glass shapes.**

   See Chapter 5 for details on how to cut glass.

6. **Use your glass grinder to remove any excess glass and to smooth out the rough edges on your glass shapes so they fit your pattern.**

   Compare the cut pieces to your pattern to make sure they fit perfectly; if any of them don't, grind them until they do. See Chapter 6 for details on grinding glass.

7. **Remove the pattern templates from the glass pieces, and use a permanent marker to transfer the pattern numbers to the glass pieces.**

8. **Cut and position the two ⅜-inch exterior lead cames into the corner of the work board; use horseshoe nails to secure the lead in place (see Figure 9-20).**

   For details on cutting lead came, check out the section "Cutting lead came," and for tips on positioning the exterior lead cames so that they frame the corner of your panel, check out the section "Framing it up."

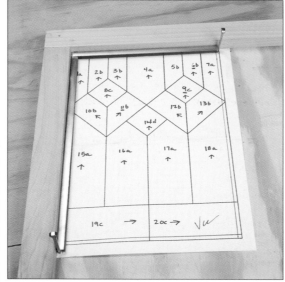

Figure 9-20: Securing two exterior lead cames in the corner of the work board.

9. **Put piece 1 into the perimeter lead came; check to make sure you can see the pattern line around the edge of the glass, and then secure it with a spacer and a horseshoe nail (see Figure 9-21).**

10. **Cut a 3-inch strip of ³⁄₁₆-inch *H*-shaped came to fit along the side of piece 1 (or the piece you just secured).**

11. **Mark the piece of lead you cut in Step 10 to allow space for another piece of lead to run along the bottom of piece 1.**

Figure 9-21:
Securing
the first
glass piece
in posi-
tion with a
spacer and
a horseshoe
nail.

The easiest way to determine the length and angle of the cut you need to make is to use a scrap piece of ⅜₆-inch came as a gauge. Place your lead knife up against the edge of the gauge. Rock the blade of the knife across the face of the lead to mark the length and angle of the cut (see Figure 9-22).

12. **Remove the marked piece of lead from the panel, and trim it to size using your lead nippers.**

13. **Place the trimmed came onto the edge of piece 1, and check that the length is right.**

Sloppy lead cuts result in sloppy solder joints. Make your cuts as accurate as possible even if that means pitching a piece of lead and starting over.

Figure 9-22:
Using a
lead knife
to indicate
where to
trim the lead
came and
the angle of
the cut.

14. **Insert piece 2 into the channel on the other side of the lead strip you put on piece 1 in Step 13, making sure you can see the pattern line; secure it with a spacer and a horseshoe nail.**

15. **Repeat Steps 10 through 13 for piece 2.**

16. **Insert pieces 3 through 7, and cut and place the lead strips that go with them by following Steps 10 through 15; then secure the side of the window with a spacer and a horseshoe nail (see Figure 9-23).**

17. **Trim and fit each piece of came along the bottom edges of all these glass pieces.**

    When you're ready to trim the piece of lead that runs along the bottom of pieces 6 and 7, you need to use a lead gauge cut from ⅜-inch *H*-shaped lead came instead of the ³⁄₁₆-inch came you use for the first six pieces because you'll be using ⅜-inch came around the outside edges of your project (refer to Figure 9-23). Be sure that the edge of piece 7 is inside the cut size.

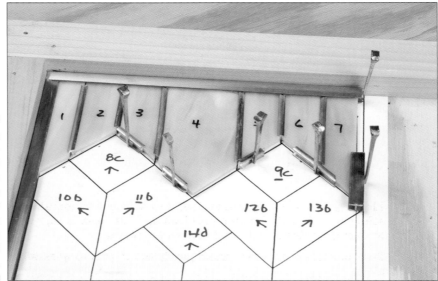

Figure 9-23: Using a ⅜-inch lead gauge to help you trim the lead along the bottom of pieces 6 and 7.

The purpose of using a lead gauge to help you trim the came in your project is to make sure you allow enough room for the next piece of came. If the next came is going to be larger, you need to allow more room for it; hence, you need to use a bigger gauge. If you always remember to use the proper gauge, your finished project will fit together perfectly.

18. **Repeat Steps 10 through 17 for the remaining glass pieces and lead cames, making sure to stay on pattern and use the proper gauges when trimming the lead.**

19. **After you place piece 20 into the panel, check to make sure all the perimeter glass pieces are inside the cut line and that the window itself is square and on the finished size line.**

    If any pieces reach outside the cut line, mark the area of glass that needs to be removed, take the piece out of your project, and use your grinder to remove the excess glass. Then refit the piece into your window.

If the window doesn't fit the finished size, it won't be square. Use your squaring bars and lead knife to gently tap the glass and lead into the correct position, if possible. If you can't make your project square by tapping it, you have to deconstruct your panel to find the glass piece that's causing the problem and repair it.

20. **Add the last two exterior lead cames to cap off the perimeter of the panel, and use two 1-inch squaring bars to hold them in place (see Figure 9-24).**

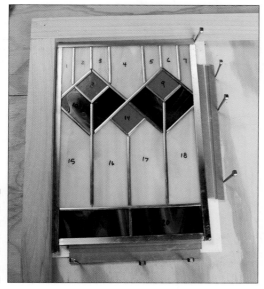

Figure 9-24:
Adding the last two lead cames to the panel.

21. **Plug in your soldering iron and set it to the right temperature for lead soldering; while it's heating up, clean up your work area, removing any scraps of lead, nails, and pattern templates.**

22. **Test your soldering iron to make sure it isn't too hot to work with lead came.**

    Turn to Chapter 7 for details on how to test your iron's temperature.

23. **Flux and solder each of the lead joints on your panel, using 50/50 solder.**

    See the section "Soldering Lead-Came Projects" and Chapter 7 for more details.

24. **When you're finished soldering the front side of the panel, carefully turn it over and solder the joints on the backside.**

25. **Cement the project by following the steps I provide in the section "Cementing your soldered panel."**

26. **Let the panel and cement dry for at least 24 hours before you clean it up using glass cleaner.**

27. **Add patina if necessary.**

    Figure 9-25 shows the finished geometric leaded panel.

28. **Place your panel in either a wooden or metal frame.**

    See the section "Framing your project" for details.

Figure 9-25:
Finished
geometric
leaded
panel in
opalescent
glass.

Project: Art Nouveau Tulip

Art nouveau designs look beautiful in leaded-glass panels. Their gentle curving lines and simple details are best expressed with straight, smooth lead lines. This tulip panel is one of my favorite beginning patterns, and I've seen it built hundreds of times using all types and colors of glass. If you select your favorite colors, I'm sure you'll love it as much as I do.

How many sheets of glass you need for this project depends on how many colors you choose and where you put them in the window. Generally speaking, you need to buy twice as much glass as you think you'll need. In other words, count up the number of pieces you want to cut from each glass color and then double that number. It's always better to err on the side of too much glass than not enough. As your cutting skills improve, so will your glass expenses!

I base this project on an 8-x-13-inch panel, but you can use a copy machine to enlarge the following pattern to whatever size fits your space. To make the 8-x-13-inch panel, you need two different sizes of lead came: ⅜-inch *H*-shaped lead for the exterior of the panel and ³⁄₁₆-inch *H*-shaped came for the interior came. To estimate how much of each size you need, measure all the edges in your pattern and then add them up. Again, it's better to have too much lead than not enough. After all, you can always use extra lead in another project.

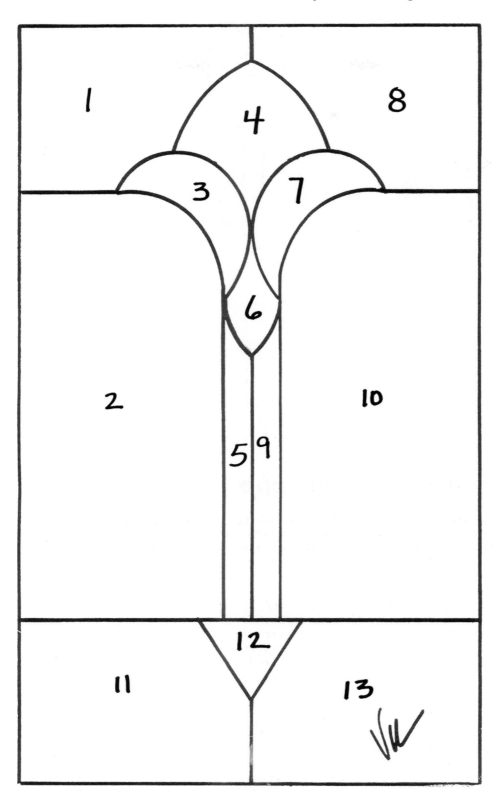

After you've gathered your glass and lead, you're ready to get started. Enlarge the pattern to be 8 x 13 inches, make three copies of it, set up your work board using one of the copies (see the section "Preparing Your Work Board and Laying Out Your Pattern" for details), and follow these steps.

Note: To make this project easier to construct, I've numbered the pattern pieces in the order you will use them in leading up this window.

1. **Using a lead vise and pliers, stretch your lead came; trim off the damaged ends and discard them.**

   See the section "Stretching lead came" for details.

2. **Mark the cut size around all four edges of your pattern.**

3. **Number and color code the pattern pieces, and indicate the grain direction for each piece.**

   See Chapter 4 for more details about working with patterns and determining grain direction.

4. **Cut out the pattern pieces using lead shears, and glue them to the glass, making sure you match the grain direction on the template to that of the glass.**

5. **Cut out all the glass shapes.**

   See Chapter 5 for details on cutting glass.

6. **Use your glass grinder to smooth out the rough edges on your glass shapes so that they fit your pattern.**

   Place the cut pieces on your pattern to make sure they fit perfectly (you should be able to see the pattern lines around the glass pieces); if any of the pieces don't fit, grind them until they do. See Chapter 6 for details on grinding glass.

7. **Remove the pattern templates from the glass pieces, and use a permanent marker to transfer the pattern numbers to the glass pieces.**

8. **Cut and position two ⅜-inch exterior lead cames into the corner of the work board; use horseshoe nails to secure the lead in place.**

   Check out the sections "Cutting lead came" and "Framing it up" for more details.

9. **Fit piece 1 into the perimeter came channel, making sure you stay on pattern; use a spacer and a horseshoe nail to secure it (see Figure 9-26).**

   If you can't see the pattern lines around the glass piece, use your grinder to remove the excess glass so that you can see the lines. Be sure to dry off your glass pieces before placing them back on your pattern.

10. **Place a 12-inch piece of ³⁄₁₆-inch came along the bottom of piece 1.**

   You have to custom cut each piece of lead came so that you have enough space for the next intersecting piece of lead. Sometimes that intersection may not come into play until the bottom of the project. To determine how much space you need, use a scrap piece of the same lead you're using in your project (³⁄₁₆-inch lead, in this case) as a gauge. Insert the glass piece into the scrap lead and mark where you need to cut your piece of came so that you have just enough space for the scrap lead to intersect the next piece of lead.

Figure 9-26:
Securing
your first
glass piece
with
spacers and
horseshoe
nails.

11. **Insert the top of piece 2 into the ³⁄₁₆-inch came that runs along the bottom of piece 1 and the side of piece 2 into the ³⁄₈-inch came that runs along the perimeter of the panel; secure the bottom of piece 2 with a spacer and a horseshoe nail.**

12. **Repeat Steps 9 through 11 to add the remaining glass pieces in numerical order (see Figure 9-27).**

    Don't forget to use your lead gauges to help you determine the exact length of each piece of lead came.

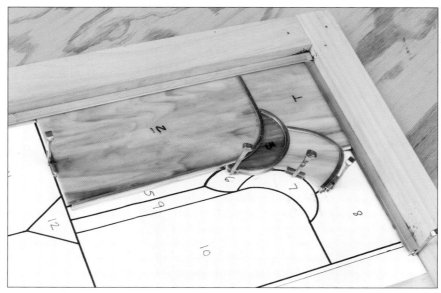

Figure 9-27:
Partially
leaded tulip
panel.

13. **Add two ⅜-inch *H*-shaped cames to cap off the project's perimeter, and secure them with squaring bars, checking to make sure the panel is the finished size and square.**

14. **Plug in your soldering iron; after it heats, test it to make sure it's the right temperature.**

    Turn to Chapter 7 for details on how to test your iron's temperature.

15. **Flux and solder each of the lead joints on the front of your panel, using 50/50 solder; then flux and solder the joints on the backside.**

    See the section "Soldering Lead-Came Projects" and Chapter 7 for more details.

16. **Cement the panel to make it airtight and waterproof by following the steps I provide in the section "Cementing your soldered panel."**

17. **Let the panel and cement dry for at least 24 hours before you clean it up using glass cleaner.**

18. **Apply black patina if needed.**

19. **Place your panel in either a wooden or metal frame.**

    See the section "Framing your project" for details. Figure 9-28 shows the finished project.

Figure 9-28:
Finished art
nouveau
tulip
window.

Project: Round All-American Panel

Building a round leaded panel can be a little tricky. Although all the steps are basically the same as the steps for creating a rectangular panel, the actual building process is a little different in that you can't use the wooden squaring bars to help keep all the pieces in place as you construct the window — because it's round and not square. To make up for the lack of squared support, you need to use a lot of horseshoe nails.

I base this project on a 10-inch circle, but you can use a copy machine to enlarge the following pattern to whatever size fits your space.

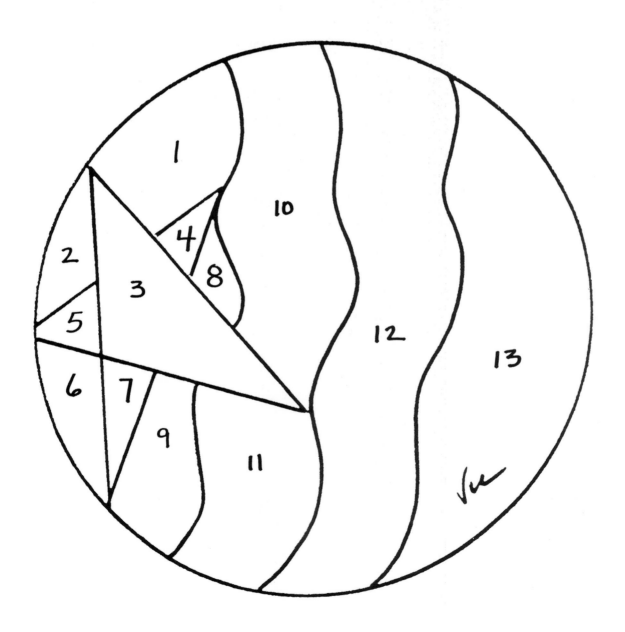

For this project, you use ⁵⁄₁₆-inch *U*-shaped came for the perimeter of the project and ³⁄₁₆-inch *H*-shaped came for the interior. As far as glass goes, select whichever colors you like. Just be sure to get twice as much glass as you think you'll need so that you don't run out. I recommend using smooth-surface glass for your first few projects because it's a little easier to work with.

When you have all the lead and glass you need for this project, you're ready to begin. Enlarge the pattern to be 10 inches in diameter, make three copies of it, lay out one of the copies in the center of the work board (see the section "Preparing Your Work Board and Laying Out Your Pattern" for details), and follow these steps.

Note: To make this project easier to construct, I've numbered the pattern pieces in the order you will use them in leading up this window.

1. **Using a lead vise and pliers, stretch your lead came; trim off the damaged ends and discard them.**

   See the section "Stretching lead came" for details.

2. **Find the center of your pattern by folding the pattern in half; mark the center with a red marker (see Figure 9-29).**

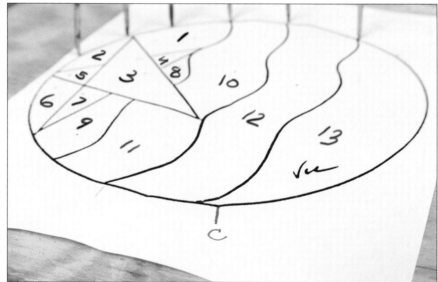

Figure 9-29: Marking the center of the pattern with a red marker.

3. **Draw the finished size on the pattern, and place horseshoe nails along that line on your pattern.**

   These horseshoe nails replace the squaring bars you use in rectangular panels. Space the nails 1 inch apart ⅓ of the way around the top of the project.

4. **Color code, number, and mark the grain direction on the pattern templates; then cut them out using lead shears and use rubber cement to glue them to your glass.**

   Make sure you match the grain direction of the glass to the directions you marked on the pattern pieces. See Chapter 4 for more details on working with patterns.

5. **Cut out all your glass pieces.**

   Turn to Chapter 5 for everything you need to know about glass cutting.

6. **Use your grinder to remove excess glass and rough edges from each glass piece.**

   Don't forget to check the pieces against your master pattern; if any glass pieces don't fit perfectly, use your grinder until they do. See Chapter 6 for details on grinding glass.

7. **Cut a strip of the *U*-shaped lead 2 inches longer than the outside circumference of the panel.**

8. **Place the *U*-shaped came that you cut in Step 7 around the top of the panel along the horseshoe nails (see Figure 9-30).**

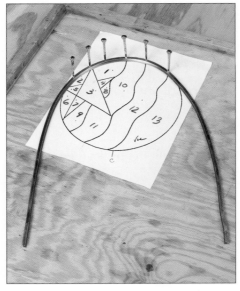

Figure 9-30:
Adding the
U-shaped
came to the
perimeter of
the panel.

9. **Fit piece 1 into the channel of the *U*-shaped perimeter lead came from Step 8; secure it with a spacer and a horseshoe nail.**

10. **Cut and fit a piece of lead along the interior edge of piece 1.**

    Use your spacer to judge where to trim the lead came so you have enough room for the next intersection of lead.

11. **Fit piece 2 into position, fitting it into the surrounding lead cames.**

    Make sure piece 2 doesn't extend over the pattern line. If it does, use your grinder to make it fit the pattern. Cut and fit another piece of lead to fit on the other side of piece 2.

12. **Repeat Steps 9 through 11 to add the remaining glass pieces and lead strips to the panel (see Figure 9-31); as you do so, add more horseshoe nails to secure the perimeter lead came around the circular boarder of the panel.**

Figure 9-31:
Partially
leaded
round panel.

13. **After you fit the last piece of glass into the project, gently wrap the ends of the came around the bottom of the panel; trim the excess lead so the intersection of the came is at the center of your panel (see Figure 9-32).**

14. **Plug in your soldering iron; after it heats, test it to make sure it's the right temperature.**

    Turn to Chapter 7 for details on how to test your iron's temperature.

15. **Flux and solder each of the lead joints on the front of your panel, using 50/50 solder; then flux and solder the joints on the backside.**

    See the section "Soldering Lead-Came Projects" and Chapter 7 for more details.

16. **Solder two wire hanging hooks onto the back of the panel along the edge of the lead came (see Figure 9-33).**

    Make sure the hooks are level to each other so the panel hangs straight.

Figure 9-32: Wrapping the ends of the came around the panel so the intersection is at the center.

Figure 9-33: The back of the panel with hanging hooks soldered in place.

17. Cement the panel by following the steps I provide in the section "Cementing your soldered panel."

18. Let the panel and cement dry for at least 24 hours before you clean it up using glass cleaner.

19. Add black patina to the solder joints if necessary.

Figure 9-34 shows the finished panel.

Figure 9-34:
Finished all-
American
panel.

Chapter 10

Making a Stained-Glass Box

Stained-glass boxes are the little treasures of the glass-working craft. They make perfect gifts for all occasions and provide infinite design possibilities. Probably the most interesting aspect of glass boxes is their three-dimensionality, but, unfortunately, that same quality is what makes building your first box a bit frustrating. Chances are, all your projects up to this point have been flat panels, so before you start making your first stained-glass box, get ready for a whole new kind of project.

Creating a functional, three-dimensional box requires that you make exact measurements. If you don't cut your glass pieces accurately, the box won't go together successfully; it's that simple. Equally important is positioning your box hinges correctly so you can open and close the box hundreds of times without damaging it. Don't worry; I cover these steps and a whole lot more in this chapter.

I struggled for days the first time I tried to make a stained-glass box. But because I wanted to make a different box for every member of my family, I knew I had to develop a technique that would ensure success every time I made a box, regardless of the design or size, and, lucky for you, that's just what I did. The process I share in this chapter is a foolproof formula that you can use over and over again to create beautiful boxes of all colors and sizes. The best part is that even after you get the hang of the process, you'll be surprised and inspired by every box you make.

Selecting the Glass for Your Box

Not all types of glass make great stained-glass boxes. If the glass is too transparent, it shows all the structure points of the box and distracts from the overall design. If the glass is too dark, it doesn't let enough light through the layers of glass, causing the box itself to lose color. For example, if you want to make a red box for Christmas or Valentine's Day, don't use red cathedral glass because the finished box will look black. A good alternative is red opalescent glass, which allows just the right amount of light through to shine red (see Figure 10-1). (See Chapter 1 for the difference between cathedral and opalescent glass.)

Figure 10-1:
Christmas box created from red opalescent glass.

When you're ready to choose the glass for your box, think about what you want the finished project to look like and what types of glass you could use to achieve that look (see Figure 10-2 for some great-looking glass boxes). The following sections cover the different types of glass you can use for the surfaces and bottom of your box, as well as a few unique objects you can use to add a bit of whimsy to the top.

Figure 10-2:
Examples of stained-glass boxes.

Art glass

When you're selecting glass for the sides of your box, choose glass based only on its surface color. In other words, don't hold it up to the light. If you love the color of the glass when it's laying on the table, you're sure to love it on your box.

In addition to color, look for glass that has an interesting pattern or finish. Many art glasses have beautiful swirls of colors or textures that add a sense of dimension and drama to anything made from them. The following three types of art glass are only a few of the many options you have when creating a stained-glass box (see Chapter 1 for many more):

✔ **Baroque glass:** This type of glass has very distinctive color streaks that run from one end of the glass sheet to the other end. Baroque glass can be clear with clear streaks, clear with colored streaks, or opal with opal streaks. The box in Figure 10-3 uses Baroque glass to create a dramatic flow from black to white to clear.

✔ **Iridescent glass:** This type of glass has a thin chemical coating on the surface that makes the glass shine and sparkle with an iridescent glow (see Figure 10-4). Although it looks expensive, this glass is very afford-able, especially when you consider the big impact it can have on your project.

✔ **Textured glass:** As its name suggests, textured glass is glass with a textured surface. Just to name a few examples, *rippled glass* has rolls of ridges running across the glass surface, *hammer-back glass* has little round knobs, and *granite-backed glass* has tiny little bumps. I like to use rippled glass just for the top of a box to spice it up a bit (refer to Figure 10-4 for an example).

Figure 10-3:
Using black and white Baroque glass to add drama to this simple box.

Figure 10-4:
Using rippled, iridescent glass to add visual appeal to the top of this black box.

When you first start making stained-glass boxes, I suggest that you work with smooth art glass because textured-glass pieces often have different thicknesses and can be a little hard to work with. After you build a few boxes, though, don't overlook the value textured glass can add to a simple box design.

Don't limit yourself to working with just one side of the glass. Sometimes the most interesting part of the glass is on the backside.

Whether you decide to use iridescent or textured glass (or some other type of art glass), get in the habit of selecting art glass for its individual beauty and the way that beauty applies to your project.

Mirrors

I love using mirrored glass for the bottoms of my boxes because it looks so pretty when you open up the lids. If you're using darker opalescent glasses on the rest of your box, adding a mirrored-glass bottom reflects the light back up and gives the dark glass more life and interest.

The most common type of mirrored glass is ⅛ inch thick and silver; however, modern glass manufacturers have really exploded your choices. Just take a trip to your local glass shop to see what I mean; you may be surprised by the huge variety of colored mirrored glass just waiting to be used in your next project.

Beveled glass

Beveled glass is glass that has angled edges; it comes in a wide range of shapes and sizes. Sheets of beveled glass are called *stock bevels,* and you can order them from any glass supplier. Adding a small, triangular piece of beveled glass to the top of a plain box design really makes a statement (see Figure 10-5).

Figure 10-5:
Adding beveled glass to the top of a plain box.

Fun and interesting objects

Perhaps the best characteristic of glass boxes is that they're such open canvases for designers. You may be surprised to see just how many different elements you can incorporate into such a simple design. For example, I love adding sea shells, agates, glass nuggets, and jewels to my boxes; they create such real dimension!

If you think you have just the object to add to your box, all you have to do is wrap the object in copper foil just like you would a glass piece and then solder it in place. You can also simply glue the object to your box's top. I like to use E-6000 glue for this purpose because it's clear, waterproof, flexible, and nonflammable; it's available at all craft and home-improvement stores. Super glues don't work because they're too brittle.

Glass nuggets make wonderful raised feet for boxes (see the section "Adding box feet" for more details).

Using Special Tools to Construct a Glass Box

The secret to successful box building is accurately cutting your glass strips. To achieve that accuracy, you need to add a strip cutter, a ruler, and a triangle to your basic stained-glass tools (refer to Chapter 2 for details on the other tools you need). The strip cutter allows you to cut as many strips of glass as you need in exactly the same size, and the ruler and triangle help you cut perfect right angles and straight strips. Figure 10-6 shows each of these additional tools.

To make perfectly straight cuts, you need to move the strip cutter along a wooden rail as you cut. Where do you get the rail? You can use the work board you use for your leaded-glass projects as long as the board along its perimeter is at least ¾ inch high.

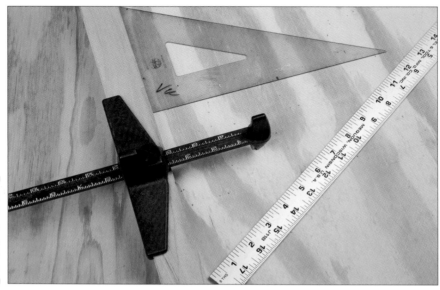

Figure 10-6:
Strip cutter, ruler, triangle, and work board rail.

Because cutting glass with a strip cutter is a little different than cutting with your regular glass cutter (see the section "Cutting the pieces using your strip cutter" for details), I recommend that you practice on less expensive clear glass until you get used to using the strip cutter.

The cutting wheel on the strip cutter isn't self-oiling, so you need to keep a small dish with an oiled paper towel handy for lubricating the cutting wheel between each score.

Visualizing the Basic Box Layout

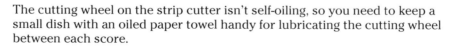

The basic box layout I describe in the following sections allows you to maximize the beauty of the glass grain with little or no glass waste. The layout and measurements I provide here are for a 6-x-4-x-2-inch stained-glass box with a solid glass top. You make the bottom of the box from another 4-x-6-inch piece of glass. Keep in mind that you can redesign the basic layout to fit almost any size box you want to make. You don't need a pattern unless you want to create a box with a decorative multipiece top.

One size fits all: Foolproof prep for cutting a perfect fit

To make a 6-x-4-x-2-inch box, you need one piece of glass that's at least 12 x 6 inches and one piece of glass that's 6 x 4 inches (see the section "Selecting the Glass for Your Box" for details on what glass to use). I recommend that you work with a piece of glass that's at least 14 x 6 inches in case you have to recut one of the pieces.

After you choose your glass pieces, you're ready to square the corners and label your glass for cutting. The following sections show you how to do both tasks.

Squaring the corners

The phrase *squaring the corners* means cutting all four corners of your glass piece so that they're 90-degree angles. If your corners aren't perfectly square, you'll have a hard time assembling your box.

Thankfully, squaring up a piece of glass is easy to do. Just follow these steps:

1. **Start with a large piece of glass, and use your triangle and ruler to lay out the 14-x-6-inch template.**

2. **Mark the perimeter lines with a permanent marker (see Figure 10-7).**

3. **Use a ruler and your regular glass cutter or strip cutter to cut out the designated 14-x-6-inch piece.**

Figure 10-7:
Marking the perimeter lines on a piece of glass.

Labeling the glass for cutting

After you square your glass, you're ready to start labeling it for cutting. At first, the layout markings I use here (*FB, BT, BB,* and so on) may seem strange, but trust me, as you work through your first box, everything will come together.

When labeling your glass for cutting, use a black or white permanent marker and the following abbreviations:

- ✔ **SBT:** Side B Top
- ✔ **SBB:** Side B Bottom
- ✔ **SAT:** Side A Top
- ✔ **SAB:** Side A Bottom
- ✔ **BB:** Back Bottom

- ✔ **BT:** Back Top
- ✔ **T:** Top
- ✔ **FT:** Front Top
- ✔ **FB:** Front Bottom

Figure 10-8 shows an example of what the glass looks like after you label it. Each glass piece needs to be 2 inches tall, so place a ruler alongside the glass to make sure you label your glass pieces every two inches. The only exceptions are the top piece (which needs to be 4 inches tall) and the bottom piece (which you make with a separate sheet of glass).

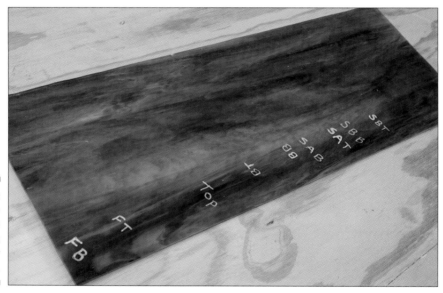

Figure 10-8:
A 13-x-6-inch piece of glass marked for cutting.

Cutting the pieces using your strip cutter

The following steps walk you through using the glass strip cutter to cut all your basic box pieces:

1. **Place the squared piece of art glass on your work board with the 6-inch side marked *FB* against the wooden rail; secure it by placing a couple of horseshoe nails against a triangle next to the glass (see Figure 10-9).**

2. **Place a ruler on top of the glass, and set your strip cutter so the cutting wheel is at the 2-inch mark on the ruler (see Figure 10-10).**

   You can also place the ruler beside the glass, if you prefer.

Figure 10-9:
Glass set up
and ready
for stripping.

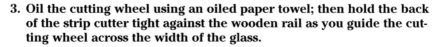

Figure 10-10:
Setting
the cutting
wheel at
2 inches.

3. **Oil the cutting wheel using an oiled paper towel; then hold the back of the strip cutter tight against the wooden rail as you guide the cutting wheel across the width of the glass.**

   Oil your cutting wheel between every score to ensure cutting success.

4. **Use your running pliers to break the glass along the line you scored in Step 3; place the cut piece on your worktable.**

   You'll cut *FT* apart from *FB* later.

5. **Adjust the width of the cut from 2 inches to 4 inches, cut the top of the box, marked *T*, and place it on your worktable.**

To cut piece *T,* slide the glass back against the rail of the work board, and score a 4-inch cut along the edge of piece *T*. Use your running pliers to break the piece along the score line.

6. **Readjust your cutter to cut a 2-inch strip, and repeat Steps 3 and 4 to cut out the back of the box (marked *BB* and *BT*).**

7. **Repeat Steps 3 and 4 to cut out the two remaining 2-inch strips for the two ends (or sides) of the box (marked *SAB/SAT* and *SBB/SBT*).**

8. **Trim the side pieces *SBB/SBT* and *SAB/SAT* to 4¼ inches by positioning them along the wooden rail as shown in Figure 10-11, setting your strip cutter for 4¼ inches, and cutting across the two strips; then break the pieces apart with your running pliers.**

   The extra ¼ inch will allow the side pieces to overlap the front and back of the box. Note that at this point piece *SBB* is still connected to piece *SBT* and piece *SAB* to piece *SAT*.

   You can toss away the extra glass.

9. **Set your strip cutter for ¾ inch, line up the four 2-inch glass strips as shown in Figure 10-12, and cut the four strips into two pieces; then break the pieces apart with your running pliers to separate the top pieces from the bottom ones.**

Congratulations! You've cut out all the art-glass pieces for your basic box. The only piece left to cut is the mirror for the bottom. The inside dimensions of the box are 4 x 6 inches, so that's how big your mirror needs to be. Use your ruler and triangle to mark a 4-x-6-inch template on the mirrored glass; then use your strip cutter or hand cutter to cut out the mirror.

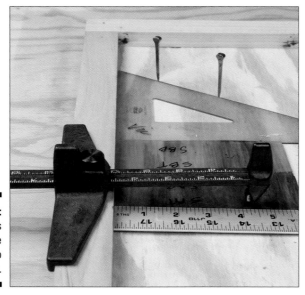

Figure 10-11:
Side pieces
ready to be
trimmed to
4¼ inches.

Figure 10-12:
Glass strips
laid out for
separating
the tops
from the
bottoms.

Laying out and foiling the pieces

As you cut the pieces by following the steps in the preceding section, you need to lay them out according to the template shown in Figure 10-13. Keep your pieces laid out this way until you start to build the project.

If your cutting is accurate, you don't have to use a grinder to smooth out your glass edges before you foil them. Just make sure the edges of the glass are free of oil and dust before you start to apply your $\frac{7}{32}$-inch copper foil (see Figure 10-14). Don't forget to foil the bottom mirror piece. Turn to Chapter 8 for all the details on how to apply copper foil to your glass pieces.

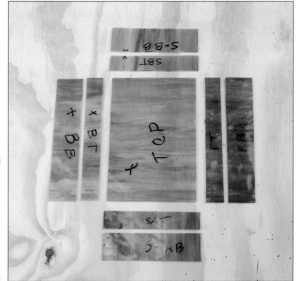

Figure 10-13:
Glass
pieces cut
to size and
laid out
ready for
assembly.

If you're using transparent glass, be sure to match your foil to the color of patina you plan to use after you solder. (See the section "Assembling the Basic Box" for details on soldering your box together and Chapter 8 for more info on applying patina to your project.)

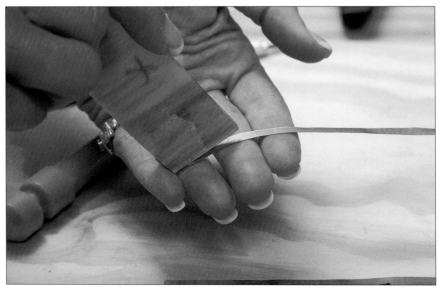

Figure 10-14:
Applying
copper foil.

Assembling the Basic Box

When you have all your pieces foiled and laid out according to the template in Figure 10-13, you're ready to start assembling your box. The following sections show you how to solder the glass pieces together, attach the hinges and chain, and add box feet.

When assembling your box, pay close attention to your glass pieces' labels. Make sure the letter labels run around the outside of the box right side up.

Soldering the box pieces together

After you've cut out and wrapped all your glass pieces in foil, the layout of the box pieces really becomes clear. Just be sure to assemble the bottom and top portions of the box as I do here so you don't mix up your pieces. As long as you follow the order I describe in this section, the grain of your glass should flow perfectly through the entire project.

To assemble the sides of your box, follow these steps:

1. **Tin all the copper-foil edges on your glass pieces by melting a thin coating of solder onto all the exposed copper foil (see Figure 10-15).**

Tinning the foil now keeps you from having to reach inside the box to finish the edges after you assemble it. See Chapter 8 for more details on tinning foil.

Be careful not to use too much solder along the edges of the glass, or you'll build up the edges, making it difficult to assemble the box pieces later.

Figure 10-15:
Foiled and tinned box pieces.

2. **To assemble the bottom sides of the box, overlap the shorter sides (marked *SBB* and *SAB*) over the longer sides (marked *BB* and *FB*), and tack solder the edges of the box, as shown in Figure 10-16.**

   Turn to Chapter 7 for everything you need to know about tack soldering.

Figure 10-16:
Tack soldering the box sides together.

3. **Place a foiled piece of mirrored glass into the bottom of the box, and solder it into place.**

4. **Turn the box over, and run a flat solder bead around the bottom of the box (see Figure 10-17).**

Figure 10-17:
Running a flat bead around the bottom of the box.

Typically, when you solder copper-foil projects, you want to run a raised, smooth bead, but here, you want to run a flat bead instead. To do so, drag the iron tip along the glass and foil surface at a medium pace, applying solder as needed. If you move too slowly, the metal will get so hot that the solder will drip through the seam.

5. **To assemble the top sides of the box, overlap the shorter sides (marked *SBT* and *SAT*) over the longer sides (marked *BT* and *FT*), and tack solder the edges of the box (refer to Figure 10-17).**

6. **Place the assembled side pieces upside down on your work board, turn the assembled top piece upside down and drop it carefully into the space created by the sides; tack solder the top in place.**

7. **Run a nice raised bead around the top edge of the box (see Figure 10-18).**

   You now have two separate, completed parts of the box — the top and the bottom. Read the next section to find out how to put them together.

Attaching the hinges

When it comes to choosing hinges for your box, you basically have two options: tube hinges or brass hinges. However, I don't recommend using the tube hinges because they're difficult to cut. Instead, I suggest that you use brass hinges because they're both efficient and affordable.

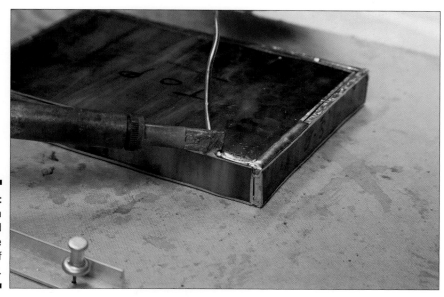

Figure 10-18:
Running a
raised bead
along the
top edge of
the box.

Attaching the hinges to your box is pretty simple as long as you don't overdo it with flux and solder. Just follow these steps:

1. **Put the top piece of the box on top of the bottom piece, and secure them together with rubber bands; position the box on its side with the backside up, as shown in Figure 10-19.**

2. **Use a small paint brush to apply a small amount of flux to the tip of the hinge.**

   Keep the flux out of the working part of the hinge. Solder doesn't flow where there is no flux, so use it sparingly.

Figure 10-19:
Tack sol-
dering the
hinge to
hold it in
place.

3. **Holding the edge of the hinge with needle-nose pliers, tack solder it to the top portion of the back of the box (refer to Figure 10-19).**

4. **Tack solder the bottom of the hinge to the bottom portion of the box.**

5. **Repeat Steps 2 through 4 for the other hinge.**

6. **Run a raised bead along the front and back side seams of your box (see Figure 10-20).**

When soldering the back of the box, be careful not to melt the solder that's holding the hinges in place.

Figure 10-20: Soldering the back and front side seams after attaching the hinges.

Attaching the chain

Although your box may look complete after you attach the hinges, it's not quite finished. You need to add a chain to secure the top of the box to the bottom when the lid is opened. Without a chain, the box lid could easily fall backward and break the glass and rip the foil. You certainly don't want that after all your hard work!

You can purchase box chain in brass, copper, or silver. Which color chain you use depends on the color of patina you plan to use on your box. If you're leaving the solder silver, select a silver-colored chain. (See Chapter 8 for more on patina.)

To measure and attach the chain, follow these steps:

1. **Open the box top to a 100- to 110-degree angle, and measure the distance between the top-front corner and the bottom-front corner; cut a piece of box chain that length.**

   You want the box to be able to open about 10 degrees past center but not so far as to place a strain on the hinges.

2. **Open the box to an 80-degree angle.**

3. **Tack solder the chain in place (see Figure 10-21).**

   Use just a small drop of hot solder to attach one end of the chain in place along the top-front corner of the box's lid and another small drop to attach the other end of the chain along the bottom-front corner. After it cools, tug lightly on the chain to make sure it's firmly attached.

Figure 10-21:
Box with chain soldered in place.

Adding box feet

You may or may not choose to add feet to your box. If you want to add feet, you have several styles of box feet from which to choose (see Figure 10-22 for some examples). The most popular box feet are simple brass balls; these feet are flat on the top so you can easily solder them to the edges of the box bottom. You can also use E-6000 glue to secure the feet to the box.

Glass nuggets make great box feet because they give a little color to your box. Nuggets are available in a wide variety of sizes, and they're easy to secure to the box using E-6000 glue.

Mixing It Up with Some Variations on the Basic Box

After you get the hang of building the basic box according to the layout I describe in the preceding sections, you can start to customize that layout to create boxes that are different sizes and styles. This section offers you two custom examples, but don't be afraid to let your imagination run wild as you come up with many more.

Figure 10-22:
Assorted
items that
can be used
for box feet.

When you're increasing the size of the box, don't forget to add the extra ¼ inch to the side pieces (marked *SBB, SAB, SBT,* and *SAT*) so they can overlap the front and back side pieces.

Project: Box with beveled top

Stock bevels make a simple box look spectacular. In this project, you use a 3-x-5-inch bevel to accent the top of a 6-x-7-x-3-inch box. To make the body of this box (everything but the bottom), you need a piece of art glass that's at least 7 x 18 inches after it's squared; to make the bottom, you need a 6-x-7-inch piece of glass.

Mirror is an excellent choice for the bottom of a beveled box because it reflects the rainbows created by the bevel.

Follow these basic steps to make the beveled-top box:

1. **Square your pieces of glass for the box and the bottom mirror piece.**

   Refer to the section "Squaring the corners" for details on how to square your glass.

2. **Label the glass using the layout abbreviations I provide in the section "Labeling the glass for cutting," except label the front piece of the top *FTF* and the back of the top *FTB*.**

   You need these two extra labels for the top of the box because you're splitting it into two pieces for this particular box.

3. **Set your strip cutter at 3 inches; then cut out six 3-inch pieces of glass (marked *FB, FTF, FTB, BB, SAB,* and *SBB*).**

   Because this box has a decorative top, you don't need to reset your strip cutter when you get ready to cut out the top piece. See the section

"Cutting the pieces using your strip cutter" for more details on cutting your glass.

Don't forget to lay out the cut pieces according to the pattern I provide in the section "Laying out and foiling the pieces." Doing so keeps you from cutting the wrong piece of glass as you start trimming sides and splitting tops from bottoms.

4. **Trim the two side pieces (*SAB/SBB* and *SAT/SBT*) down to 6¼ inches.**

5. **To separate the sides into two pieces, set your cutter at 1 inch, line up the side pieces along the wooden rail of your work board, and cut one piece at a time.**

6. **Cut out a 6-x-7-inch piece of art glass or mirrored glass for the bottom of the box.**

7. **Center the bevel on top of the two 3-inch strips you cut for the top of the box; trace around the bevel with your permanent marker (see Figure 10-23).**

8. **Use your hand-held glass cutter to cut along the line you drew around the bevel in Step 7.**

9. **Foil each piece of glass in ⁷⁄₃₂-inch copper foil.**

   If necessary, use your glass grinder to smooth out any rough edges before you apply foil. See Chapter 8 for everything you need to know about foiling glass pieces.

   Most bevels are clear, so make sure you match the backing on your foil to the patina color you plan to use on the box. If you plan to leave the solder in its natural silver color, you need to use silver-backed foil on the beveled piece of glass.

10. **Solder the sides of the box together.**

   Refer to the section "Soldering the box pieces together" for details.

Figure 10-23:
Tracing the shape of the bevel onto the box's top pieces.

11. **Attach the hinges to the backside of the box.**

    Refer to the section "Attaching the hinges" for details.

12. **Attach the chain to secure the lid on the box when it's opened.**

    Refer to the section "Attaching the chain" for details.

13. **Add box feet and/or patina if desired.**

    Refer to the section "Adding box feet" for details on adding feet and Chapter 8 for details on adding patina.

    Refer to Figure 10-5 to see what the finished project should look like.

Project: Box with a 3-D flower

This project is fun to make and can be as simple or as elaborate as you desire. The size of the box is 4 x 6 x 2 inches, and you cut and assemble it the same way you do a basic box. The only difference is the floral accent that that you add to the top of the box.

To create this project, build the box according to the steps I provide in the sections "Visualizing the Basic Box Layout" and "Assembling the Basic Box." When you're finished, follow these simple steps to create the floral accent for the top of the box:

1. **Trace the designs shown in Figure 10-24, and make several copies of each shape.**

   You can cut out as many petals as you like. I cut out eight for this project.

2. **Use regular scissors to cut out each pattern template.**

3. **Glue the templates to three different shades of compatible glass; then cut out the shapes using your hand-held cutter.**

4. **Remove the paper templates from your petals.**

5. **Use your grinder to smooth the rough edges of the petal pieces.**

6. **Clean the petals with a damp cloth and dry them; then foil them with ³⁄₁₆-inch copper foil.**

   I recommend using this smaller foil because it's thinner and doesn't look as bulky as the ⁷⁄₃₂-inch foil you use for the rest of the box. See Chapter 8 for more details on foiling your glass pieces.

7. **Create a circle on top of the box using the larger petals and making sure that at least two petals touch the solder seam around the edge of the box.**

   These larger petals create the first layer of the flower.

   Try lifting one or two of the petals up at a slight angle to the top to give the flower more dimension.

8. **Tack solder the larger petals in place (see Figure 10-25).**

   See Chapter 7 for details on how to tack solder.

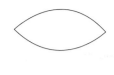

Figure 10-24:
Three
templates
for floral
accent.

Figure 10-25:
Box with the
first layer
of petals
soldered in
place.

9. **Arrange the middle-sized petals on top of the first layer you created in Steps 7 and 8; tack solder them in place (see Figure 10-26).**

10. **Finish the flower by arranging the smallest petals on top of the second layer and tack soldering them in place.**

11. **Use copper wire to create stamens for the center of the flower, if desired.**

For tips on working with wire, turn to Chapter 8.

Figure 10-26:
Box with
the second
layer of pet-
als soldered
in place.

12. **Clean the box with warm, soapy water, and dry it gently with a cloth.**

    If you plan to apply patina to your box, don't use soap with ammonia or
    lemon.

13. **Add patina to the box as soon as it's dry, if desired.**

    For more about patinas, check out Chapter 8. Figure 10-27 shows the fin-
    ished box. I added a butterfly as another embellishment. If you want to,
    use the pattern in Chapter 8 to make your own butterfly. You just need
    to reduce the size.

Figure 10-27:
Finished box
with a floral
accent.

Chapter 11

Shedding Some Light with a Basic Panel Lampshade

· ·

In This Chapter

▶ Looking at different lampshade styles

▶ Picking out the glass and hardware you need to make a lampshade

▶ Cutting out and foiling your glass pieces

▶ Laying out the glass panels according to your pattern

▶ Assembling the lampshade and adding a few finishing touches

· ·

Aside from windows, Tiffany-style lampshades are likely what many people think of when they hear the term *stained glass.* In this chapter, I walk you through the steps you need to take to create your own basic panel lampshade. Using the basic panel design I provide here, you can create countless different styles and shapes of lamps. All you have to do is let your imagination run free!

Different Styles of Lampshades: Panel versus Dome

Panel lampshades, like the one in Figure 11-1, are created out of straight panels of glass. The panels can be highly decorative or very simple. Either way, they're easy to design and make because they don't require a mold or form. As an added bonus, you can use a panel design to fit any size lamp. This style is what I show you how to make in this chapter.

Dome lampshades, on the other hand, require a form or mold to make. The basic process goes like this: You cut the glass pieces to a pattern, foil them, and then position them onto a styrofoam or fiberglass lamp form or mold. The form is what gives the lamp its shape. Most of the original Tiffany lampshades were built on wooden forms. The glass pieces were tacked in place around the form, creating a curved shade of art glass.

Figure 11-1:
Stained-glass panel lamp.

To make the construction process a little easier, several manufacturers now produce lamp kits that include both a pattern and a form. Some forms are full, while others are only sections. When working with just a section of a form, you have to make separate sections of the lampshade and then solder them together to create a complete shade. I recommend that you work only with full forms because sections are difficult to handle and don't always yield the best results. Figure 11-2 shows an example of a dome lamp made using a full form.

Figure 11-2:
A stained-glass lamp built from a full form.

A little history on Louis C. Tiffany and his lamps

The best-known stained-glass lampshade maker of all time is Louis C. Tiffany. In the early 1900s, his studio created stained-glass shades by the thousands. Electricity was a new addition to the American household at the time, and people bought Tiffany shades to draw attention to the fact that they could afford the new luxury.

So how did these highly sought-after status symbols come to be? Tiffany began creating his lampshades because he needed a productive use for all the scrap glass that his studio produced when it made its beautiful, large, stained-glass windows. Essentially, he turned the scrap glass into stained-glass lampshades. To save money, he employed women to create the shades at a lower wage than the men who worked in his window departments. Ironically, Tiffany became famous for a product that was manufactured from recycled glass and designed and built by low-paid women.

Selecting the Glass and Hardware for Your Lampshade Based on Your Pattern

A panel lampshade is a great project for a beginning stained-glass artist because it's so fun and easy to make. To help you get started, I provide a basic eight-panel lampshade pattern here. The best part about this pattern is that you can adjust it to fit your own design tastes. For example, you can choose which accents (beads, wire, or the glass accent shown in this pattern) to add to give your lamp a look of its own, and you can enlarge it to fit your lamp base.

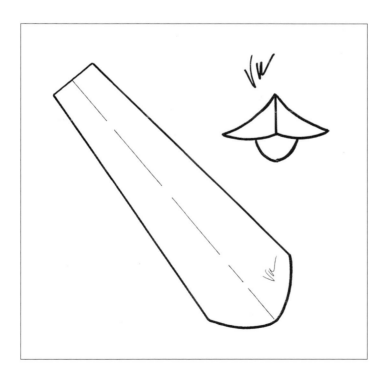

If you already have a pattern you want to use, feel free to do so. You can find hundreds of books with beautiful stained-glass panel lampshade patterns and designs. I just recommend that you work with a pattern for your first few shades; then, after you get some experience, you can try your hand at creating your own lampshade design.

When you're ready to select the glass for your lampshade, think about how that glass will look on the lamp you plan to put it on. Also consider where you plan to place the lamp when you're finished with it; make sure the glass matches that particular room's décor. In the following sections, I provide some tips and suggestions to help you choose your lampshade glass based on your pattern.

Deciding what kind of glass to use and how much

Opalescent glass is the glass of choice for most lampshade projects because it hides the working parts of the lamp. Although you can't see through it, opalescent glass is designed to catch the light and let it illuminate through the glass, casting a warm glow on everything around it — which is why it makes such beautiful lampshades. Lucky for you, opalescent glass comes in thousands of beautiful colors, so the possibilities for your lampshade are endless!

When selecting glass for a lampshade, I recommend using a light box because it represents exactly how your finished glass shade will look when you place it on the lamp base. Don't try to choose your glass by holding it up to a natural daylight source, such as a window, because the glass doesn't look the same when it's in front of the sun as when it's in front of a light bulb.

Never hold glass over your head when checking the color. The glass may contain a concealed crack that could give way, causing the glass to break over you and cut you. Ouch!

Don't steer away from glass that has a textured surface. Rippled, stippled, mottled, and cat's-paw are just a few of the different types of textured glass that can look really stunning in a lampshade. The textured surface catches the light and bounces it back against the surface of the glass, giving your lampshade sparkle and interest. When you assemble your lampshade, just make sure the textured side of the glass faces the light source.

To determine how much glass you need to make your lampshade, multiply the number of panels by the bottom width of the panels and by the top width of the panels; add those two numbers together. Divide the sum by 2. The number you get is the minimum width of the piece of glass you need. The length of the glass you need is the same as the length of your panels. For example: For a panel lampshade that has 12 panels that are 3 inches wide at the bottom and 1 inch wide at the top and 10 inches long, you'd need a strip of glass that's 24 x 10 inches.

Choosing the right lampshade hardware

Different styles and sizes of lamps require different hardware for display. Hardware gives strength to the shade and secures the shade onto the base of the lamp. Figure 11-3 shows some of the various pieces of hardware available.

The most common piece of hardware is the round vase cap. The *vase cap* secures the panels together and attaches the shade to the lamp base. Vase caps are generally manufactured out of brass and come in a wide variety of sizes and shapes, including round, square, hexagonal, and octagonal. For the project in this chapter, I recommend a 3½-inch round vase cap. Some caps have a single row of holes stamped around the edges of the cap and some are made with lacy design motifs. The holes are both decorative and functional in that they both add a touch of texture to the cap and allow the excess heat from the light bulb to escape.

Figure 11-3: A variety of lamp hardware, including vase caps and spiders.

Heat can damage a stained-glass lampshade, so make sure your shade is always at least 2 inches from the light bulb. Also never use more than a 60-watt bulb.

Sometimes lamp makers use spiders and bars in place of a vase cap. A *spider* is a brass or zinc metal frame with a center washer and three or more posts extending from it to the edge of the shade. A *bar* is a flat strap of metal with a hole drilled into the middle. These hardware items are more common on hanging lampshades than on table lamps. Before you use spiders and bars, you have to trim them to fit your lamp by using a hacksaw or a power saw.

Prepping Your Pattern and Cutting Out Your Glass Pieces

After you choose the glass and hardware for your project, you need to enlarge the pattern I provide earlier in this chapter to be the size you want for your lamp base and then make a copy of it for each panel in your lamp. You can make your copies on paper like you do for most of the other projects in this book; however, paper templates wear out rather quickly when you're making a lampshade, especially when you use a glass grinder to shape the pieces. For that reason, I like to trace my pattern templates onto Mylar, a thin sheet made of plastic that you can find at any art store. The main benefit of using Mylar patterns is that you can use them over and over again. If you're using Mylar, you don't need to make any extra copies of your pattern.

When you have your patterns cut out, it's time to adhere them to your glass. You can use double-sided tape or rubber cement to attach the Mylar or paper template to the glass surface. Then you're ready to cut!

Simply follow these steps to cut out your lampshade panels:

1. **Use your plastic square and a permanent marker to draw a line on the glass that's perpendicular to the bottom edge of the glass.**

2. **Position your pattern template's top edge along the top edge of the glass so that the line you drew in Step 1 runs down the dotted line on the center of the pattern (see Figure 11-4a).**

3. **Cut out the panel piece by following closely to the pattern's edge.**

   Check out Chapter 5 for everything you need to know about cutting glass.

4. **Flip your pattern template around, and line the top edge of the template along the bottom edge of the glass and the side edge of your pattern piece along the newly cut side of the glass (see Figure 11-4b).**

   By flipping your pattern template after each cut, you maximize your glass usage and speed up the cutting process.

5. **Continue cutting and flipping your template until you've cut out all the panels (see Figure 11-4c).**

Figure 11-4:
Flipping your pattern after each cut.

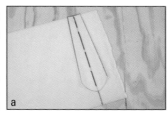  

a   b   c

Foiling the Glass Pieces

Before you begin foiling, I recommend that you use your grinder to smooth out all the edges of your lamp pieces. Grinding glass helps the foil adhere better to the glass edges, which is especially important because lamp construction puts additional demands on the foil.

Next, you need to make sure you remove all the dust and dampness from the glass surface. I like to foil my lamp pieces after they have air dried for a couple of hours or overnight.

Then follow these basic steps to foil your glass pieces (refer to Chapter 8 for a lot more details on copper foiling):

1. **Position the glass in the center of a strip of $\frac{7}{32}$-inch foil, and peel back the paper backing on the foil, exposing the adhesive side.**

   If your panels have lots of small pieces, consider switching to a smaller-sized foil like $\frac{3}{16}$ inch. Using too large of foil can make your lampshade look bulky and add too much weight to the shade.

2. **Keep the glass centered on the foil as you rotate the glass piece (see Figure 11-5).**

   Be careful not to apply too much pressure to the foil along the glass panel edges. If you do, the foil will simply pull off the glass edges, and you'll have to start all over again.

3. **When you reach your starting point, overlap the foil about $\frac{1}{4}$ inch, and trim the foil using your craft knife.**

4. **Burnish the foil tightly to the edge of the glass with a Foilmate roller; then crimp the foil over the edges and roll both sides tightly to the glass surface.**

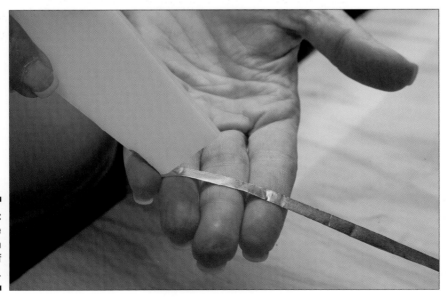

Figure 11-5: Glass piece centered on the strip of copper foil.

If you're having trouble getting your foil to stick to the glass, make sure the glass is clean and dry. If you live in an area with high humidity, make sure you store your foil in a sealed container so the adhesive doesn't lose its stickiness over time.

Laying Out Your Pieces for Lamp Assembly

My favorite part of making a lampshade is laying out all the pieces to get ready for assembly. Although the process looks scary, it turns out perfectly every time, trust me. Before you get started, gather up your Homasote work board, masking tape, push pins, and vase cap (see Chapter 8 for details on how to set up your work board for a foil project).

If you plan to start soldering your lampshade together as soon as you're finished laying it out, I recommend that you get all your soldering equipment (including 60/40 solder) ready before you start laying out your project. You also want to start heating your soldering iron to a medium setting.

When you have all your foiled glass pieces and other supplies handy, follow these steps:

1. **Lay out your glass panels on your work board with the back side of the glass facing up; line up the top and bottom edges evenly.**

2. **Tape the panels together using masking tape (see Figure 11-6).**

   Don't be afraid to use a lot of tape. The more tape you use, the easier it'll be to pick up the lamp.

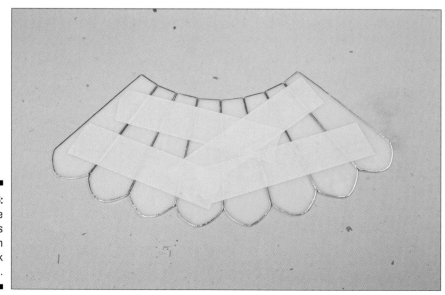

Figure 11-6:
Taping the lamp panels together on the work board.

3. **Grasp the top of the lamp on each side, and in one motion, lift the top of the lamp up and toward you while keeping the center of the bottom edge of the lamp against the work board (see Figure 11-7a).**

4. **Bring the two side panels together, and place tape along the outside of the lamp where the two edges meet (see Figure 11-7b).**

5. **Place the vase cap on the top of the lamp, and use it to help you round out the shape of the lamp (see Figure 11-7c).**

6. **When you're happy with the lamp's shape, stabilize the panels by adding more tape.**

Figure 11-7: Creating the lamp's round shape.

Soldering for Stability

After you tape your panels together so they look like a lampshade, it's time to start soldering. Before you do, though, you need to gather a few supplies: a preheated soldering iron (set at medium heat), 60/40 solder, flux, and a strip of 18-gauge prestretched copper wire (see Chapter 8 for more details on working with wire). When you have everything ready, you first need to add the foundation to your project by tack soldering; then you have to run beads of solder along all the seams of your project to hold it together. The following sections walk you through both of these soldering steps.

Tack soldering

Tack soldering is like having an extra pair of hands to help you assemble your lampshade. It adds a lot of stability to your project. To get started, set your lamp on your work board, and follow these steps:

1. **Remove the vase cap from your lamp, flux the foil around the top of the shade, and tack solder the top edges of the individual panels together.**

   Be sure to use enough solder that the pieces are secure.

2. **Place a piece of copper wire along the top edge of the glass panels, and tack solder it in place (see Figure 11-8); overlap the wire about ½ inch when you reach the place where you started, and trim away the excess wire.**

The wire provides extra support to the fragile foil and helps hold the lamp's shape.

3. **Re-flux the entire top of the lampshade, and add additional solder, burying the wire with solder (see Figure 11-9).**

4. **Turn the lampshade upside down, and place it on the work board; make only slight adjustments to the shape, making sure you don't put too much pressure on the foil.**

5. **Flux the entire bottom of the shade, and tack solder each panel's intersection with the next panel (see Figure 11-10).**

6. **Repeat Steps 2 and 3 to place and solder a piece of wire around the bottom of the lampshade.**

If the bottom of the shade is contoured, make sure the wire follows tightly to the glass edge. You definitely don't want to have a gap between the wire and the foil.

At this point, your shade should be very stable. You can remove the masking tape from the inside of your lamp. Just be careful not to pull any of the foil off the glass edges.

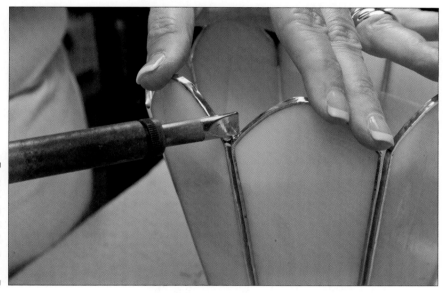

Figure 11-10: Tack soldering the bottom panel intersections together.

Running smooth beads along your lamp's seams

Before you can finish the soldering process, you need to make sure you give plenty of support to the shape of the lampshade. In other words, don't lay down the shade on its side because the weight of the glass will cause it to sag. Instead, support your shade with blocks of wood, small sandbags, or folded towels (see Figure 11-11).

To finish the soldering process, you need to run beads along each of your lamp's seams. Just follow these steps, and refer to Chapters 7 and 8 for details on soldering copper-foil projects:

1. **Flux the inside seams of your lamp.**

2. **Run a bead of solder along the length of each inside seam.**

Melted solder is like water, so you have to continuously make adjustments to the position of your lamp as you solder to keep all your seams level. Unless your seams are completely level, gravity will keep you from being able to solder smooth, even beads.

Figure 11-11:
Supporting your shade's shape with wooden blocks and towels.

3. **Turn the shade over, and flux all the seams on the outside of the lamp.**

4. **Run a bead of solder along each of the outside seams (see Figure 11-12).**

   Your biggest job here is to keep the seams level while you're soldering. If you have a cardboard box that fits your lamp perfectly, use it to secure the lamp while you finish soldering.

   Don't use crumpled newspapers or other materials that might catch on fire during the soldering process to support your lamp. Spray your cardboard box with a little water to keep it cool and safe while you're working.

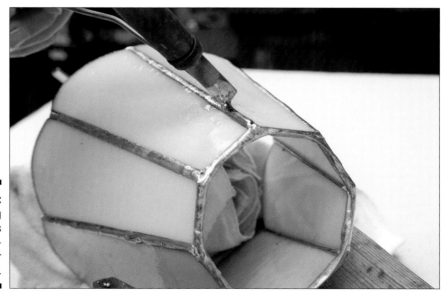

Figure 11-12:
Soldering the seams on the outside of your lamp.

Always allow the seam to *set,* or cool, before you try to rotate the shade to solder more seams; if you don't, the molten solder will roll off the seam and you'll have to start over.

If your solder drips through from the outside seam to the inside seam as you work, try these three fixes:

✔ Turn down the temperature of your iron.

To cool your iron quickly while you work, wipe the hot tip on a clean, wet sponge.

✔ Don't keep working in the same area for a long time. If you've tried to run a particular bead two or three times, stop and let the seam cool off, and then return to try it again.

✔ Place a damp towel inside the shade, making sure the towel is touching the backside of the seam you're soldering. The moisture of the towel helps to cool both the solder and the glass, eliminating the frustrating drip.

Capping Off, Cleaning Up, and Adding Patina

After you finish soldering your lamp together, it's time to attach the vase cap to the top of your shade. To do so, follow these steps:

1. **Set the soldered shade on your work board, making sure it's level.**

2. **Place the cap on top of the shade, and use a small line level to make sure the cap is level.**

3. **Use masking tape to temporarily secure the cap in place (see Figure 11-13).**

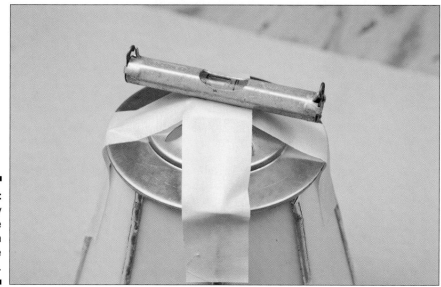

Figure 11-13:
Temporarily securing the vase cap on top of the shade.

4. **Turn the shade onto its side, and tack solder the inside of the cap securely to the top edge of the glass (see Figure 11-14).**

   Don't be shy with the solder; the cap must be securely soldered to your shade.

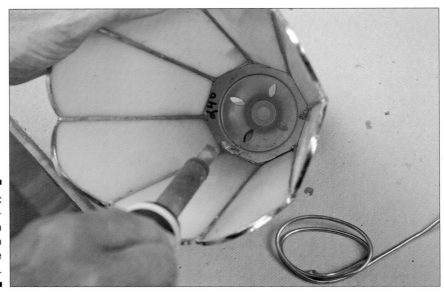

Figure 11-14:
Tack soldering the cap to the top edge of the glass.

When you're finished adding the cap, mix up a sink full of soapy, warm water and give your lampshade a good bath. Make sure you remove any remaining flux and residue left from the masking tape, and then gently dry off the shade.

If you want to add a little color to your solder, you can apply patina to your clean lampshade. *Patina* is a chemical that turns the solder from silver to black or copper, depending on the type of patina you use. I prefer using black patina for my lampshades because black solder lines blend well with the lamp design when illuminated.

To apply patina to your lampshade, be sure to wear rubber gloves. Then saturate a small, clean cloth with patina, and wipe the patina over all the solder seams and the vase cap. Apply as much patina as you need to get a deep, rich finish. Let the shade sit for a few minutes; then wipe the excess patina off the glass surface with a clean, damp cloth.

To get that rich, shiny, black finish that you see on Tiffany lamps, do what the museums do: Dust them with a little lemon oil at least twice a year.

When you're finished, your lampshade should look something like what's shown in Figure 11-1. Note that the lamp in the photo has a few added embellishments, including some beads and small pieces of glass that have been soldered between the panels.

Chapter 12

Putting Your New Skills to Work: Project Patterns

*I*t's time to put all your newly developed glass-cutting, grinding, and soldering skills to work. In this chapter, I offer you eight project patterns to consider for your next project. The first four designs are for copper-foil projects, while the last four are for lead-came projects. To help you get started, I provide a few tips upfront for enlarging patterns to fit your space needs and estimating how much glass you need for each design.

Note: Several of these projects can be constructed using either lead or foil techniques; I've added a note to those particular projects. The projects that don't include a note lend themselves to only one technique.

Project Tips and Tricks

Before you get started on the fun projects I include in this chapter, take a look at the following sections, which offer you some tips to keep in mind when working on these and other projects.

Enlarging a design

You may see a design in this chapter (or any other stained-glass book you happen to pick up) that looks great, but you think the finished piece would work better if it were larger. Here are some tips for enlarging patterns successfully:

✔ **Be realistic.** Don't jump into a large, complicated project when you're just beginning your stained-glass hobby. Give yourself some time to build your skills before you try to tackle your dream window.

✔ **Consider the size of your work board.** Don't make a project bigger than the work board you plan to use. Your entire project has to fit on the work board during the construction phase.

✔ **Make sure your lines are straight and your pattern is square.** If you use a copy machine to enlarge your design, remember that it can distort some of the geometric pattern lines. Use your ruler and square to check the lines and make any necessary adjustments. (You can also use an opaque projector to enlarge patterns; see Chapter 4 for details.)

A quick way to determine whether a pattern is square is to hold it up to a light and fold the pattern in half, matching the four corners. If the paper doesn't fold smoothly, you know your pattern is out of square.

Selecting your glass

One of the greatest benefits of creating your own stained-glass projects (including the ones in this chapter) is that you can use any color of glass you want. So make the projects in this chapter fit you and your space; if you plan to hang your finished window in your yellow and green kitchen, incorporate those colors and others that go well with them into your project. In general, I recommend steering clear of heavily textured glass until after you've created a few projects; it's a little more difficult to work with than less-textured glass.

To determine how much glass you need for any project, measure the finished size of your window, multiply the width times the height, and divide that number by 144. Your answer is the square footage of the project, which is a good place to start when deciding how much glass you need for the background area. Be sure to measure the larger individual pattern pieces, too, so you don't buy a 12-inch-long piece of glass when you have a 13-inch-long pattern piece.

Always buy at least 20 to 25 percent more glass than you think you'll need in case you have to recut a few pieces. You can always recycle the leftover glass in another smaller project.

Copper-Foil Projects

Although many stained-glass patterns can work with either copper foil or lead came, the following projects are all best suited to copper-foil techniques. Refer to Chapter 8 for detailed guidance on creating copper-foil projects.

Hummingbird panel

Hummingbirds come in all colors. Study photos of real hummingbirds to help guide you when you're selecting your glass for this project. You can add an eye on your bird by using any high-quality glass paint from your local craft store. You may also choose to use ladder-back chain to finish off the outside edges.

Mr. Buzz sun catcher

I recommend that you use black, yellow, and white glass for this project. To add a little buzz to these bees, you may also want to use a few pieces of white iridized glass for the wings. You can create the antennas out of wire and add eyes using glass paint, if you wish.

Before you solder the hooks to the various pieces of this sun catcher, double-check to make sure it'll hang straight on your wall or window. You may have to adjust the placement of the hooks a couple of times.

Floral panel

If you want to enlarge this design, try making two copies of the pattern and then taping them together either side by side or one on top of the other. This design works using either copper-foil or lead-came techniques.

Lily panel

This project is great for practicing your glass-cutting skills because it has so many inside curves. Don't forget to add the wire stamens after you construct the panel itself. If you need more details on working with wire, refer to Chapter 8.

Lead-Came Projects

Although many stained-glass patterns can work with either lead came or copper foil, the following projects are all best suited to lead-came techniques. Refer to Chapter 9 for detailed guidance on creating lead-came projects.

Wright-inspired panel

Frank Lloyd Wright's work is the inspiration behind this design. The lines are clean and balanced. You can construct this window out of several different types of clear glass, or you can add in a few touches of color.

This design wouldn't work well in copper foil because it contains too many straight lines to match up.

Picture-perfect panel

This geometric project is a little more detailed than the Wright panel, but its many straight lines still make it perfect for lead-came construction.

Use clear glass for the large diamond in the center of the window so you can display a picture behind it. All you have to do is transfer a photograph to clear contact paper and apply it to the back of the clear glass. If you're unsure how to do so, see your local photo shop for help.

Landscape panel

Landscapes make great stained-glass projects because you can use so many different types and colors of glass to create them. The colors you use depend on what type of landscape view you're trying to achieve. For instance, using the pattern I include here, you can create a lake, desert, farm land, or icy mountain range based on the glass you select.

You can construct this panel using either copper-foil or lead-came techniques, but I include it here in the lead-came section because it offers a great opportunity to practice working with flowing lead lines and sweeping lead joints. Although it includes a lot of straight lines, they flow together and aren't geometric in form.

Sunshine panel

Although this pattern looks pretty advanced, if you study it closely, you can see that most of the cuts are fairly easy to make. The flow of the lead lines makes this project a lot of fun to build, and it gives you great practice working with your lead knife. Note that you can use foil instead of lead, if you want.

I recommend using several shades of yellow glass for the sun and the rays in this panel. As for the background glass, you can use blue, red, orange, or just about any other color, depending on how you want your finished sunset to look.

Hummingbird panel

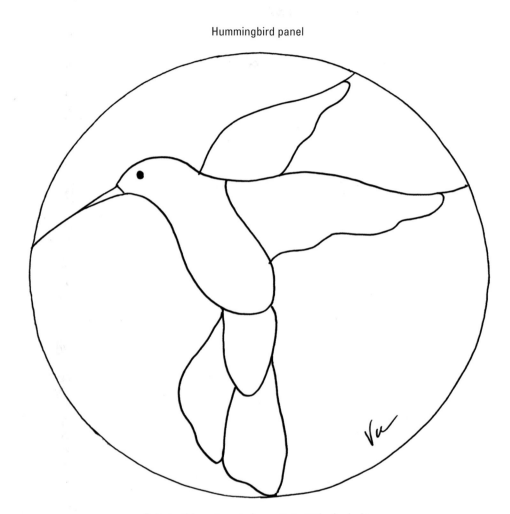

Enlarge this pattern to be an 8- to 10-inch circle.

Mr. Buzz sun catcher

Use this pattern in its actual size, or reduce it by 30%.

Floral panel

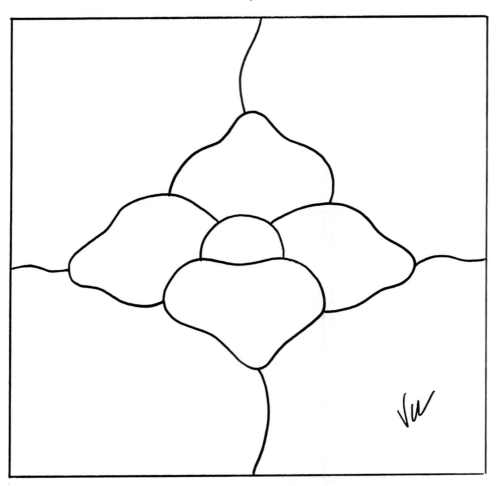

Lily panel

Enlarge this pattern to be an 8-x-10-inch rectangle, so you can use a standard-sized frame.

Wright-inspired panel

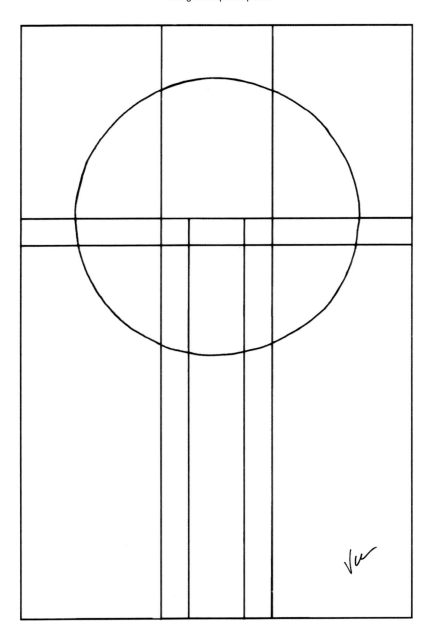

Picture-perfect panel

Landscape panel

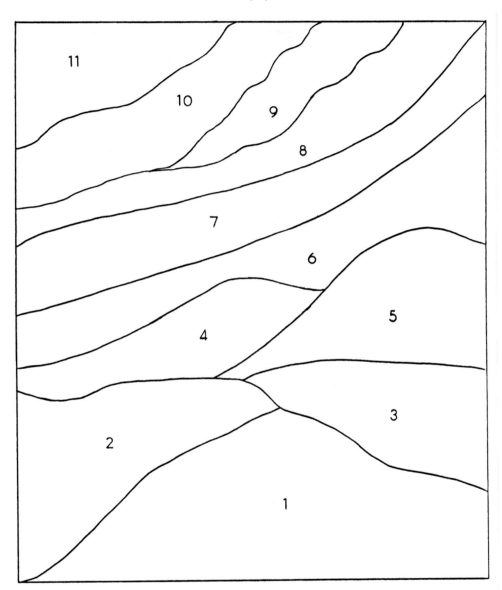

Sunshine panel

If you plan to frame this panel (or any round panel) in wood, purchase the frame first,
and then enlarge the pattern to fit the frame. Custom wooden round frames can be very expensive.

Part IV

Adding a Little Heat to the Mix: Working with Warm Glass

The 5th Wave   By Rich Tennant

"This is where I create all my glass work from scratch, so to speak."

In this part . . .

Glass fusing, an increasingly popular art form, is the perfect technique to add to your portfolio of glass-working skills. If you don't do traditional stained glass, don't worry. You can still jump right into this part of the book and have lots of fun.

Here, I introduce you to kilns and all the other supplies you need to get started with this magical art form. I guide you through the processes of heating, shaping, and then cooling glass, and I show you how to use these processes to create beautiful projects. Then I help you put your new skills to the test as you create coasters, vases, and other timeless treasures that you and your family are sure to love.

Chapter 13

Getting Your Studio Ready for Warm Glass

The term *warm glass* describes the glass-working techniques that require glass to be reheated and formed into different shapes. The two glass-working techniques that I focus on in this book are fusing and slumping. (Don't confuse warm glass with *hot glass,* which refers to the techniques used in glass blowing.)

Although many of the glass-cutting techniques you use to make stained-glass projects (see the first three parts of this book) also apply to your warm-glass projects, the techniques you use to connect the glass pieces are quite different. Instead of using metal and solder to hold a project together, you reheat the cut pieces of glass to the point that they fuse together into one solid mass.

Perhaps the best reason to use warm-glass techniques is their versatility. Because warm glass doesn't involve any metal, you can use it to create platters, bowls, dinnerware, and other objects that will come in contact with food — something you definitely wouldn't want to do with regular stained glass. Plus, depending on the size of the glass kiln you're using, you can create large decorative glass windows and even door panels.

In this chapter, I show you how to set up your warm-glass studio and describe the special tools and equipment you need to add to it. Fusing and slumping glass requires working with specific types of art glass, so I cover those here, as well. Although the equipment is fairly expensive, the fusing process is easy to learn and the project possibilities are endless.

Knowing What Makes a Good Warm-Glass Studio

If you already have a stained-glass studio, you may be able to set up a fusing center right there in your current work space. If you don't have a working studio or if your current studio is too small to fit another hobby, you'll just have to set up a new work space. Either way, you need to keep in mind the considerations I cover in the following sections as you set up your warm-glass studio.

Space requirements

The largest piece of equipment in your warm-glass studio is your glass kiln, which means your space has to at least be big enough to hold your kiln and everything that goes with it. (In case you're wondering, a *glass kiln* is the heating chamber you use to reheat and shape your glass pieces; see the section "Adding the Right Tools and Supplies to Your Warm-Glass Toolbox" for more details.) The larger the kiln, the larger the glass projects you can create, and, of course, the more space you need in your studio.

Most home studios work with kilns that are 3 x 3 feet or smaller. But because kilns get so hot, you need an additional 2 feet of space around the outside of your kiln to keep it away from anything flammable. In other words, your studio needs to be at least 5 x 5 feet to fit the average-sized glass kiln. But don't settle on a space that's exactly large enough for your kiln. You need room for fusing supplies, shelves for molds, and glass racks on which to store your fusing glass. (It's important that you don't mix this glass with your other art glass.) When all's said and done, I recommend finding a studio space that's at least 10 x 10 feet.

In terms of flooring in your studio, you want a hard surface that you can clean easily with a damp mop.

Electrical requirements

Electric kilns require a lot of power, so they definitely need their own plugs and circuits in your studio. Smaller kilns require 120 volts and 10 to 20 amps. The larger, full-size kilns require 220 to 240 volts and 20 amps. (In case you're curious what all that electricity does, these larger kilns reach a maximum temperature of 2,300 degrees!)

Be sure to follow your kiln manufacturer's electrical requirements and have a licensed electrician install the proper electrical outlet for your kiln. Never use an extension cord to operate a kiln, no matter what size it is. Doing so can cause fires.

Kilns are red hot, so be sure to keep a fire extinguisher close by, and don't use the top of your kiln to store anything! Someone can easily accidentally turn on a kiln without your knowledge, so always keep the kiln unplugged when you're not using it.

Ventilation

Good ventilation is important for any glass-working studio, including warm glass. When you fuse glass together in a kiln, you release quite a few glues, fibers, and paints into the air, and you need to have a way to get rid of them. You can choose from several ways to ventilate your studio, including the following:

- ✔ **Open the doors and windows to allow fresh air into your studio.**
- ✔ **Use exhaust fans to help remove the fumes released by the fusing process.**
- ✔ **Attach vent hoods and down-draft ventilation systems to your kiln.**

  You can purchase these ventilation attachments from your kiln manufacturer.

If money is no object and you have the right kiln and setting for vent hoods and down-draft systems, you can use both ventilation options in your studio. Just be sure to check with the vent manufacturer for specific requirements before selecting the system for your studio. For more details on adding the proper ventilation to your studio, turn to Chapter 3.

If your studio has overhead fire sprinklers, make sure you don't place your kiln directly below one of the sensor heads. If you do, you may be surprised by an unexpected shower from above when you open the lid on your hot kiln!

Adding the Right Tools and Supplies to Your Warm-Glass Toolbox

If you're a stained-glass artist, you already have all the basic glass-cutting tools, design and drafting supplies, and glass grinders and saws you need to start creating warm-glass projects. (If you decided to start with warm glass instead of stained glass, flip to Chapter 2 for details on the glass-working supplies you need.) But before you can get started, you have to add a few other important pieces of equipment to your studio. The following sections explain what you need.

Choosing the right kiln for your studio

A kiln is a must-purchase because it's what you use to heat up your glass in order to work with it. Most glass kilns are made of firebricks and metal, and they have electrical heating elements positioned in their tops and sides. Kilns come in a variety of sizes, shapes, and styles, and, in general, they're priced according to their size and operating systems. The following sections take a quick look at the different options you have when buying your first glass kiln.

Glass kilns are different from ceramic kilns in two main ways: where the heating elements are positioned and how the temperature is controlled. You can adapt a ceramic kiln to fuse glass, but it's much easier to work with a glass-specific kiln.

Selecting the right size kiln for your needs

To determine what size kiln you should purchase for your warm-glass studio, ask yourself the following three questions:

- **How much space do I have in my studio?** You need a minimum of 2 feet clearance around all sides of the kiln to keep it away from any combustible walls or materials. (See the section "Space requirements" for more details about studio space.)

- **Do I want to fire one shelf or multiple shelves of glass at the same time?** If you want to create a set of dishes, you'll want to fire more than one plate at a time and may need more than one shelf in your kiln. If you're mass-producing jewelry, one shelf may provide plenty of room.

- **Where will my hobby take me in the next five years?** Kilns are a major financial investment ranging in price from a few hundred dollars to over a thousand dollars. You don't want to be stuck with a small kiln if you have big plans for your warm-glass future. However, it costs more to operate a larger kiln, so you may want to invest in a smaller kiln until your skills, interest, and talent increase; then, when you're ready, you can purchase a larger kiln.

Considering style and shape

Most kiln manufacturers offer a wide variety of kiln shapes and styles. The major difference between these styles is the way you load the kiln before you fire it up. The three basic styles are

- **Top loaders:** The lids on these kilns lift off or open and allow the user to lower the project into the kiln from the top.

- **Front loaders:** These kilns have a side door that's hinged and opens much like a cabinet door. You simply load your project into the kiln like you load a casserole into a kitchen oven.

- **Clam-shell kilns:** These kilns open like a clam. The lid is hinged to the back of the kiln like a top loader, except that the heating elements are all located in the lid. The firing shelves are completely exposed when the lid is raised, allowing you complete access to the project being fired.

Kiln shapes vary from square, round, and octagonal, to the granddaddy of all, the coffin kiln. This kiln is 3 x 6 feet and can accommodate almost any project that you might want to create.

I recommend that you purchase a top-loading kiln that sits on a floor stand. In terms of size, a medium kiln with an 18- to 22-inch firing chamber that's at least 9 inches deep works great for almost any type of project you want to make.

Considering controls

Fusing glass pieces together requires perfect timing and temperature. After all, your ability to control the reaction between glass and heat determines the results of your warm-glass projects. As the glass starts to heat up and melt, you need to have a way of adjusting that temperature so you don't overfire your projects. To help you control this reaction, you can choose a kiln with either manual or automatic controls; however, I recommend an automatic controller because it'll save you time and costly firing mistakes down the road. The difference between the two controls is simple.

✔ **Manually controlled kiln with basic power switch and pyrometer:** The basic controllers for any manually controlled kiln are the On/Off switch and the pyrometer. A *pyrometer* is a thermocouple connected to a temperature gauge. The thermocouple consists of two wires that are inserted into the kiln. As the temperature in the kiln changes, the thermocouple registers the change on a gauge mounted to the outside of the kiln (see Figure 13-1).

Fusing glass in a kiln that's manually controlled requires a digital timer and your careful attention. You have to keep great firing charts and stay with your kiln at all times (see the section "Keeping firing charts" later in this chapter for details). Glass-fusing cycles can take several hours, so this manual technique can be pretty intense.

If you don't have a digital timer and you plan to operate your kiln manually, go out and buy one now. I use a small one that slips into my pocket so that I don't forget when I'm supposed to be watching the kiln.

Figure 13-1: A temperature gauge mounted to the outside of a kiln.

✔ **Kiln with automatic controllers:** A few years ago, kiln companies introduced automatic controllers for glass kilns (see Figure 13-2 for an example). This invention really liberated the glass artists because they no longer had to sit idly next to the kiln while they waited for the kiln to fire their glass. Artists can basically set their projects in the kiln, fire it up, and forget about them until they're finished. Plus, automatically controlled projects turned out much better than those that were manually controlled, and they could be repeated with perfect accuracy time and time again.

Figure 13-2:
Automatic controller mounted on a glass kiln.

All automatic controllers work the same way. Computerized programs turn the kiln on and off and regulate the firing temperatures during the firing process. Controllers come with specific instructions for how to set the program for each type of firing procedure.

Although automatic controllers take much of the guesswork out of glass fusing, most glass artists will tell you that it's still important for you to monitor the fusing processes and keep excellent firing records until you're really familiar with your kiln's operating system. After all, you need to figure out how glass reacts at your kiln's different temperature settings so that when you program your automatic controller for your projects, you know exactly what settings you need to use to achieve a particular fused appearance.

Furnishing your kiln

Using the term *furniture* in conjunction with glass working always cracks me up. It sounds like you're getting ready to play with your dollhouse and dolls. But in all honesty, without certain kiln furniture, you can't do any fusing.

Kiln furniture includes a variety of shelves, supports, molds, and other items that you use while working with warm glass. Why do you need furniture? Kilns are made out of either firebricks or ceramic fibers, and neither of these materials can come in contact with hot, molten glass because the glass would stick to the kiln floor or walls when it cooled, causing damage to the integrity of the kiln. If hot glass touches a heating element in your kiln, it'll burn out the element, causing you to have to replace it. Now do you see why you need furniture?

Shelves

Kiln shelves are made from cordierite, a material that's designed to withstand temperatures of 2,350 degrees. Lucky for you, this means they won't warp or break during the firing process.

Shelves come in a variety of sizes and shapes to fit your specific kiln design (see Figure 13-3). I recommend that you purchase several shelves in full and half sizes so you can accommodate a variety of different project sizes.

Even though kiln shelves seem invincible (with the high temperatures they can withstand), you need to make sure to protect them from the molten glass by covering them with kiln wash or fiber paper (see the later section "Gathering a few other tools and supplies" for more details).

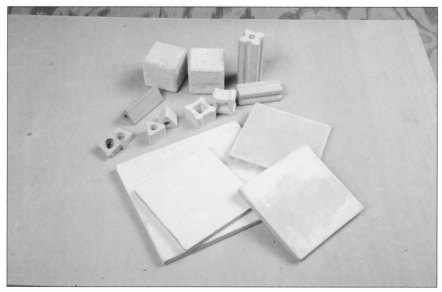

Figure 13-3:
Various shapes and sizes of kiln shelves and posts.

Posts

You have to elevate your kiln shelves off the floor of the kiln so that air can circulate around the shelves during the firing process. To elevate your shelves, you can use linear pillars of hard ceramic material, called *posts*. Posts come in various lengths and shapes (refer to Figure 13-3 for some examples). If you're planning to fire multiple shelves of glass at one time, you need additional posts to elevate the extra shelves. For this reason, I recommend that you purchase at least four posts in each of the following lengths: 1 inch, 2 inch, 3 inch, and 4 inch. You can get whatever shaped posts you want.

Molds

One reason why people fuse glass together (instead of using lead, foil, and solder like they do in stained glass) is that they want to shape it into various forms, such as bowls, vases, and platters. Shaping molten glass is called *slumping,* and to do it, you need a mold into or over which the glass can lay. The two traditional styles of molds are ceramic and stainless steel, each shown in Figure 13-4. Ceramic molds are designed for the glass to slump into the shape when the glass reaches a certain temperature. Stainless steel molds, on the other hand, are designed to allow the molten glass to slump over the form, thus creating the desired shape. (Turn to Chapter 16 for a lot more details on shaping warm glass.)

Figure 13-4: A collection of ceramic and stainless steel molds for slumping glass.

You can't slump glass into stainless steel molds because the metal contracts when it starts to cool. This contraction process would shatter any glass that's hardened into the mold. Ceramic molds are made from cordierite (the same material from which kiln shelves are made). Cordierite doesn't contract or expand when heated or cooled.

Don't forget to cover both ceramic and metal molds with kiln wash or firing paper to protect them from molten glass (see the next section for more details).

Gathering a few other tools and supplies

Melted glass sticks to any unprotected surface. To protect molds and kiln shelves from that melted glass, glass artists coat them in special fiber paper or kiln wash. I introduce you to these supplies in the following sections.

Fiber paper

Fiber paper refers to a type of ceramic fiber sheet that you can use for a variety of purposes when firing glass. It comes in various thicknesses from paper-thin to 2 inches thick. The thicker sheets are called *fiber blankets.* You can cut the larger papers and blankets to create your own molds and shapes for countless fusing projects.

Fiber boards are stiff versions of fiber blankets; you can use them to create mold shapes, elevate designs, and provide support to various fusing projects. You can also use fiber boards in place of kiln shelves for lighter-weight projects.

You can use thin fiber paper in place of kiln wash on shelves and some molds, especially when you're in a hurry and don't have time to allow kiln wash to dry properly.

Kiln wash

Kiln wash (also called *shelf primer*) is a dry, powdered compound made up of kaolin clay and alumina hydrate. Before you can use the powder, you have to mix it with water until it's the consistency of buttermilk. Then you can cover your kiln shelves with it. The wash is normally pink when mixed, but it turns white after firing so that you know whether your shelf is primed and ready to be fired or it has already been fired and needs to be primed again.

Don't reuse shelves or molds that have already been fired without cleaning them and reapplying kiln wash. Allow the wash to air-dry completely before using the shelves or molds.

Fun gadgets

You may be surprised to find out how many different tools — glass formers, racks, and combs, just to name a few — you can use in your warm-glass studio (see Figure 13-5 for some examples). The best part about these tools is that they've all been specifically designed to be used to manipulate hot molten glass.

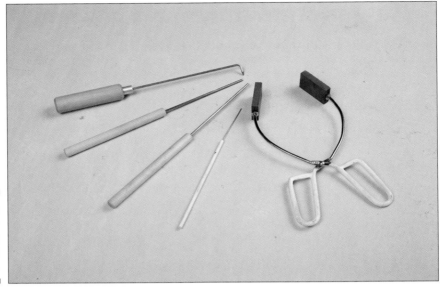

Figure 13-5:
Glass-
working
tools for kiln
work.

When you have a variety of warm-glass tools in your studio, the possibilities of what you can create are endless. Check out Figure 13-6 to see a glass bracelet that an artist created using a stainless steel bracelet former and a pair of graphite tongs. The next time you're at a gallery or museum, try to determine how the featured artists created their fused-glass pieces, and then ask someone from the gallery to see if you're right!

Figure 13-6:
Fused-glass
bracelet and
the tools
used to
create it.

Wearing the right safety gear

All glass artists (but especially those who work with warm glass) use products, tools, and processes that can be very dangerous if handled improperly. For example, if you don't wear the right protection gear, opening a 2,300-degree kiln filled with red-hot molten glass can be very hazardous to your skin and eyes — ouch!

Here are just a couple of the accessories you must wear anytime you work with warm glass:

- **Gloves:** Specially designed fusing gloves are available at all your glass suppliers (see Figure 13-7). You can choose from quite a few different styles, but I prefer the gloves with longer cuffs because they protect my arms when I reach into the kiln to pick up and move my warm-glass pieces.

- **Glasses:** You never want to look at hot, molten glass without wearing safety glasses because the heat that comes off the glass can severely damage your eyes. To protect yourself, you need to wear didymium-coated safety glasses anytime you look into your kiln — even if it's just for a quick peek.

  You can find quite a few varieties of didymium-coated glasses at your local glass shop or online, and some are definitely more stylish than others. I'm sort of attached to my old "superman" style didymium glasses (refer to Figure 13-7), but as long as you wear your glasses when looking into the hot kiln, you can choose whichever style feels comfortable for you.

Figure 13-7:
Safety gloves and glasses for kiln work.

Avoid wardrobe catastrophes! Always wear close-toed shoes, long pants, and short sleeves in your glass studio. If you have long hair, be sure to pull it back with a clip or elastic band. After all, you don't want your hair or clothing to touch the super-hot kiln, and you definitely don't want any hot glass to touch your legs or toes.

Selecting Fusible Glass

When it comes to choosing glass for your warm-glass projects, you have to consider a little more than just color. Most important, you have to select glass that's both *fusible* (able to be fused together in a kiln) and compatible. In addition, you have to choose the right sizes and shapes of glass to fit your project needs. The following sections explain these important considerations in more detail.

Determining glass compatibility

Before you start fusing different pieces of glass together, you need to make sure they're compatible with each other. To find out whether two pieces of glass will fuse together well, you need to look at the *coefficient of expansion* (or COE) of the glass. The COE of a piece of glass is the rate at which the glass starts and stops moving when heated. If you're using two or more different pieces of glass in a project, you must make sure that all the glass pieces will move and stop moving at the same rate. If they move at different rates, your project will crack.

Over the years, glass manufacturers have tried to take the guesswork out of glass compatibility by categorizing glass into two major groups: 90 COE and 96 COE. As long as you work only with glass in one range or the other, you'll have fairly consistent results when fusing. These categories have really helped beginners be successful in warm glass.

As your skills develop and your projects expand in complexity, I recommend that you find out more about how to test your own glass for compatibility. Although this process takes time, the results you get will be worth it. Check out www.bullseyeglass.com for details on how to test for glass compatibility.

Different artists prefer different COEs, so I recommend that you do one project using 90-COE glass and one using 96-COE glass. Find out which one works best for you and your projects, and then stick with it for all your other projects. If you want to use 90-COE glass, check out Bullseye Glass at www.bullseye glass.com. Bullseye provides one of the largest selections of glass colors and materials. If you want to use 96-COE glass, visit www.spectrumglass.com.

Note: Many hard-core, highly experienced fusers believe that more than just the COE determines whether one glass will be compatible with another. However, the other factors that contribute to glass compatibility are too detailed for me to discuss here and they're not as critical as the COE, so when choosing your glass, just focus on the COE.

Choosing the right glass size to purchase

Fusible glass comes in 3-millimeter-thick sheets and ranges in size from 4 square feet to 8 square feet. You can purchase either full sheets or smaller pieces, depending on both your current and future projects. If you like the color of a particular glass, I suggest that you always purchase the larger sheets. They're cheaper, and you can get more projects (and less waste) out of an 8-square-foot sheet than you can with a 1-square-foot sheet. If you don't think you'll use a particular color often or if you're working on a small project, feel free to buy a smaller sheet of glass.

Because some glass shops carry limited amounts of fusing glass, you may have to check online or in store catalogues if you can't find what you need locally. Just remember it's always more accurate and fun to select your glass in person.

 I like to keep a record of all the glass I have in my studio, including the color, manufacturer's stock number and the project(s) I've used it for. That way, I know exactly which glass I really love, and I can easily reorder it when I start to run out.

Spicing things up with glass shapes and characters

Glass makers have created lots of fun glass pieces that you can incorporate into your work to add a little zing to your projects. These pieces come in the following two basic formats (see Figure 13-8 for examples of each):

Figure 13-8: Using fusible glass shapes and pieces to add some variety to your projects.

✔ **Stringers:** You can add these thin strips of glass to any fusing project. They make great borders for designs, and you can use them to divide sections of designs or to create curved shapes in your project by bending them with the heat of a candle flame.

✔ **Fractures:** These thin layers of glass are already broken into random shapes called confetti, chips, and ground-up glass (also known as *frit*). Imagine what you can do with shapes like these!

Like regular glass sheets, these glass pieces need to be compatible with each other and the rest of your glass if you want them to work in your projects. Make sure you check the COE of each stringer and fracture before you purchase it.

Preparing to Fire and Use Your Kiln

Getting your first batch of glass into the kiln is very exciting, but before you do so, you need to take a few safety precautions in your studio, get your kiln furniture ready for the first firing, and have a test firing to make sure everything's working right. The following sections show you how to do all that, and, as an added bonus, they explain how to keep firing charts so your projects turn out perfectly every time.

Making sure your studio is safe

Safety is an important part of any hobby, which is why I harp on the many safety considerations to keep in mind when working with art glass throughout this book. Here I provide some safety tips you absolutely must follow whenever you work with warm glass. Many of these tips go for stained glass, too, but some of them are warm-glass specific, so be sure to read each tip carefully before you start your first warm-glass project. Review these tips often, and make sure you (and any visitors you bring with you) practice them every moment you spend in your studio.

✔ Keep your work areas neat and tidy — especially the floor so you don't slip on chips of glass.

✔ Place a heat-resistant pad on your worktable so you have a place to set down any hot items you use when working with your fused projects.

✔ Don't use an extension cord on your kiln. Always have the wiring installed and checked by a licensed electrician.

✔ Keep a fire extinguisher near your kiln in your studio.

✔ Always wear your regular safety glasses when working in your studio, and always switch to your didymium-coated glasses when you're looking into a hot kiln.

✔ Wear your heat-resistant gloves whenever you're working around a hot kiln. Be sure to check the gloves for any damage often, and replace them if necessary.

✔ Never leave a hot kiln unattended. If you don't have time to stay in your studio through a complete heating cycle, don't fire up the kiln!

✔ Always unplug your kiln before you use tools inside it. If metal makes contact with any of the heating elements, the contact will cause an electrical shock.

✔ Make sure your studio is well ventilated (see the earlier section "Ventilation" for details).

Preparing shelves and molds

You have to prepare your kiln shelves and molds with kiln wash before you can use them in your kiln. Every time you fire the shelves or molds, you have to clean off the old wash and reapply a new coating before you can use them in the kiln again. This cleaning process is very easy to do, but you need to make sure you do it ahead of time so your shelves and molds have plenty of time to dry before you want to use them.

The preparation process is the same for shelves and molds. For it, you need the following supplies:

✔ Kiln wash

✔ Plastic mixing container

✔ Water

✔ *Hake brush* (a very soft-haired brush that doesn't leave marks on the shelf or mold)

✔ Flat metal scraper or wire mesh sanding sheet

✔ Newspapers

✔ Respirator

To prepare your shelves and molds, follow these simple steps:

1. **Follow the manufacturer's direction to mix water with the kiln wash powder.**

   Don't make the mixture too thick because it'll crack and stick to the back of the glass during firing. I like the consistency to be more like buttermilk than pancake batter.

2. **Place your shelf or mold on newspaper; use your hake brush to apply a coat of kiln wash to the surface of the shelf, moving the brush in a horizontal direction from side to side (see Figure 13-9).**

3. **Use your hake brush to apply a second coat of kiln wash to the shelf or mold, this time moving the brush in a vertical direction from top to bottom.**

4. **Repeat Step 2 to apply a third coat of kiln wash in a horizontal direction.**

5. **Allow the shelf or mold to dry completely.**

   I like to prepare my shelves the day before I plan to fire up my kiln so they have time to dry completely before I load my glass into the kiln.

Note: When preparing stainless steel molds, lightly sand the metal surface, and then apply three layers of kiln wash by following the preceding steps.

Figure 13-9:
Applying the first coat of kiln wash to a shelf.

Certain brands of kiln wash mix colorants into their powders so they look pink when they're fresh and white after they've been fired. If you're working with a mixture that doesn't have colorant in it, just add a few drops of food coloring to the water-powder mixture. The food coloring will change to white after you fire it.

Don't stack your shelves or molds on top of one another after you apply kiln wash to them. They can get damaged, and the kiln wash can be scraped off. If you have several shelves and molds, a shelving unit with narrow shelves provides an excellent storage space.

Test firing

Before you use your kiln for the first time, I recommend doing a test fire in an empty kiln. When you transported your kiln to your studio, small pieces of fire brick may have jiggled loose and you don't want them to drop into your fused-glass project. When you do a test fire, the heating elements expand and contract, dislodging any of those little pieces. The test fire also burns off any residue or dampness inside your kiln. As an added bonus, test firing lets you get more familiar with your kiln and its controls, which will come in handy when you go to fire your first project. Figure 13-10 shows a new glass kiln being test fired. Notice that the lid is vented about 1 inch to let fumes and moisture escape during the initial heat-up; refer to your kiln's manual for specific test-fire details about your kiln.

Each kiln manufacturer has its own instructions for test firing, so I don't cover the procedure here. Just follow the steps in your kiln's owner's manual. If you can't find your manual, check online. All kiln makers have their owner's manuals available on their Web sites.

Even if you purchased a used kiln, you need to test fire it before you use it for the first time because you need to know how it operates. And it's always a good idea to read through the owner's manual before you fire your first project.

Figure 13-10:
Test firing
a new
glass kiln.

Ventilation is important whenever you're working in your warm-glass studio, but especially the first time you test fire your kiln. So open all your doors and windows, turn on your exhaust fan, and let the fresh air flow. See Chapter 3 for more details on properly ventilating your studio.

Keeping firing charts

To get the best results from your kiln, you need to keep firing charts for each of the projects you fire. A *firing chart* is basically a record of what temperatures the glass project was subjected to, how long the kiln took to reach those temperatures, and how long the kiln remained at them. Most kiln manufacturers provide a suggested firing chart for a basic project with their kilns. Keep in mind, though, that this chart is a set of guidelines, not strict rules. Every kiln is a little different, so you have to chart your own projects and keep track of the results. You can then use this information to make adjustments to your future firing schedules.

For each of your projects, you can either create your own firing chart or use the layout I provide in Table 13-1. Either way, your firing chart needs to contain the following information:

- ✔ The thickness of the glass being fired
- ✔ The type of glass you're using (96 COE or 90 COE)
- ✔ The overall dimensions of the project
- ✔ The power setting, temperature, and amount of time the piece was held at that temperature setting
- ✔ A record of the results each time you adjust the power and/or firing time and how each change affects the temperature inside the kiln

Table 13-1		Example of Firing Chart		
Segment	*Settings*	*Desired Temperature*	*Soak Time*	*Action*
Heat-up				
Ramp-up				
Flash-cool				
Anneal				
Cool-down				

Here's a quick look at what the terms in the firing chart mean:

- **Segment:** Each firing involves the following five segments, or time periods. How long each segment lasts depends on the type of glass you use and the size and thickness of your project. (See Chapter 14 for more details on what happens during each segment.)

    • **Heat-up:** The segment during which the kiln temperature goes from room temperature to 1,000 degrees

    • **Ramp-up:** The segment during which the kiln temperature goes from 1,000 degrees to the desired highest temperature

    • **Flash-cool:** The segment during which you cool the glass down as quickly as possible from the highest temperature to 1,000 degrees

    • **Anneal:** The segment during which you slowly cool the glass to its annealing range (see Chapter 14 for more details)

    • **Cool-down:** The segment during which you cool the glass back down to room temperature

- **Settings:** These settings are either on the dials on your kiln or programmed into the automatic controller.

- **Desired temperature:** This temperature is what you need to reach at each segment of the fusing process.

- **Soak time:** The soak time refers to the extended amount of time you need to maintain a consistent temperature during a particular segment of the fusing process.

- **Action:** This part of the firing chart refers to any actions you take during the fusing segments, including turning up the temperature, opening the kiln to vent, and turning off the kiln.

Chapter 14

Starting Simple with Basic Fusing Techniques

The easiest way to begin your fusing journey is to take a piece of base glass, add some fun-shaped glass, such as noodles, stringers, or confetti (refer to Chapter 13 for more on these), and then fire the pieces so they become one. The end result is impressive without a lot of work.

In this chapter, I explain how glass reacts to heat (so you understand how your glass pieces unite to become one beautiful project), and I show you how to prepare your glass pieces for the kiln and then fire them properly. I also walk you through your first fused-glass project: a sun catcher.

Remember to have fun and enjoy experimenting with this new glass technique by starting simple and working your way up to more complex projects and firing procedures (see Chapter 15 for advanced fusing techniques). Grab your fusing gear, and get ready to heat things up! (Turn to Chapter 13 for details on the supplies you need to get started.)

Understanding the Firing Process for Fusing Glass

The glass-fusing process requires a lot of heat and, if you want it to go smoothly, a lot of detailed firing records (see Chapter 13 for details on how to keep good firing charts). The hotter the glass gets, the more changes that take place within the glass itself and the way it looks. In general, glass is very susceptible to stress; it expands when heated and contracts when cooled. Each time you fire up a fused-glass project, you need to allow ample time for the glass to gradually readjust to those temperature changes so it doesn't crack, ruining your project.

To understand the firing process, you need to understand what happens to your glass pieces when you heat and cool them. The following sections cover the five basic cycles or segments your glass projects need to transition through during firing.

Both sheet glass and decorative glass pieces like noodles and stringers are available in either 90 or 96 COE. (*COE* stands for *coefficient of expansion* and is the rate at which the glass starts and stops moving when heated.) You can't mix glass with these two COEs when fusing, so make sure you use only glass with the same COE for any given project. Accidentally mixing even a very small piece of 90-COE glass with a piece of 96-COE glass can cause cracking and project failure. (See Chapter 13 for more info on COE.)

Initial heat-up segment

During the initial *heat-up segment,* you're heating the glass, kiln, and mold from room temperature to 1,000 degrees. The most important thing to remember is not to heat the glass too quickly; doing so can cause stress on the glass, resulting in cracks.

In general, the thicker and larger the mass of glass you're firing, the slower this initial heating segment needs to be. If you're firing your glass for the first time, you want this segment to gain heat at a rate of 10 to 20 degrees per minute until the kiln reaches 1,000 degrees or so. If you can't hit that rate exactly, err on the slower side; you can never heat up too slowly.

If you're firing thicker glass, you need to slow down the heat-up speed because thick glass absorbs heat more slowly than thin glass. Try heating up at 4 to 6 degrees per minute.

You need to vent your kiln about ½ to 1 inch during this initial heat-up segment to let any moisture, fumes, and toxins escape from the kiln. Some kilns come with a metal brace for venting (see Figure 14-1); if yours doesn't, you can place a 3-inch kiln post on its side to prop open the kiln. When the temperature reaches 1,000 degrees, make sure you remove the vent and close the kiln.

Ramp-up segment

During the *ramp-up segment,* you're heating the glass from 1,000 degrees to the desired working temperature. When you heat glass, the changes that occur are very obvious. I recommend charting these changes and the temperatures at which they occur so that you can create similar effects in other projects. For the most part, the changes that take place when you heat glass fall into the following three basic fusing stages:

✔ **Tack fusing:** Glass layers are fused together with very little deformation of the glass shape (see Figure 14-2a). The edges of the glass pieces become slightly rounded. Tack fusing occurs between 1,225 and 1,250 degrees.

Figure 14-1:
Venting the
kiln during
the initial
heat-up.

✔ **Dimensional-surface fusing:** The glass edges are soft and rounded when
the layers are fused together, but the surface of the project retains
dimension (see Figure 14-2b). This fusing stage occurs between 1,300
and 1,350 degrees.

Dimensional-surface fusing can occur anytime between tack fusing and
full fusing, depending on the type of glass you're working with.

✔ **Full fusing:** The glass layers completely melt into each other to form a
single mass. The glass surface is smooth, and the edges are completely
rounded (see Figure 14-2c). This stage occurs between 1,475 and 1,550
degrees.

Figure 14-2:
Tack fuse,
dimensional-
surface
fuse, and
full fuse.

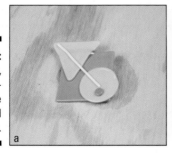

a   b   c

The temperature ranges I provide here are generalizations based on firing a
piece of 96-COE glass. Temperature rates can change based on the type of glass
you're working with, the color of the glass, and the number of layers you're
using in your project. I include several firing charts for various thicknesses and
sizes of glass projects throughout Part IV, but the key to setting up your own
firing schedules is experience. So read through your kiln manual for guidance,
start fusing your projects, and make sure you keep good firing charts.

Flash-cool segment

After you maintain the desired ramp-up temperature for your particular project, it's time to cool it down again. The *flash–cool segment* is when you open the top of the kiln and let as much heat escape as possible, reducing the temperature inside the kiln very, very quickly.

Although some glass artists don't include the flash-cool segment in their fusing processes, I like to flash cool for two reasons:

- ✔ **When I'm shaping glass, I want the glass to stop moving when it looks exactly the way I want it to look.** As soon as the glass starts cooling, it stops moving. See Chapter 16 for details on shaping glass.

- ✔ **Flash cooling helps prevent *devitrification*, which is when the glass gets a scummy haze or film on the surface of the glass.** Devitrification occurs when you hold the glass temperature between 1,330 and 1,400 degrees for extended periods of time. Note that 90-COE and 96-COE glasses don't seem to have much of a problem with devitrification.

If you're using a kiln with a digital controller, you don't flash cool. You simply set the controls and let them do the work.

Anneal segment

Annealing is the process of slowly cooling the glass to remove internal stress and strain. You have to anneal your glass properly to keep it from cracking and breaking during (and after) the fusing process.

Different thicknesses of glass require different annealing temperatures. The *annealing point* is the temperature at which glass is most readily annealed; it's the point in the middle of the *annealing range* — the range of temperatures in which the annealing process can take place.

Different colors and categories of glass have different annealing points. In general, the annealing point for opalescent glass tends to be several degrees lower than the annealing point for transparent, hot–colored (red, yellow, and orange) glass. Most COE-96 glass varieties anneal best between 940 and 965 degrees, and most 90-COE glass varieties anneal best at about 960 degrees.

Always check with the manufacturer of your glass to find out the exact annealing point for the glass you're working with. You may need to make minor adjustments in your firing charts depending on the type of glass you use for each project.

The amount of time you have to maintain the annealing temperature for a given project is called the *soaking time*. The larger and thicker the glass, the longer you need to soak the glass at its annealing point. The following chart offers some general guidelines for how a project's size relates to its soaking time. Although this chart is meant to be a good starting point for you, as you fuse more and more projects, you'll need to make adjustments to match your individual kiln and glass pieces.

Size of Project	Anneal/Soaking Time
Small pieces for jewelry and sun catchers	Turn the kiln off and let it cool down on its own.
3- to 6-inch pieces with two layers	Hold at annealing temperature for 45 minutes.
6- to 10-inch pieces with two or three layers	Hold at annealing temperature for 60 minutes.
12-inch pieces (or bigger) with three or more layers	Hold at annealing temperature for 90 to 180 minutes. For each additional layer of glass over three, add a minimum of 20 minutes per layer.

Cool-down segment

Small projects like jewelry or 2- to 4-inch projects don't require as much careful attention during the cool-down process because they're not under as much stress as larger projects. For that reason, when you reach the cool-down segment for a small project, you can simply turn everything off and let it cool naturally. Just be sure to keep the lid closed.

If you're firing a larger project, you need to cool it slowly after you finish the anneal segment. Set your digital controller to cool off at a rate of 4 to 6 degrees per minute until it reaches 700 degrees. If you don't have a digital controller, set an egg timer to remind you to monitor the temperature gauge on your kiln every 10 to 15 minutes so you can maintain the proper cool-down rate. Then just let everything cool off at its own rate until it reaches room temperature.

Preparing the Glass for Fusing and Firing Up the Kiln

Before you can assemble your warm-glass project and fire it up in the kiln, you have to cut out your glass pieces. If you're new to cutting glass, take a look at Chapter 5 before you start your first fused-glass project.

Several glass manufacturers now make clear, fusible, precut glass pieces in various sizes and shapes. I love working with these glass pieces because they're consistent in size and really speed up the prep work for certain projects. Some of the most common sizes available are 8-inch, 10-inch, and 12-inch round disks, which are perfect for dinnerware, and 4-x-4-inch squares, which are perfect for coasters. Like any other fusible glass, you can decorate and fire these shapes.

How a fusing project turns out depends on several factors, the two most important ones being the number of glass layers you're working with and the firing temperatures you set your kiln to. I discuss these two factors and more in the following sections.

Working with multiple layers of glass

Most fusing projects are created using two or more layers of glass. The exact number of layers you use depends on your project's design. Generally, the first layer is made up of clear glass because it's affordable and provides a great base for most projects. The other layers can be made up of single layers of colored glass, individual pieces of glass that have been cut into a particular design, or glass shapes like noodles, stringers, or frit (see Chapter 13 for more on these glass shapes). The following sections explain everything you need to know about working with multiple layers of glass.

I recommend always working with at least two layers of glass because glass changes shape when heated; using a base layer reduces the amount of shrinkage and distortion. The hotter the firing temperature, the more the glass will change shape. Keep this fact in mind when you design your projects. If you need to use higher temperatures to fuse your selected glass pieces together, consider adding more than two layers to your project so the glass's basic shape doesn't get too distorted.

Assembling your multi-layered project

When it comes to assembling your multi-layered projects, you have two options:

- ✔ If you're working with a smaller kiln, assemble the project on the fusing shelf. (Then you can load the whole shelf into the kiln; see the next section for details.)

- ✔ If you're working with a larger kiln, assemble the project on your worktable. (Then you can load your project and shelf separately into the kiln; see the next section for details.)

To assemble your project, start with the base glass. Then add each additional glass element, layer by layer. If your glass pieces are difficult to stack and keep shifting or rolling off the base glass, add a little glue to hold them in place.

Almost any white, water-based glue will work. Simply use a wooden toothpick to apply the glue to the base glass and tweezers to arrange small stringers and frit. Just keep in mind that too much glue can cause problems in your project and leave a carbon residue on the glass. For this reason, I like to dilute my glue with a little water before applying it to the glass.

If you don't add glue to your project, any components that aren't glued down (like stringers, frit, and other glass shapes) may shift as the glass expands and contracts from the heat of the kiln — and those shifts can ruin your project.

Keeping your glass pieces clean and free of fingerprints and residue is critical during project assembly. When you fire your project, any oil from your hands on the glass can actually make your fingerprints permanent, so make sure you remove any grinder dust and oil before you assemble your project. I wear a pair of white cotton gloves when assembling my glass-fusing projects because they eliminate the fingerprint issue altogether.

Keep a small paint brush handy to whisk away any unwanted glass chips and debris created as you assemble your project.

Reducing air bubbles during firing

One of the quirks you have to deal with when you're fusing glass together is that glass slumps or sags when heated. If you're working with multiple layers of glass, the edges can slump faster than the interior, trapping air bubbles between the layers. You can reduce the number of bubbles you get by slowing the rate of heating and adding a half-hour of soaking time when the glass reaches 1,220 degrees (*soaking* just means to maintain a particular temperature for a set amount of time).

Loading the kiln

If you're working with a small kiln, you can simply remove your shelf from the kiln, load your project onto the shelf, and then return it to the kiln (see Figure 14-3). The shelves in larger kilns are pretty heavy, so if you're using a larger one, you may need to load your project onto the shelf after you position it in the kiln. That way, you don't have to try to pick up the shelf and your project at the same time.

Regardless of the loading method you use, however, you need to make sure you've properly prepared your kiln shelves with kiln wash before you use them. (See Chapter 13 for details.)

Make sure you place all your projects in the center of the shelf. If your projects are too close to the heating elements along the sides of the kiln, they'll get hotter than they're supposed to, resulting in irregularly shaped glass pieces. If you're firing multiple projects at one time, make sure to leave 2 to 3 inches of space between each project. If you don't, your projects could fuse together.

Figure 14-3:
Placing a project on a small kiln shelf in the kiln.

All projects being fired at the same time have to be created from the same type of glass and made up of the same number of glass layers, and the projects themselves need to be about the same size. If they aren't, some projects will turn out perfectly while others will either over or undercook.

Working with a table-top kiln

For basic fusing projects, I recommend using a small, hot-box-style kiln, like I use to create the sun catcher project at the end of this chapter, because it heats up quickly and is easy to operate during the firing process. It runs on a standard 120-volt, 15-amp house current, and it's controlled by an infinite switch that can be dialed to low, medium, and high settings. A pyrometer measures the temperature inside the kiln. (For more about the different kinds of kilns you can use for your warm-glass projects, check out Chapter 13.)

Make sure you keep a journal and firing chart for all your firings — even the seemingly simple ones. That way, when something goes wrong — and it will from time to time — you'll have your notes to help you figure out what happened so you can adjust your firings for your next project. (Check out Chapter 13 for more details on keeping firing charts.)

Table 14-1 shows a firing chart for a small hot-box-style kiln. These particular settings and temperatures are for small two- to three-layer projects that are tack fused.

Table 14-1	Firing Chart for Small, Tack-Fused Projects with Two to Three Layers			
Segment	**Settings**	**Desired Temperature**	**Soak Time**	**Action**
Heat-up	Low/Medium	1,000 degrees	1 minute	Remove vent.
Ramp-up	Full/High	1,350 degrees	10 minutes	Monitor.
Flash-cool	Off	1,000 degrees	0 minutes	Open the lid, and close it when the temperature reaches 1,000 degrees.
Anneal	Medium/Low	955 degrees	10 minutes	Adjust controls to keep the kiln at 955 degrees during this phase.
Cool-down	Off	100 degrees	0 minutes	Turn everything off, and let it cool naturally. Don't open the lid!!

Never leave a hot kiln unattended, and make sure you always follow the kiln-related safety procedures I describe in detail in Chapter 13, such as wearing the right heat-resistant gear and not using your tools in your kiln until after you unplug it.

No peeking!

Although you can open the kiln and check the progress of your work without damaging the end results at times (after the kiln reaches above 1,000 degrees), don't even think about peeking inside the kiln when the temperature falls below 1,000 degrees. No matter how curious you are, keep the kiln shut! A sudden blast of cool air or a quick drop in temperature can cause thermal shock to the glass and break your project.

Wear your heat-resistant gloves and didymium-coated fusing glasses whenever you look into a hot kiln. (See Chapter 13 for more safety precautions to follow whenever you operate a kiln.)

After your kiln has passed through the annealing temperatures and the kiln has been turned off, you can leave the kiln unattended. I like to do firings in the evening so the glass has plenty of time to anneal and cool down during the night. I love admiring my work over my morning coffee the next day.

Project: Fused Sun Catcher

Before you can create this simple fused-glass project — a sun catcher — you need to purchase a small piece of clear glass (at least 2 x 2 inches) and a 6-x-6-inch piece of brightly colored, transparent fusing glass. Then prepare your kiln shelf for firing by following the instructions I provide in Chapter 13.

Note: In place of the 6-x-6-inch piece of glass, you can use larger scrap pieces and some stringers, confetti, or frit to add a little zing to your project (I use scraps of dichroic glass for my sun catcher).

Always use compatible glass to create your projects. In other words, don't mix COE-96 glass with COE-90 glass.

After you pick out your glass, follow these steps, be safe, and have fun:

1. **Cut a small 1- to 1½-inch square of glass for the base of your sun catcher. You can use clear or colored glass.**

2. **Cut five to eight pieces of your brightly colored glass about 2 to 3 inches long, making sure the tips of the curves come close to each other when you place them in a circle on top of the base glass (see Figure 14-4).**

   For tips on glass cutting, refer to Chapter 5.

3. **Clean the glass, making sure you wipe away all the dust and oil.**

4. **Assemble your glass pieces, and use a small amount of white glue to secure them together.**

   See the section "Assembling your multi-layered project" for details.

5. **Use glass stringers to decorate your project, if desired; cut the stringers and place one stringer on each of the glass strips radiating out from the center base piece.**

Figure 14-4:
Overlapping the tips of the glass curves.

To give the stringers more shape, you can bend them by holding them over a candle flame (see Figure 14-5). Just make sure you remove any carbon residue from the bent glass before adding it to your project.

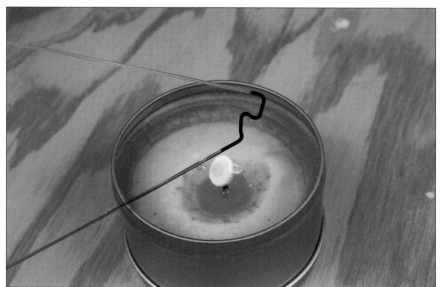

Figure 14-5:
Bending a glass stringer over a candle flame.

6. **Allow the glue to dry for a few minutes.**

7. **Lay your project on the prepared kiln shelf, place the shelf into the kiln, and vent the lid open about ½ inch with a kiln post.**

   The purpose of venting the kiln during the initial heat-up is to allow any moisture from the glue, the kiln wash, and the kiln to escape.

WARNING!

Don't ever put anything wet into your kiln. Doing so will not only cause the glass to explode but also ruin your kiln. Always let the glue dry completely before putting your project into the kiln, and let all the moisture escape during the heat-up stage of firing.

8. Follow the firing chart in Table 14-1 to fuse your project.

Figure 14-6 shows the finished sun catcher.

Figure 14-6:
Fused sun catcher decorated with stringers.

Chapter 15

Heating Things Up with Some Advanced Fusing Techniques

In This Chapter

▶ Designing your own fused-glass projects

▶ Creating advanced projects using fun techniques and multiple layers of glass

▶ Adding wire and fiber paper to your glass projects

▶ Trying out your new fusing skills on a set of coasters

*A*fter you successfully finish your first few fusing projects, you may be ready to kick it up a notch, which is where this chapter comes in. Here, I show you how to work with more complex techniques than the ones I cover in Chapter 14. I explain some of the basic design elements you need to consider when designing your own project patterns, and I show you how to use multiple layers of glass to create eye-catching effects and wire and fiber paper inclusions to make your projects more functional. So, if you're up for a fiery-hot challenge, read on!

Note: The focus of this chapter is on expanding the firing experience by working with a larger glass kiln than the smaller hot-box-style kiln you use for the simple projects in Chapter 14. But don't worry if you don't have a larger kiln — the projects and firing charts I include here will still work in your smaller kiln. You may just have to adjust the project size.

Creating Your Own Project Design

Compared to stained glass, the process of fusing glass is a lot more abstract, which means you have more freedom to see where your creativity takes you. One area where you can exercise this freedom is in the design pattern (or lack of one). For example, you don't even need a pattern for the sun catcher project I show you how to make in Chapter 14; all you have to do is layer random cut shapes and pieces together to create the desired finished product. (If you're the type who prefers to follow a design, countless books are available that contain pre-made designs and patterns.)

As your fused-glass skills increase, however, you may want to create more complex designs and projects of your own. You may also want to be able to repeat a design over and over again if, for example, you're creating a set of dishes or a matching pair of vases. In either case, you need to use a paper design template to create your project to ensure that all the pieces match up and that the last dish or vase you make looks like the first one. In the following sections, I explain what you need to know to design a workable project pattern and to choose the right glass to fit it.

Overthinking a project can take the fun out of fusing if you aren't careful. After all, the most appealing aspect of fusing is its free-form nature. So be sure to let your creativity lead you as you design your project's pattern and then create your project.

Considering your project's size

The size of your kiln determines the size of the project you can make. A small kiln is perfect for jewelry, coasters, sun catchers, and ornaments, but if you want to make anything larger than 4 inches square, you'll need a bigger kiln. When you're ready to make a larger project, I recommend using a kiln that has a 14- to 20-inch firing chamber and that's at least 9 inches deep because it can accommodate such a large variety of great projects.

In general, your project needs to be at least 2 inches smaller in diameter than your kiln shelf. To make sure your project will fit in your kiln, start by drawing out the size of your project on a piece of paper. After you draw the size of your project, you're ready to start adding the details of the design to your paper template (see the next section for details).

Focusing on layers

Unlike stained-glass projects, fused projects are made up of layers of glass fused together by the heat of the kiln (as opposed to being connected by metal). This concept is important to keep in mind as you start to plan your design. The more complicated your design is, the more important it is to have a paper pattern, so go ahead and draw out a design on paper if it makes you feel more confident. You can also make a copy of that pattern and cut out your pattern *templates* (the individual pieces of your pattern) just as you do for stained-glass projects. (For more information about working with patterns and templates, check out Chapter 4.)

After your design is more or less finished, take some time to study it. Think about what kind of glass you want to use for which layers and how the different glass pieces will affect each other. For example, if you layer red transparent glass over yellow glass, you may end up with orange glass on your finished project. On the other hand, if you layer a piece of colored glass over a clear piece of base glass, you don't have to worry about changing colors.

I recommend using at least two layers of glass for all fused-glass projects. The first layer should be one, solid piece of clear fusible glass because it provides a consistent base on which to build your design; plus, it's affordable. If you're not supporting your project with clear base glass, you need to extend the size of your glass pieces so they can be stacked onto each other to keep your project together when it fuses.

Make sure you use glass with the same *COE* (the coefficient of expansion or rate at which the glass starts and stops moving when heated) in your project. You can't mix COEs, or else your project will crack and break during firing.

Figure 15-1 shows a finished fused-glass disk for a wall sconce and the pattern used to create it. This project provides a great example of how different glass layers affect each other because it contains so many layers of glass. All the glass used in this project is COE-96 fusing glass. The base of the disk is clear glass, the background is made up of two main pieces (one blue and one tan), and the palm tree (made up of brown and green glass) is layered over the sky and sand.

As with the simple projects in Chapter 14, I recommend that you add a small amount of white, water-based glue during project assembly to hold all your pieces in place. (See that chapter for more details on adding glue to your project.)

Figure 15-1:
A fused-glass disk and the pattern used to create it.

You can add stringers, frit, and other decorative glass elements to your project to give it more pizzazz; see my palm tree wall sconce in Figure 15-2 for an example of how to incorporate these accent elements into your glass work. (Turn to Chapters 13 and 14 for more on stringers and other types of glass you can include in your fused-glass pieces.) Again, the key to creating a well-blended project is layering each component so that it fits with all the others, whether you're working with large, flat pieces of glass or fine frit.

If you have a stained-glass pattern you think would make a great fused-glass project, feel free to use it. Just make sure you keep the layering concept in mind throughout the project.

Figure 15-2:
Layering
different
components
to create a
well-blended
fused-glass
project.

Understanding the effects of stacking glass

When you fire your project, one layer of glass shrinks while the other two or more layers expand. What your finished project looks like depends on which glass layers shrink and which ones expand, which is why you may want to practice stacking glass (and seeing what happens when it's heated) before you choose which glass to use for your more complicated projects.

To see some of the effects you can create by stacking different sizes and shapes of glass, follow these steps:

1. **Cut out five 2-inch squares of colored glass, three 2-inch squares of clear glass, and one 2-x-6-inch strip of clear glass.**

   Turn to Chapter 5 for everything you need to know about cutting glass.

2. **Place one 2-inch square of colored glass on a dry kiln shelf that has been prepped with kiln wash.**

   Turn to Chapter 13 for details on how to prepare your kiln shelf for firing.

3. **Make two separate stacks of glass on the same kiln shelf you used in Step 2; leave at least 2 inches between each stack.**

   For the first stack, place one square of clear glass on the bottom and one square of colored glass on the top; for the second stack, place two squares of clear glass on the bottom and one square of colored glass on the top.

4. **Place the 2-x-6-inch strip of glass on the kiln shelf so that it's 2 inches away from the squares you placed in Steps 2 and 3; place one 2-inch colored square on each end of the strip.**

   Your shelf should look something like Figure 15-3.

Figure 15-3:
Laying
out your
glass for a
firing test.

5. **Follow the firing chart for small, two- to three-layered projects I provide in Chapter 14 to fire your glass stacks.**

6. **Let the glass cool completely; then measure the stacks of glass.**

   Notice how the pieces changed in size and appearance after being fired (see Figure 15-4). The single layer of glass is smaller in width than the double- and triple-layered stacks. The clear strip with two pieces stacked on each end is thinner in the middle because it is only one layer at that point.

You can create great effects by stacking layers of glass. Using the results from your testing batches, you can determine the effects that different colors and shapes will have when the glass is stacked and fired. As you choose the glass for the different layers of your fused-glass project,

- ✔ Don't forget about the color changes that will occur when you stack pieces of translucent glass. What you see isn't always what you get!

- ✔ Don't forget you can use clear glass to add bulk to your projects and to help thinner strips keep their shape during firing.

Figure 15-4:
The results
of test firing
various
layers of
glass.

Weaving Glass

When you're ready to start putting your self-designed, fused-glass project together, you can layer your glass any way you want — let your creativity be your guide. One of my favorite more-advanced layering techniques is weaving two different colors of glass together. This technique works great for sun catchers, picture frames, trivets, and dishes.

Try your hand at glass weaving by following these steps:

1. **Draw a pattern template for a 6-inch square; draw ½-inch stripes across the template, as shown in Figure 15-5.**

   See the section "Creating Your Own Project Design" for details on how to draw a pattern template.

2. **Cut out a 6-inch square of clear glass for the base.**

3. **Cut out five ½-x-6-inch strips of one color of transparent glass and five strips of another color.**

4. **Glue one layer of the same color of glass strips to the clear glass base so that all the strips are going in one direction and are evenly spaced across the base glass; make sure the first and last strips are at the edges of the base glass (see Figure 15-6).**

   Don't overdo it with the glue. Too much glue can leave a carbon residue on the fused glass. See Chapter 14 for details on how to glue your layers to the base and to each other.

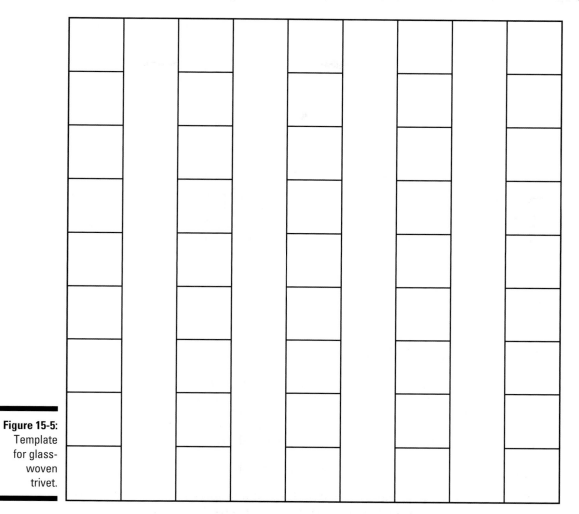

5. **Glue a layer of the second color of glass strips on top of and perpendicular to the first layer, creating the look of a woven design (see Figure 15-7).**

   As you did in Step 4, make sure to space the bars evenly and line the first and last strips up against the edges of the glass base.

Figure 15-6:
Laying out
and gluing
your first
layer of
glass.

Figure 15-7:
The perpen-
dicular layer
of glass
creates
the woven
design.

6. **Place the project in the kiln, and fire it according to the firing chart in Table 15-1.**

   See Chapter 14 for more details on how to load and fire the kiln.

Figure 15-8 shows what the finished woven trivet looks like.

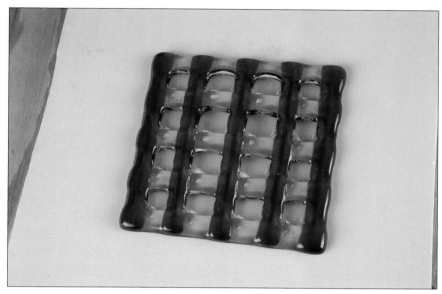

Figure 15-8:
Finished
glass-
woven
trivet.

Table 15-1   **Firing Chart for Full-Fused, Medium-Sized Projects with Two to Three Layers**

Segment	Settings	Desired Temperature	Soak Time	Action
Heat-up	Low/Medium	1,000 degrees	1 minute	Remove vent.
Ramp-up	Full/High	1,480 degrees	10 minutes	Monitor.
Flash-cool	Off	1,100 degrees	0 minutes	Open the lid, and close it when the temperature reaches 1,000 degrees.
Anneal	Medium/Low	955 degrees	30 minutes	Adjust controls to keep the kiln at 955 degrees during this phase.
Cool-down	Off	100 degrees	0 minutes	Turn everything off, and let it cool naturally. Don't open the lid!

Bringing out the big guns, I mean kilns

Most large kilns are equipped with digital controllers that allow you to preset them to automatically complete just about any firing cycle without much hands-on intervention from you. I have one of these kilns in my studio, and although I find it very helpful, nothing beats hands-on experience. I recommend that you fire your first few projects manually before you start relying on the automatic system. That way, you can really see what different temperatures do to your glass pieces.

Playing, testing, and experimenting are what make glass fusing so creative and fun. After you've fired a few projects manually, you can set it and forget it! Well, sort of. You never want to leave a kiln firing when you're not nearby just in case something doesn't go according to plan.

Adding Wire and Other Inclusions to Your Projects

If you want to hang up your fused projects after you finish them, you need to use wire, fiber paper, or some other design technique to add a hook or hanger. The most common and simplest technique is to design your project so that two glass pieces fuse together leaving a small open space between the pieces through which you can string fishing line, wire, ribbon, or chain. However, some projects don't allow you to use this technique; for those projects, you must rely on inclusions or metal hooks.

An *inclusion* is something that you add to a project primarily for displaying; it can be wire for a hook or fiber paper to create a hole. I discuss the different types of inclusions you can use in your projects in the following sections.

Wiring to hang

When it comes to adding wire to your project, you have several types of wire to choose from. Some artists use 18-gauge copper wire for hooks, but I've found that copper wire sometimes leaves a residue of carbon powder that stains the glass. Plus, the wire becomes very brittle when heated. As a result, the wire can break under very little strain, which, as you can imagine, is quite destructive for your glass project.

I prefer to use *Nichrome wire,* a nickel-chromium, nonmagnetic, corrosion-resistant wire that can withstand high temperatures. It's available for purchase from most fusing suppliers and glass shops.

To connect the wire to your glass project, first use a pair of needle-nose pliers to shape the wire into a hook or loop. Then glue it to a small ½-inch piece of clear glass, and place it under your fusing project (see Figure 15-9). Position the wire at the top of the glass piece so that your project hangs correctly after firing. As the clear glass fuses into the project when heated, it encases part of the hook, connecting it to the project.

Figure 15-9:
A wire hook glued to a piece of clear glass and placed under your project.

Using fiber paper to create holes in glass

Fiber paper is an extremely versatile tool that you always want to have on hand in your glass studio. Not only can you use it to cover your kiln shelves in place of kiln wash, but you can also use it to keep certain sections of glass open during the fusing process. The paper creates a tube or tunnel in the glass through which you can thread a piece of fishing line, chain, or rope. Because the fiber paper doesn't stick to the glass, all you have to do is rinse it away after the project has been fired and cooled. You can then hang the finished project on a wall or, in the case of a necklace like the one in Figure 15-10, on a neck.

Figure 15-10:
Fused-glass necklace charm with a tunnel for the chain.

Gluing hangers to fused projects

To display a larger wall hanging, you need to attach metal hooks to the back of the project. I suggest that you use E-6000 glue to do so. Just make sure you clean the surfaces of both the glass and the hooks with rubbing alcohol (and then let them dry completely) before you glue them together.

Project: Creating a Set of Four Glass Coasters

The best thing about this project is that you can create it out of any of your favorite glass colors. Depending on how big your kiln is, you can either fire the coasters one at a time or all at the same time. If you're firing them one at a time, be sure to follow your firing charts exactly for each coaster so all four coasters turn out the same.

For this project, you need the following supplies:

- ✔ Four 4-square-inch pieces of clear glass
- ✔ 6 square feet of pink, black, and lime-colored glass (Feel free to replace these colors with your own favorites.)
- ✔ White, water-based glue
- ✔ Glass-cutting tools (See Chapters 2 and 5 for more details.)
- ✔ Drafting supplies (See Chapters 2 and 3 for more details.)

After you have your supplies handy, follow these steps to create four fused-glass coasters:

1. **Draw a 4-square-inch pattern template on a piece of paper.**

   If you want to use a different design for each coaster, draw four separate templates.

   Keep your design elements to at least 1-inch squares and 1-inch-wide strips to eliminate glass waste.

2. **Cut out your glass pieces, and trim them to fit your design template.**

   For more info on how to cut glass, check out Chapter 5.

3. **Using a toothpick and glue, attach your glass pieces to the 4-inch clear glass base, making sure to keep the glass clean and free of fingerprints.**

4. **Repeat Step 3 for each coaster.**

   Figure 15-11 shows what the coasters look like prior to being fired.

Figure 15-11:
These
coasters are
ready for
firing.

5. **Load the four coasters into the kiln, leaving about 2 inches between each coaster on the kiln shelf.**

   Make sure your kiln shelf has a fresh, completely dry coating of kiln wash on it. For tips on how to prepare your kiln shelves, turn to Chapter 13.

   When making sets of items like these coasters, try to fire all the items at one time, if possible. If your kiln isn't large enough, make sure you keep good firing records so you can re-create every detail of the firing procedure for each item so all the pieces of your set turn out the same.

6. **Fire the kiln by following the settings, times, and actions listed in the firing chart in Table 15-1.**

   You're firing the coasters to a temperature of 1,500 to 1,600 degrees, depending on the type of glass you're using. This temperature range results in a full-fused project in which all the edges of all the glass pieces fuse into each other, creating a solid glass mass that has a smooth, flat surface with no definition between pieces or layers. This effect is perfect for coasters. (See Chapter 14 for more details on full fusing.)

   Figure 15-12 shows the finished set of fused coasters.

Figure 15-12:
Finished
fused-glass
coasters.

Chapter 16

The Art of Shaping Warm Glass

F lat-glass fusing (which I discuss in Chapters 14 and 15) is great for creating sun catchers, jewelry, and trivets. But what if you want to make something with a little more shape to it? You've come to the right place! Slumping glass is one of the most empowering processes in the art of warm glass because it gives you the opportunity to reshape glass (including prefused glass) into bowls, lampshades, platters, and three-dimensional glass sculptures.

In this chapter, you get familiar with glass slumping. You discover how to select and prepare your molds for various projects, how to prefire your glass for slumping projects, and how to master the basics of manipulating warm glass into functional shapes. At the end of the chapter, you can put your new-found knowledge to work by completing two glass-shaping projects.

When you start making glass projects that may come in contact with food and your mouth, you may be concerned with safety and health issues. Rest assured. All glass manufacturers have their glass tested to make sure it's completely safe to touch your food (or mouth). However, you do need to make sure you don't add just any stain or paint without checking its package to make sure it's safe to use on dinnerware and the like.

Gathering the Tools You Need to Start Shaping Glass

Glass slumping (also called *glass shaping*) is the process of sagging or shaping hot glass over a mold; it works because hot glass continues to move until it touches a solid surface. As the glass cools, it becomes the shape of that surface. So, for example, if you want to create a bowl with scalloped edges, you need to use a bowl mold with a scalloped design.

Glass slumping generally involves a two-step firing process. After you decorate your glass piece, you fuse it at a temperature between 1,400 and 1,550 degrees, depending on your project's size, thickness, and design, to create a solid glass disk. You then place that disk on a glass mold and refire it at a lower temperature between 1,100 and 1,300 degrees. When heated, the glass disk slumps down and contours to the shape of the mold.

Sounds fun, right? Well, before you can start slumping glass, you need to make sure you have a kiln that works for both fusing and slumping glass and a mold that helps you shape the glass. The following sections explain what you need to know about these two key tools. Turn to Chapter 13 for details on the other basic glass-fusing supplies you need to have in your studio.

Using the right type of kiln for slumping

When you're picking out what type of kiln to use for your glass-slumping projects, consider the following factors (check out Chapter 13 for more details on kilns):

- ✔ **Size:** Because slumping glass requires a lot of space, you need to use a larger kiln than the small hot-box-style kiln you use in Chapter 14. I recommend that your kiln have a firing chamber that's at least 12 inches wide and 9 inches tall. Using anything smaller really limits the types of projects you can create, and you certainly don't want that!

  Your glass always has to be at least 2 inches away from the kiln's heating elements, and your kiln shelf has to be at least 1 inch above the kiln floor. In other words, if your kiln is only 6 inches deep, you can't create any slumped project that's more than about 2 inches tall. Although that height works fine for a shallow bowl or platter, it's not nearly big enough for a vase or larger bowl.

- ✔ **Door or lid placement:** You can slump in either a front-loading kiln or a top-loading or clam-shell kiln. I prefer the top-loading version because it makes positioning the glass evenly on the mold easier for me to do.

- ✔ **Controls:** You can do your glass slumping in a kiln that's either manually or automatically controlled, although I strongly recommend purchasing a kiln with a digital controller, such as the one in Figure 16-1, if you can afford it. Kilns with automatic controls make it easy for you to create wonderful projects time and time again.

No matter which type of kiln you use, make sure you have the basic firing charts for general fusing projects that go with it. These charts should include instructions or tips for slumping projects. If you can't find your owner's manual, check the Internet. Most kiln companies post their manuals online as free downloads.

Figure 16-1:
A large, top-loading kiln with a digital controller.

Picking out and preparing glass molds

A *mold* is what gives slumped glass its desired shape. When you're beginning a glass-shaping project, you have several types of molds to choose from, and you need to treat each one a little differently. For example, some molds slump glass inside the mold, and others slump glass around the outside; some are made of clay, while others are made of metal. You'll likely want to work with all types and shapes of molds because they all yield different types of projects.

Molds, especially large ones, can be expensive, so be careful when working with them. I recommend storing them on a shelf where they'll be out of the way and protected from most accidents. Whatever you do, don't stack your molds on top of each other; doing so can quickly cause unrepairable chips or dents in their surfaces.

Hot glass sticks to everything! Just like the walls and shelves in your kiln, you have to protect your molds from hot, molten glass. If you don't prepare them properly for each firing, the hot glass will permanently stick to any unprotected surface. If you accidentally get some hot glass on the mold, don't try to remove it until the kiln and glass have cooled completely.

The following sections cover the different types of molds and the methods you need to follow to prepare them for firing.

Always wear a respirator when working with kiln wash, molds, fiberboard dust, glass powders, and firing paper.

Ceramic molds

Ceramic molds (see Figure 16-2) are made up of clay that's been bisque fired. You can find hundreds of different sizes and shapes of ceramic molds for jewelry, dishes, and everything in between. They work great for creating bowls, platters, and any other concave shapes because you can slump glass into the molds. The surfaces of ceramic molds are also smooth, so they don't leave any rough textures on your projects.

Figure 16-2:
A collection
of ceramic
molds.

When applying glass to your ceramic mold, you always slump it into the mold. Never drape glass over a ceramic mold.

Ceramic molds come with a few small vent holes in their bottoms to let the air escape during the slumping process. When glass starts to slump, the edges of the glass are the first to make contact with the rim or edge of the mold. As the middle of the glass starts to fall, air can be trapped in between the glass and the mold. The vent holes are critical to keeping large air bubbles from forming.

If your mold doesn't have any or enough vent holes, you can drill more with a ⅛-inch carbide drill bit. Place the holes in the lowest point of the mold, where they'll be most effective.

To prepare ceramic molds for firing, you follow the same process you do to prepare the kiln shelves with kiln wash. Follow the directions on the package to mix your powdered kiln; then apply two to three coats of the kin wash to the surface of your ceramic mold. After the kiln wash has dried, use your hand to gently sand off any excess kiln wash and remove any ridges or bubbles from the surface of the mold. Allow the mold to dry completely before using it in the kiln. I also like to give the mold a light dusting of dry kiln wash before firing. Check out Chapter 13 for more info about kiln wash.

Fiber molds

Although you can find hundreds of different ceramic molds, many glass artists like to create their own free-form molds, which is where fiber molds come into play. Fiber molds, which have become increasingly popular over the years, are made of *alumina-silica fiberboard* (a porous, rigid board that can be cut, carved, and shaped), and come in a variety of thicknesses from 1 to 2 inches. So if you can't find a mold for the type or size of project you want to create, like a wall sconce or uniquely shaped dish, a fiber mold is a good choice. You can slump into or drape over a fiber mold. Unlike ceramic molds, fiber molds don't absorb or retain heat, so the glass cools more evenly after it has been slumped or draped.

Most brands of fiberboard require some preheating prep work to burn off the organic bonding agents that hold the fibers together before you can use them as molds for your projects. Unfortunately, this preheating process can cause the fiberboard to become soft and less rigid than you might want your mold to be. The exception is Kaiser Lee Board, which doesn't require any prep work and can be used over and over again, as long as you handle it with care.

You don't need to apply liquid coats of kiln wash to these molds. You can simply spread a fine layer of dry kiln wash powder on the surface of your fiberboard mold to protect it from *glass spiking,* or the little pointed edges that often occur on the fiberboard during firing thanks to the expanding and contracting glass. As glass heats, it expands, and then, as it cools, it contracts. As the glass contracts, the edges of it catch on the fibers in the mold, resulting in glass spiking.

I recommend filling a mesh sock or part of a pair of panty hose with kiln wash so that you can apply a quick dusting of kiln wash on molds and shelves.

Stainless steel molds

Stainless steel is a very durable mold material that can be used over and over again. Molds made from this material don't chip and are easy to store. They're perfect for creating vases and glass bracelets. Unlike ceramic molds, you have to drape your glass over the outside of stainless steel molds.

Never slump glass into a steel mold because the metal mold loses its heat faster than the glass; if you slump your glass into the mold, the mold will contract during cooling and crack the glass.

The most popular stainless steel mold is the *floral former,* an inverted mold over which you drape glass so that it forms a vase shape as the hot glass softens. If you want to make something other than a vase using a stainless steel mold, I recommend checking out a few flea markets; there you can find a lot of different stainless steel shapes that work great as draping molds.

Preparing a stainless steel mold for firing is much the same as preparing a ceramic mold (see the preceding section for details). All you have to do is apply several coats of kiln wash with a brush or airbrush and let them dry completely. If you're coating a new stainless steel mold, you may find that the kiln wash adheres better if you lightly sand the surface first. (If you go this route, make sure you use a damp cloth to wipe off any dust or residue before you apply the kiln wash to the mold.)

Make sure your stainless steel mold doesn't have any inside curves or rims. Remember that the mold will be completely coated with a rigid layer of glass after the firing. You need to be able to slip the glass off the form without it getting stuck on any inside curves or rims.

Opting for Fancier Glass

In Chapter 13, I introduce you to the basic types of glass you can use for your warm-glass projects and discuss the importance of making sure all your glass is compatible. Refer to that chapter if you need a refresher.

As your warm-glass skills improve and you start using molds to create bigger, more three-dimensional glass projects, you can also expand your glass selection. Here I show you several fancier specialty glasses that work great for slumping projects. Get to know these glasses a bit so you can consider them for future projects.

Most slumping projects look nicer when you use two or more pieces of glass. I recommend that you use a piece of clear glass cut to the same size as your original glass blank (the term *blank* refers to the glass being slumped). Where you position the clear glass in relation to your glass blank in your project affects the final look of your project. For example, if you place the clear glass under your colored art glass, you add more weight to the project but don't affect how the color of the art glass looks. But if you place the clear glass over the top of the colored art glass, you deepen the hue of the art glass and enhance the depth of the piece. Experiment with these two effects before you use them on a major project so you know how to create them and which one you like best.

Thin fusing glass

Standard sheets of fusing glass (the glass I talk about in Chapter 13) are about 3 millimeters thick. *Thin fusing glass* is a type of specialty glass that's between 1.8 and 2 millimeters thick. Using this thinner glass provides the added capacity for delicacy, weight reduction, stacking precision, and color overlay you need in some fusing projects, such as jewelry. Thin fusing glass comes in dozens of different colors as well as in both transparent and opalescent.

Iridescent fusing glass

To create *iridescent fusing glass,* glass makers flash-fire the glass with a micro-thin layer of metallic crystal, creating a mother of pearl finish. When you fire iridescent glass as part of your slumping project, the surface can sometimes burn off at high temperatures. For this reason, if you're firing two pieces of iridescent glass, don't place the iridescent sides facing each other. If you do and the surfaces burn off, the two pieces won't fuse properly. Figure 16-3 shows a slumping project that uses iridescent glass.

Figure 16-3:
Example of
iridescent
glass used
to create a
fused-glass
fish.

Dichroic glass

To create *dichroic glass,* glass makers use electron beams in a vacuum chamber to apply ultra-thin layers of quartz and metallic coatings to already-manufactured fusible glass; the results are the most vibrant, space-age colors you can imagine. Dichroic glass is very expensive and can be used for slumping projects as well as any other fusing project to which you want to add sparkle and shine. Not surprisingly, it's a favorite of jewelry artists and torch workers.

Dichroic glass is available in both 90 coefficient of expansion (COE) and 96 COE. Just make sure your dichroic glass is compatible with the other glass in your project (see Chapter 13 for more details about COE and glass compatibility). Figure 16-4 shows a piece of jewelry made with dichroic glass.

Glass frit

Although you can use different glass fractures (including noodles and confetti) in any fused-glass project, *frit,* or finely ground glass, works especially well in slumping projects. You can use it on any of your fused-glass surfaces to add a little texture and color. Frit is available in dozens of colors and a variety of grits from powder to mosaic chips. You can use a stencil to apply the powder and small frit to the surface of your glass like paint; you can use glue to hold larger frit in place. Either way, the results you get from adding frit to your slumping projects are stunning.

Figure 16-5 shows a plate that displays the design effect you can achieve by using glass frit on clear glass. To create the plate in the figure, the artist first decorated a clear piece of glass using a stencil and frit, then placed another layer of clear glass over the decorated glass blank to incase the colors, and finally fired and slumped it (see the section "Fire It Up! Fusing and Slumping Your Glass" for more details on this process).

Figure 16-4:
Examples
of jewelry
made of
dichroic
glass.

Figure 16-5:
Fused and
slumped
glass plate
decorated
with glass
frit.

Preparing Your Glass for Shaping

Before you can fire up your glass-slumping project, you have to prepare the glass to be slumped. The three steps you need to take to prepare your glass are:

1. **Cut your glass to fit the mold.**
2. **Clean the glass.**
3. **Decorate the glass.**

I discuss each of these steps in the following sections. (Chapter 14 offers more details on preparing and assembling your fusing glass before the first firing, so go there if you need more details.)

If you're working with more than one layer of glass or you're incorporating a design of any type in your glass-slumping project, you have to do two firings. The first firing creates the glass blank, which is the glass disk you later place on the mold and reheat to create your project's finished shape. If you don't do the first firing, the decorations and individual glass pieces you put together as part of your project design will start to move and fall off the glass during the slumping process. Think of the first firing step as permanently attaching all the glass pieces together so they can be shaped together as one glass piece.

Cutting your fusing glass to fit your mold

After you select which fusing glass you want to use for your slumping project, you have to cut it to fit your mold. You may be curious about how to measure for the extra glass you need to slump down into the mold. Lucky for you (and me), you don't have to worry about that extra glass because the glass stretches when it gets hot.

To measure a piece of glass to fit a mold into which you slump the glass, turn the mold upside down on top of the glass piece, and trace around the edges of the mold, as shown in Figure 16-6. Then just cut out the fusing glass as you'd cut any other art glass (see Chapter 5 for everything you need to know about cutting glass). If you're using a floral former or other mold over which you drape the glass, simply measure the outside surface of the mold (refer to the section "Project: Glass Vase Draped Over a Floral Former" for details).

As long as you cut the glass properly, you won't need to grind the edges. When the glass is heated, the edges automatically round out nice and smooth.

Cleaning the glass

Before you start putting your glass pieces together, make sure you clean both sides of your glass to remove any dirt, dust, or fingerprints. After your glass is clean, handle it by the edges to keep new fingerprints from appearing on it.

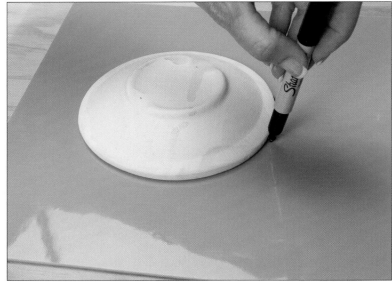

Figure 16-6:
Tracing the
shape of
a ceramic
mold onto
the glass
surface so
you know
where to cut
your glass.

Decorating the glass

To create a design on your glass-shaping project, you can add either cut glass
pieces or embellishments, such as frit and stringers, to the top or bottom
piece of glass, depending on the types of glass you're working with. For example, if you're using clear glass as the base glass and opalescent glass for the
top glass, you need to decorate the top piece. If you're using clear glass over
the top of your design, you need to decorate the bottom glass.

When decorating your glass, remember to start small and experiment with
any new materials before you incorporate them into a large project. You
certainly don't want to open your kiln to find that the big platter or bowl you
spent hours decorating with little pieces of iridescent fusing glass and frit
cracked in half and not know why.

Fire It Up! Fusing and Slumping Your Glass

Most slumped-glass projects require a minimum of two firings because
glass slumps at a lower temperature than it fuses. So if you want your project to stay together when you finish it, you have to first fire the glass flat to
the temperature that yields the fusing results you want — tack- or full-fuse
effects, for example. (That temperature is likely between 1,400 and 1,550
degrees; for more information about tack and full fusing, see Chapter 14.)

After this first firing process has been completed and the glass has cooled completely (perhaps the day after you fuse it), you can slump the glass any way you choose.

The following sections take a closer look at the fusing and slumping processes.

First firing: Fusing the glass

After you've selected your fusible glass, decorated it (if you chose to do so), and prepped it for firing (see the sections "Opting for Fancier Glass" and "Preparing Your Glass for Shaping" for details), you're ready for the first firing. Chapter 14 walks you through the firing process as it pertains to all fused-glass projects, so turn to that chapter for detailed instructions.

Here are the basic steps you need to take to complete the initial firing of your slumping project:

1. **Lay your project flat on your washed and dried kiln shelf, and then place it in the kiln (see Figure 16-7).**

   Whether you're working with just one piece of glass or multiple layers and pieces, everything is assembled together at this point. See the section "Preparing Your Glass for Shaping" for specifics on decorating your glass blank and Chapter 14 for details on working with multiple layers of fusible glass.

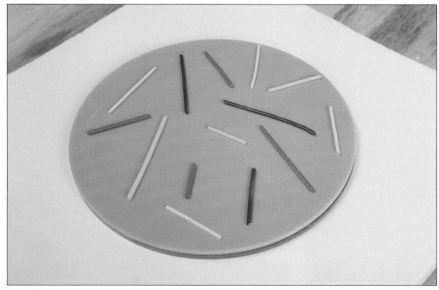

Figure 16-7: Project centered on the kiln shelf.

2. **Follow the firing chart in Table 16-1 for the first firing.**

3. **Let your glass cool completely for at least 12 hours; then move on to the second firing (see the next section).**

Table 16-1		Firing Chart for First Firing of Large Projects with Two to Three Layers		
Segment	**Settings**	**Desired Temperature**	**Soak Time**	**Action**
Heat-up	Low/ Medium	1,000 degrees	10 minutes	Remove vent.
Ramp-up	Full/High	1,440 degrees	15 minutes	Monitor.
Flash-cool	Off	1,100 degrees	0 minutes	Open the lid, and close it when the temperature reaches 1,000 degrees.
Anneal	Off*	955 degrees	90 minutes	Adjust controls to keep the kiln at 955 degrees during this phase.
Cool-down	Off	100 degrees	10 minutes	Turn everything off, and let it cool naturally. Don't open the lid!

*__*Note:__ You may need to turn the kiln back on to keep the temperature at 955 degrees for 90 minutes, depending on the kiln and the project.*

Second firing: Slumping the glass

When you've fused your glass and cooled it completely, you're ready for the second firing, which is when you actually slump your project.

To complete the second firing, follow these steps:

1. **Apply a new coating of kiln wash to your slumping mold and kiln shelf, and let them dry completely before moving on to Step 2.**

    Any moisture left in your mold or kiln shelf will create steam during the fusing process and destroy your project. See Chapter 13 for details on how to prepare your molds and shelves to be fired.

2. **Place the kiln shelf in the kiln, making sure to elevate it 1 inch off the kiln floor using posts; then place your mold in the center of the kiln shelf (see Figure 16-8).**

    Make sure the mold is at least 2 inches away from the top and sides of your kiln; you need to have plenty of room for the glass to sit freely on top of the mold.

3. **Position your already-fired glass project on the mold, and measure its placement to make sure it's exactly centered on the mold (see Figure 16-9).**

    If the project is the least bit off center, your project will end up lopsided.

    If you're slumping into your mold, look at the edges of the mold to see if the glass is centered. If you're slumping over a mold, use a small ruler to measure out from the edges of the mold to the edges of the glass to check whether the blank is exactly centered on the mold.

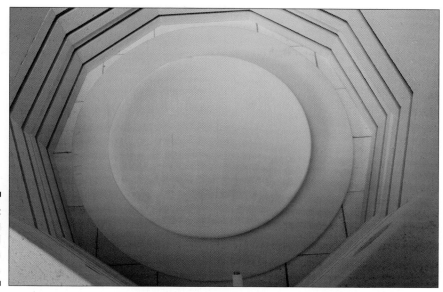

Figure 16-8:
Positioning
the mold
on the kiln
shelf.

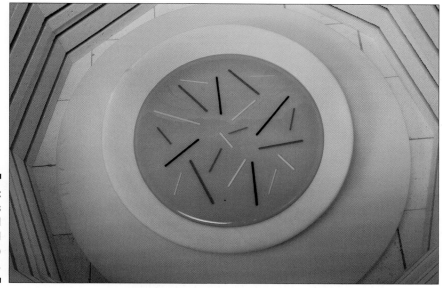

Figure 16-9:
Glass
centered
on the mold
and ready to
be fired.

4. **Follow the firing chart in Table 16-2 for the second firing.**

Don't try to use the firing chart in Table 16-1 for this step. Your already-fused glass doesn't fire the same as the individual pieces did during the first firing because it's already been fired and it's twice as thick as it was before.

Note: If you're draping your glass over a mold instead of slumping it into a mold, follow the firing chart in Table 16-2, but make your highest desired temperature during the ramp-up segment 1,210 degrees instead of 1,280 degrees.

Figure 16-10 shows the finished and cooled plate.

Note: Don't ever try to slump two projects at once. Glass blanks may look the same, but some blanks are heavier and will slump faster or slower than others.

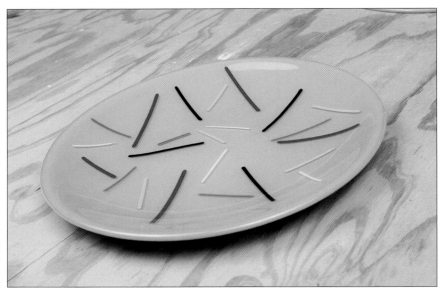

Figure 16-10: Finished plate.

Table 16-2		Firing Chart for Second Firing (Slumping) of a Two- or Three-Layer Project		
Segment	*Settings*	*Desired Temperature*	*Soak Time*	*Action*
Heat-up	Low/ Medium	1,000 degrees	10 minutes	Remove vent.
Ramp-Up	Full/ High	1,280 degrees	10 minutes	Monitor.
Flash-cool	Off	1,000 degrees	0 minutes	Open the lid, and close it when the temperature reaches 1,000 degrees.
Anneal	Off*	960 degrees	90 minutes	Adjust controls to keep the kiln at 960 degrees during this phase.
Cool-down	Off	700 degrees	10 minutes	Turn everything off, and let it cool naturally. Don't open the lid!

*Note: You may need to turn the kiln back on to keep the temperature at 955 degrees for 90 minutes, depending on the kiln and the project.

Project: Tropical Bowl Slumped into a Mold

For this project, I use the same design I use in Chapter 15 for a wall sconce except that I slump the project to make a bowl here. To make this bowl, you need a bowl-shaped ceramic mold that's at least 10 inches in diameter, a square foot of clear glass for the base, and one 12-x-6-inch piece of glass in each of these colors: sky blue, cream, brown, and green. You also need tan and blue frit and green stringers for accents.

Although I've chosen a tropical design for my bowl, you can create any design you want to. No matter how you decorate your bowl, the basic fusing and slumping steps look like this:

1. **Apply a coating of kiln wash to your kiln shelf; let it dry completely.**

   See Chapter 13 for details on how to prepare your kiln shelf for firing.

2. **Trace around the edge of the mold on a piece of paper to determine what size you need to cut your clear base piece of glass.**

   My bowl is 10 inches in diameter.

3. **Design your project within the dimensions of this circle.**

   You can use my tropical design or create your own using a stained-glass pattern, frit, stringers, or random shapes of fusing glass.

4. **Cut a circle of clear fusing glass that's the same size as the one you traced in Step 2; also cut out any other glass shapes you need to decorate your project.**

5. **Use a small amount of glue to decorate your glass circle with the glass pieces you cut out in Step 4 (see Figure 16-11).**

6. **Load the project onto the kiln shelf, and follow the firing chart in Table 16-1 to fire your project for the first time; let it cool completely.**

   See the section "First firing: Fusing the glass" for more details.

7. **Apply a coating of kiln wash to your slumping mold and your kiln shelf; let them dry completely.**

8. **Place your mold on the center of the kiln shelf, and position your prefused glass on top of the mold, making sure the glass is centered evenly on the mold (see Figure 16-12).**

9. **Follow the firing chart in Table 16-2 to slump your glass.**

   See the section "Second firing: Slumping the glass" for more details.

REMEMBER

Each project will react a little differently, so you want to be sure you don't overheat your project. Always check the progress of your slumping or draping project as the heat approaches the desired annealing temperature. Just be sure to always wear your safety fusing glasses when looking inside the hot kiln. If your kiln doesn't have a peep hole, you have to lift the lid a few inches to check your project's slumping progress. Always wear your safety gloves and glasses, and don't keep the kiln open for more than a few seconds; gently close the lid when you're done.

Figure 16-13 shows the finished project.

Figure 16-11:
Decorating the glass before the first firing.

Figure 16-12:
Getting the glass and mold ready for the second firing.

Figure 16-13:
Finished
tropical
bowl.

Project: Glass Vase Draped Over a Floral Former

The first time you use a floral former, I recommend using a fairly simple design. Because you have to drape the glass around the former, detailed designs sometimes get lost in the firing. For this project, you need a stainless steel floral former and one or two pieces of glass the size of the vase you want to make, depending on whether you want to work with one or two layers. You may also choose to incorporate some decorative glass pieces, like frit, stringers, or other shapes, into your vase. Whatever glass you use, make sure it's all compatible, fusible glass (see the section "Opting for Fancier Glass" for details). No matter how you decorate your vase, the basic fusing and draping steps look like this:

1. **Apply a coating of kiln wash to your kiln shelf; let it dry completely.**

2. **Measure the height and width of the base of the stainless steel floral former (see Figure 16-14); subtract ½ inch from each measurement.**

   The number you get is the largest size circle you can cut for your vase. If you want to make a smaller vase, simply cut a smaller circle in Step 3.

3. **Cut out two circles of glass the size you determined in Step 2.**

   Although you can make a vase with just one layer of glass, using two makes your finished project much more durable and richer looking.

   You can cut both circles out of the same glass, or you can use clear glass for one and colored glass for the other. If you're feeling adventurous, try cutting out two circles from different colors of glass to create a vase that's one color on the outside and another color on the inside. (See Chapter 5 for details on cutting glass.)

Figure 16-14:
Measuring
a floral
former.

4. **Clean all the glass using glass cleaner; then use a little glue to hold your glass pieces and any decorative glass accents together.**

5. **Load the project onto the kiln shelf, and follow the firing chart in Table 16-1 to fire your project for the first time.**

6. **The next day, apply a coating of kiln wash to your floral former mold and your kiln shelf; let them dry completely.**

7. **Place your stainless steel floral former mold in the center of the kiln shelf.**

8. **Place your already-fired glass project on top of the mold, making sure you have plenty of space around the top and sides of the glass edges for it to move freely as it heats.**

   Use a ruler to make sure the circle is centered over the former.

9. **If you're using two layers of glass, follow the firing chart in Table 16-2, except reduce the desired temperature during the ramp-up segment to 1,210 degrees.**

Make sure you reduce the highest desired temperature when you're creating a draping project. If you overheat the glass, it'll continue to sag on the mold, thinning out the thickness of the bottom of the vase and making your finished project very fragile.

If you're making a single-layer vase, I recommend that you fire polish the vase's edges. *Fire polishing* is heating a piece of glass to the point that the edges round out and shine. The temperature range for fire polishing is 1,375 to 1,400 degrees, and you do it during the first firing. To fire polish, keep an eye on the glass as the kiln starts to approach 1,350 degrees. When the edges of your vase start to round out, your fire polishing is complete. Turn off the kiln, and flash cool down to the annealing temperature; then continue through the rest of the firing segments.

Figure 16-15 shows the finished project.

Figure 16-15:
Vase
created
using a
stainless
steel floral
former mold.

Part V
The Part of Tens

In this part . . .

You can't have a *For Dummies* book without the Part of Tens. Here, I offer you ten ways to improve your all-important soldering skills and introduce you to my ten favorite stained-glass works of all time. Take time to visit and study these works if you can; you may be surprised by how much your skills improve after a simple study session or two!

Chapter 17

Ten Strategies to Improve Your Soldering Technique

In This Chapter

▶ Understanding how to use your equipment

▶ Controlling the flow of the solder and the size of your intersections

▶ Practicing to gain confidence and familiarity

As you may have already discovered, soldering is one of the most difficult skills to master in stained glass. Most instructors believe the only way to improve your soldering skills is to solder a lot as often as possible. Although I agree that practicing is certainly important, I believe that understanding how metals, heat, and chemicals react to each other is even more important. After you figure out how to control these factors, your skills will improve in no time.

In this chapter, I cover ten strategies you can follow to help you gain the understanding and control you need to get better at soldering. So grab your iron, solder, and flux, and get ready to heat things up! (Turn to Chapter 7 for plenty more details about soldering.)

Understand How to Control Your Soldering Iron's Temperature

Your soldering iron is one of the most important tools in your stained-glass studio; it has to perform perfectly every time you use it if you want to perfect your soldering techniques (and create good-looking, sturdy projects at the same time). You and your projects depend on your soldering iron to perform exactly the same every time you set it at a particular setting. In other words, when you increase or decrease your iron's temperature, you need to know that it's going to deliver a consistent working temperature every time.

Every iron and rheostat/thermostat combination works a little differently, but that's okay — as long as you understand exactly how yours works. (Check out Chapter 2 for details on the different types of irons you can use for stained glass.) Take time to test your iron at each of its settings, and record your findings. Retest it again and again until you know for certain which settings on your rheostat work best for which soldering tasks (use a medium to high setting for running beads on copper-foil projects; use a low to medium setting for creating joints on lead-came projects). Indicate those settings on the rheostat so you can make dependable temperature adjustments quickly and accurately for every project you work on.

Keep Your Soldering Tip Clean

You can dramatically improve the quality of your soldering if you make a habit of wiping off the tip of your soldering iron on a clean, wet sponge as you solder. If you're working with lead came, wipe the tip after every one or two joints; if you're working with copper foil, wipe it after every few minutes. Why do you have to keep your iron's tip clean? It's simple: Only a clean soldering tip will deliver constant, clean heat to your soldering surface and, in turn, create perfectly soldered joints and beads.

When you're working with a hot soldering iron, check out the soldering iron tip periodically. Notice the dark spots and small partials that form on the tip as you solder a project. Dirt builds up on the iron tip as a result of dirty solder, corrosive flux, and the oxidation that occurs on the surface of the hot metals, and you need to clean it off.

Figure Out How to Hold Your Iron

If you've ever participated in golf, tennis, or baseball, you know how much time you have to spend just learning how to hold your club, racket, or bat. Well, the sport of soldering is no different. If you want to succeed at soldering, you first need to figure out how to hold your iron.

When it comes to holding your soldering iron, the most important thing to remember is to hold your iron like you hold a bat — with your hand wrapped around the handle — not like you hold a pencil. That way, the weight of the soldering iron is directed downward onto the soldering joint or seam, helping you steady your hand and eliminate small ripples and ridges from your soldering seams. If you hold the iron like a pencil, the soldering seam will pick up the tension and pulse of your body, making it impossible to solder a smooth, even seam or joint.

Specifically for copper-foil projects, be sure to turn the soldering tip on its side. Compared to the tip's flat edge, the side of the tip is narrower and heats up a smaller area, allowing you to better control the temperature of the solder. On the other hand, when you're soldering lead came, remember to rotate your iron tip and use the flat edge for larger joints. The larger flat edge of the tip heats a larger area, allowing you to heat the entire joint at once.

Be Loyal to Your Brands

When it comes to flux and solder, you have quite a few types and brands to choose from. I recommend that you try out several brands until you find the one that performs the best for you. Although you may decide to switch brands at some point (to switch to a less-toxic version of flux, for example), don't make a habit out of constantly switching back and forth. After all, to have the most success in soldering, you need to use soldering tools and supplies that perform consistently time after time.

The varieties of flux range from organic to highly toxic. Unfortunately, most of the best flux performers over the years have been the more-toxic varieties; however, each year manufacturers lower the amount of toxic chemicals in their flux varieties and improve their performance. When you find a flux that's less toxic than yours, give it a try; if it works just as well or better, feel free to switch to it.

In terms of solder, some brands are purer and cleaner than others, but the majority of stained-glass solder is comprised of both tin and lead. Because tin is a lot more expensive than lead, however, some manufacturers skimp on the amount of tin to save money. So how do you know if your solder is pure and clean enough to use? Look for little specks of dirt in your solder seams and joints; if you see them, you need to get a purer, cleaner solder.

The perfect solder blend for copper-foil projects is 60/40 (60 percent tin and 40 percent lead) because it melts quickly and cools quickly, resulting in a nice, round bead. For lead-came projects, you need to use 50/50 solder, which has an even mix of tin and lead, because it stays molten longer, thus allowing the lead joint to flatten and blend better with the came. If you're working in a lead-free studio, you can use a lead-free version of solder for all your projects.

To keep consumer prices down, most stained-glass supply stores purchase large quantities of solder from a local supplier. Because your local store may carry only one brand of solder, staying loyal to your solder is pretty easy to do if you purchase it in a store.

If you purchase your solder online, make sure you choose a good-quality brand that you've personally tested, and stick with that brand. Don't be lured to buy a poor-quality solder just because it's on sale.

Know That You Can Never Use Too Much Flux

Flux is a cleaner that you absolutely must apply to your project before you solder to remove the oxidation that occurs when you heat metal. (In case you're wondering, oxidation puts a thin crust on top of the solder, restricting its ability to flow evenly.) If you don't flux, your project's pieces won't bond together, so be sure to apply flux to all your project's seams and joints every time you solder or re-solder them.

Find the Right Flow and Rhythm

The *flow* of solder is the liquid movement it makes when melted. Figuring out how to control that flow is the key to soldering successfully. The first step in controlling your solder's flow is finding the right rhythm as you move your iron and solder along your project's seams and joints. Just like playing the piano or painting, after you get into the rhythm and start to control the solder's flow, you can relax and enjoy the experience.

To help you feel more comfortable as you solder, I recommend listening to your favorite music while you work.

Work on One Area at a Time

Staring at a fresh project ready to be soldered is both exciting and daunting when you're just getting started with stained glass. Don't let your emotions dictate how you solder your project; the worst thing you can do is jump around from one area to the next, soldering a little here and a little more there. If you follow that technique, pretty soon all your joints and seams will look bad and you won't have a clue how to fix them.

Always start soldering at the top of your project. For lead-came projects, apply flux to two or three joints, and solder them first; then work your way down the panel. For copper-foil projects, study the flow of the design. Flux a 4- to 5-inch area, and work on that section until you're happy with the way it looks; then move on to the next spot. Never leave an area until you're happy with it.

Note: Sometimes when you're working on a large lead-came panel with a lot of straight lines, you may need to tack solder the major intersections to keep them from shifting as you solder the project together.

If your solder gets too hot and starts to heat the glass, take a break, let the area cool completely, and then re-flux and re-solder the area. To cool off your iron temporarily, wipe your iron on a clean, wet sponge.

Keep Your Intersections Clean and Low

The way you approach soldering joints and intersections depends on the type of project you're working on.

- **Lead-came projects:** Your goal is to create solder joints that blend flawlessly into the face of the lead. In other words, they're consistent in size and flat; they don't look like buttons. If your joints are too tall or have ridges where they meet the came, re-flux the area, clean off your soldering tip on a clean, wet sponge, and reapply the flat side of your soldering tip to the joint. Hold the tip on the joint until the solder starts to glow and spread out onto the face of the came.

You want your solder joints to be the same width as the came you're soldering. Applying flux only to the area you want to solder can help you control the size of your joints because the solder doesn't travel where there isn't any flux.

If you've applied too much solder, re-flux the area, reapply heat with the iron, and, when the solder starts to melt, lift your iron straight up off the joint and wipe the tip on the wet sponge to remove the excess solder. Continue to repeat this process until you've removed all the excess solder from your project. Then re-flux each joint and reheat it until it smooths out.

✔ **Copper-foil projects:** Your goal is to create intersections that are the same width and height as the other seams in the project. Try to control the amount of solder you apply to your seams at any given time. Keeping the melted puddle of liquid solder under your soldering tip consistent in size allows you to keep your seams and intersections even in size. When the puddle starts to get too small, melt more solder; just make sure you don't overdo it.

Solder has a tendency to build up wherever two or more glass pieces join. To keep the intersections from building up, always solder away from the intersections, never into them.

Mentally Visualize the Size of Your Lead Joints

The key to creating the perfect joint on a lead-came project is controlling the joint's width, and the easiest way to do so is to visualize the size and appearance of each joint before you start soldering it.

The perfectly sized lead joint extends out in all directions the same distance as the width of the came you're soldering. For example, if you're using ⅜-inch lead on the perimeter of the project, your perimeter joints need to be ⅜ inch wide in each direction. If you're using ³⁄₁₆-inch lead for the interior of your panel, your interior joints need to be ³⁄₁₆ inch wide in each direction.

When you're first starting out, you may want to mark the ideal width of each joint on the face of the lead came so you know exactly how much solder to add. Over time, you can start to visualize the size of your project's joints in your mind. Think about how big the joint should be, and apply only enough solder to spread out and cover that particular distance. Remember that adding more solder is easier to do than removing excess solder.

Practice, Practice, Practice

The more you work in your stained-glass studio, the more familiar you'll be with your soldering tools and the better you'll get at making them respond to your demands. For instance, the more you solder, the more you'll understand how flux impacts your project and why you need to use a lot of it.

Each stained-glass project you do is an opportunity to practice and gain more familiarity and confidence. Every time you solder, try to improve your quality of craftsmanship. Challenge yourself to do a better job on your current project than you did on the last one.

Chapter 18

Ten Glass Works You Must Study

*T*he best way to understand any art form is to study its masters. In stained glass, the most famous artist is Louis C. Tiffany. He invented or refined many of the techniques that have become commonplace today, including using opalescent glass, copper foil, overlays, and mosaics to create beautiful and unique stained-glass works. In this chapter, I examine Tiffany's works and explain the impact they've had on the modern stained-glass movement.

Selecting only ten works for this chapter was quite a challenge, but the windows I describe here represent the vast, somewhat incomprehensible legacy he left to everyone who aspires to become a great glass artist, including you! Most of these windows are available for viewing online and in public art collections, museums, and buildings. The Morse Museum of American Art in Winter Park, Florida, houses the biggest collection of Tiffany windows (check out www.morsemuseum.org for more details), and the book *Tiffany Windows* by Alastair Duncan (Simon and Schuster) provides some beautiful pictures of Tiffany's greatest works.

The Bathers

Considered by most glass-art enthusiasts to be one of the finest Tiffany windows of all time, this window was massive and featured eight full-size women. In addition to its size, the window's most outstanding characteristic was the way Tiffany manipulated the light in it. Tiffany was a master at selecting and using glass that would create the effect of natural sunlight. Having been installed in Tiffany's home, Laurelton Hall, this window was destroyed in the 1957 fire that gutted the home, destroying many of his best windows.

When you study one of Tiffany's windows, always pay attention to where Tiffany positioned the light source. To create a realistic landscape or floral window, you have to decide where the source of light, be it the sun or artificial light, is positioned in a particular scene. Ask yourself, "Is the sun rising over that hill in the background or shining through the trees to the right?" Doing so can help you decide how to select glass colors so you can properly shade your windows.

The Entombment

This window depicts Jesus being placed in the tomb after his crucifixion. Its uniqueness is in the painting of the faces, hands, and bodies of the figures. (The face of one of the saints was modeled after Charles Lewis Tiffany, Tiffany's father.) In his windows, Tiffany allowed only the hands and faces to be painted; everything else had to be created from glass. This window is now a part of the McKean collection at the Morse Museum of American Art.

Feeding the Flamingoes

This window is one of the best examples of Tiffany's plating technique. In case you're wondering, *plating* is the process of layering one or more pieces of glass on top of each other to create a unique color.

Tiffany designed this window for the 1893 Chicago Columbian Exposition. The exposition booklet described it as "more realistic, more elaborate, and showing more clearly the possibilities of American glass than any window in our exhibit." After the exposition, the window was installed in Tiffany's home, Laurelton Hall. It's now a part of the McKean collection at the Morse Museum of American Art.

The Four Seasons

Tiffany designed four windows depicting the four seasons — summer, fall, winter, and spring — to demonstrate the beauty of *Favrile glass* (a type of glass created by Tiffany that has a warm internal glow, giving color and life to the glass). In addition to the Favrile glass, the windows incorporate jewels, drapery glass, fracture and streamer glass, and lettering. If you ever get a chance to see these windows in person, don't miss the impressive techniques Tiffany used to create the geometric borders and to encase the hundreds of nuggets and jewels in them. These windows are now in the Morse Museum of American Art.

The presence of Favrile glass is the single characteristic that experts use to determine whether or not a window is truly a Tiffany; however, it isn't always the final factor because workers in Tiffany's studio often moonlighted, making windows using glass they'd stolen from the studio.

Magnolia and Irises

Tiffany developed many glass-manufacturing processes that produced different textures and colors of glass. One of the most unique is *drapery glass,* a type of glass created by manipulating glass while it's still hot and soft. When finished, drapery glass resembles the way fabric looks when it's draped, hence its name.

Tiffany used drapery glass to represent the robes and dresses in many of his portrait windows and flowers and other details in his landscape windows. Magnolias were a popular theme for him, and he used creamy, white, lush drapery glass to create this delicate flower. The irregular thickness of the glass required Tiffany to use both copper foil and leaded glass to accommodate the glass in these projects.

Minnehaha Window

This window, designed by Anne Weston from Duluth, is a wonderful example of how art can be used to express another art form. The window's theme comes from Henry Wadsworth Longfellow's epic poem *The Song of Hiawatha*. It shows the Indian maiden, Minnehaha, standing in front of the laughing waterfall after which she was named. The window embodies important national symbols and provides a picture into this historic era.

The Minnehaha window was displayed in the Minnesota Building at the 1893 Columbian Exposition in Chicago and then presented to the Duluth Public Library located in the old Masonic Temple Building.

Mosaics

Tiffany used many mosaic techniques in his windows, lamps, and decorative accents. He even mixed mosaic techniques with blown-glass daffodils to create the cement columns for his home, Laurelton Hall. Part of a column survived the fire in 1957 and is now part of the Morse Museum of American Art's collection.

Two of my favorite mosaic windows are the pebble-cluster panels created for the Maxwell Plum restaurant in New York City. Using thin slices of natural stone, Tiffany leaded the windows together to create clusters of five-petal flowers. The geometric border treatments on these windows provide balance and structure to the design.

If you'd like to find out more about the mosaic technique, check out www. americanmosaics.org.

Peacock Windows

Tiffany created many famous windows depicting peacocks. My personal favorite is one he created in 1920 for Mr. Hill's residence in Tarrytown, New York. The window is an excellent example of how to incorporate both natural and manmade objects into a landscape image. In addition to peacocks, the window incorporates some of Tiffany's favorite themes: sailing ships, balustrades, wisteria, and sunsets. Tiffany didn't use any painting in this window; he created all the images using glass in unique and clever ways.

Another important peacock window is *Peacock and Peonies.* Tiffany used hundreds of glass shades and colors to create this realistic landscape, and the lead work in the peacock's feathers is fantastic. This window is now part of the Morse Museum of American Art's Tiffany collection.

Wisteria Lamps and Windows

Wisteria may have been one of Tiffany's favorite plants. After all, he incorporated its flowers and leaves into his windows, transoms, skylights, screens, and lamps by way of mottled glass. *Mottled glass* has dark and light spots that add movement to the glass, allowing artists to cut only one piece of glass and have it appear as if they've used multiple pieces.

In the backgrounds of many of his windows, especially the wisteria-themed panels, Tiffany used *fractured glass,* also called *confetti.* Fractured glass is created by dropping small, thin pieces of glass onto the backside of a hot sheet of clear- or neutral-colored glass. When used as background glass, fractured glass looks like dense foliage.

Many of today's glass makers still manufacture variations of fractured, confetti, and streamer glass. If you're interested in incorporating these unique types of glass into your stained-glass projects, study Tiffany's windows to figure out how to use them to their fullest potential.

Woman and Cupid Window

Pinpointing my all-time favorite Tiffany piece is nearly an impossible task because I love them all and have learned so much from studying them. However, I do have a special place in my heart for one particular window. It doesn't have an official name, and it isn't necessarily unique. So why do I love it? I love it because I found it.

Years ago when I lived in Detroit, my husband Chris and I owned a large stained-glass studio and learning center. Detroit has several great Tiffany windows, and I was on the lookout for one more. Listed in Alastair Duncan's book *Tiffany Windows* (Simon and Schuster) was a Tiffany window supposedly located in Wayne County Community College. The window featured a woman teaching a cupid how to play a flute and two white doves. I looked all over the city for it with no luck.

A few years after I'd given up my search, I passed an old stone mansion on Wayne State University's campus. Through a layer of yellowed protective plastic, I caught a glimpse of a large stained-glass window with two white doves in the corner. I couldn't believe my eyes. I'd actually found the window from Duncan's book!

Index

• *G* •